Hurricane R4118
Revisited

Hurricane R4118
Revisited

The extraordinary story of the discovery and
restoration to flight of a Battle of Britain survivor:
The adventure continues 2005 – 2017

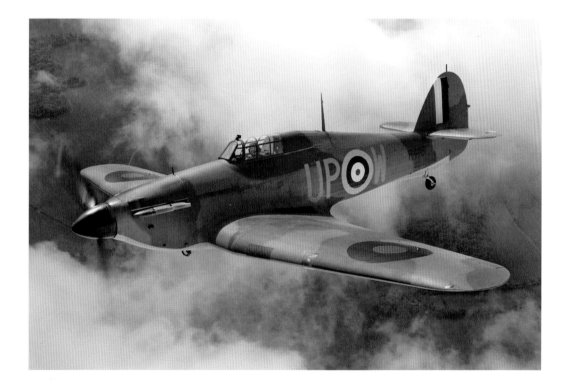

Peter Vacher

Grub Street • London

Published by
Grub Street
4 Rainham Close
London
SW11 6SS

First published as *Hurricane R4118* in 2005
Copyright this new edition © 2017 Grub Street
Text copyright © 2017 Peter Vacher

ISBN-13: 9781910690437

Design and artwork by Roy Platten
roy.eclipse@btopenworld.com

Printed and bound in the Czech Republic by Finidr

Contents

Foreword

OVER the past half century many books have been written about the Battle of Britain, the whys and wherefores, the ifs and buts and rights and wrongs.... With the blessed vision of hindsight, we now know how both sides should have fought the battle. Unfortunately, those of us at the sharp end at the time knew none of this. All we knew was that day after day enemy bombers and fighters were crossing the South Coast to attack our airfields, factories and cities, and we had to destroy as many as possible to survive.

Winston Churchill once said, albeit at a different time and in a different context, "Give us the tools and we shall finish the job." We had the tools and started to finish the job with two great fighter aircraft, the Hurricane and its younger – and some say – prettier sister the Spitfire. The latter has received most of the publicity over the years, but the Hurricane played an equal, if not greater part in the victory. Simply but robustly built, she could absorb as well as hand out punishment, and we had an implicit faith in her ability to get us home, if at all possible.

This story concerns one such, R4118. But the book is not only about one Hurricane, it is also about one man, Peter Vacher, whose single-minded determination saw this project through to the end.

A passing interest in an old wreck, then to a more detailed study and the realisation that here was something historically unique, led to an obsession that was not to be denied. Peter rightly pays tribute to all those who have helped him over the years and in all parts of the world, but it is his own enthusiasm, inspiration and passionate zeal that saw the project through to its satisfactory conclusion. Truly, like the fairy story of the Ugly Duckling, transferred back into a Princess.

Last year I sat in the cockpit of UP-W for the first time in nearly sixty-five years; the last time was the morning of 2 October 1940. It was all there as I remembered it. Odd thoughts passed through my mind of those hectic days of long ago, and for no particular reason, one small incident. It was a beautiful sunny afternoon in September, and we were taking off from Croydon Airport across the Purley Way. Below was a sports club and four people playing tennis.

As we flew over, they stopped playing and waved their rackets in salute, maybe they shouted "Good luck and a safe return" – who knows? They then returned to their game and we to ours.

Many years have passed since then, and we now live in so-called peaceful times. However, if one day you hear the distinct sound of a Merlin engine and, looking up, see good old UP-W flying overhead, raise your hand and say loud and clear, "Good luck, good flying and thank you."

Wing Commander Bob Foster DFC

An Appreciation of the Hurricane

I FLEW this fighter aircraft almost daily for just short of three years, from December 1938 until August 1941. At this time I took command of a Spitfire squadron in Hampshire.

The Hurricane was a magnificent warhorse, with its unsurpassed gun platform in the leading-edge of the wings, which had a deadly promise. It had no vices whatsoever with superb reliability and was so easy to fly in any weather conditions.

Totally trustworthy in every respect. A confidence-giving aeroplane, loved by all who flew it.

Wing Commander Bunny Currant
DSO, DFC and Bar, CdeG

Peter Thompson, Bunny Currant and Bob Foster reunited with R4118 after sixty-one years.

Acknowledgements

SO many old friends have helped with the rescue of R4118, but it has also proved an opportunity to make new ones. Enthusiasts from all over the world have offered advice and guidance. To each and every one, thank you.

The responsibility for the discovery of R4118 lies squarely with John Fasal. Without his knowledge of, and enthusiasm for all things Indian, the day when we first set eyes on that dilapidated British aircraft would not have dawned. He joined me on six subsequent visits and was untiring in his encouragement when it seemed we would never rescue this historic machine. I remember the sweat pouring off him as we battled to load the aeroplane in the heat of that Indian summer – a good friend indeed.

My research was prompted by Hugh Smallwood, who introduced me to the intricacies of the Public Record Office and the library at the RAF Museum at Hendon. These in turn led to my interviewing pilots who had flown R4118 in the Battle of Britain. Bunny Currant, Bob Foster, Alec Ingle, Archie Milne and Peter Thompson all patiently put up with my questions whilst a tape recorder ran. Their memories and log books filled in gaps in the history of R4118, and provided an insight into the conditions that had made them such characters. My especial thanks go to Bunny who, at the age of 93, not only has amazing powers of recall, but continues to relate amusing, mostly breathtaking, stories of his time in the RAF. It has been a pleasure meeting and corresponding with the families of Skid Hanes and Denis Winton who flew the aircraft with Treble One Squadron, and also with F J M Palmer who famously hit the lorry on the runway.

Bill Bishop hails from Australia, regularly flying a Qantas 747 to London. Yet he seems to have been working full time on the project. When not dismantling the airframe, he has browsed the web from his hotel bedrooms around the world looking for parts and information. Back home he has built models of R4118 to ensure every detail on the real thing is completed accurately, especially the colour scheme and markings. He has even organised 'down under' the manufacture of some parts. Another Qantas captain, Ross Kelly, has spent his time in the UK helping whenever possible.

Armed with his video camera, Roy Noble has faithfully recorded the Hurricane as found in India, and then on, week by week, as the stripping and rebuild have progressed. Apprenticed at De Havilland, Roy has been equally at home taking the aircraft apart as well as helping in countless other ways. From all that has happened, Roy has made various films which brilliantly capture the story of our great survivor.

ACKNOWLEDGEMENTS

Working with Bill, Ross, Roy and myself has been Roger Andrews. Roger, the most patient, uncomplaining of people, has spent days, no, weeks chipping away at corroded parts to enable their reuse or for patterns. Condemned for hours to the noisy, hot blasting room, we only let him out for the occasional piece of bread and water, then sent him home for a good bath! Robert Benson, our local farmer, spent hours loading and unloading lumps of aircraft and engine with his remarkable Sanderson. What a wonderful group of friends.

John Elvins not only located a rare TR1133 radio, but gave weeks of his time to rebuild the entire wireless and IFF systems. It is a credit to his tenacity and patience that the ageing electrical components were brought back to life.

My thanks go to the Director of the RAF Museum at Hendon, Michael Fopp, and to his team, especially Henry Hall, Peter Elliott and John O'Neill. Their support over the loan of an engine, and allowing frequent access to the library and the museum's early Hurricane has advanced the project immeasurably. Ernie Cromie and the committee at the Ulster Aviation Association have helped greatly with propeller problems. Gerry Morrison and his staff at the Aerospace Museum in Calgary kindly released a spare engine which the RAF most helpfully shipped in a C130. I am grateful to Ivor Jones for information on 52 MU at Cardiff, and to Graham Crisp for allowing me to quote from his work on Drem Lighting.

In the search for parts and information on the Mk I Hurricane, especial mention must be made of Guy Black at Aero Vintage. Also thanks are due to Barry Parkhouse, Iain Arnold, Hedley Griffiths, Mark Biggs whose uncle flew with 605 Squadron in the Battle, James Black, Peter Brown, Paul Cole, Peter Croser, Neville Cullingford, Lewis Deal of the Medway Aircraft Preservation Society, John Elgar-Whinney, Ken Ellis from *Flypast*, Martin Espin at the Fighter Collection, Mike Evans and Peter Kirk from the Rolls-Royce Heritage Trust, Chris Morris and Steve McManus at the Shuttleworth Collection, Chris Radford at the Jet Age Museum, Al Watts from Retro Track and Air, Rick Roberts, Graham Wimbolt and Peter Wood. Commercial sponsorship was greatly appreciated from USF Surface Preparation Ltd, Adaptaflex Ltd, and English Abrasives and Chemicals Ltd.

Bearing the brunt of the restoration of R4118 was Tony Ditheridge and his quite fantastic group at Hawker Restorations Ltd. Their dedication and enthusiasm for the project was beyond the call of duty. When I was being at my most pernickety, they took it all with good humour. The proof of their workmanship is flying in R4118 today. To Bob Cunningham and his team at Bournemouth goes great admiration for the meticulous rebuilding of the wings, metal panelling and much of the tailplane.

Maurice Hammond undertook the rebuilding of the Merlin III engine. This was not easy, largely because, being such an early mark of Merlin, there was a dearth of technical information and parts were not easy to source. Maurice welcomed me into his workshop to strip the engine, which I am sure was a nuisance for him but I thoroughly enjoyed it, now being acquainted with every part of the engine. Himself a highly competent pilot, he attended to every tiny detail as if he was going to fly the aircraft himself.

We were fortunate in our three pilots, Pete Kynsey, Stuart Goldspink and Andy Sephton who displayed a high degree of professionalism during the crucial test period. At the same time huge support was provided by Terry Holloway, Malcolm Gault and their team at Marshall Aerospace at Cambridge. Squadron Leader Al Pinner, a close friend from the Battle of Britain Memorial Flight, was a source of sound advice. Superb air-to-air photography was taken by John Dunbar.

My sister, Janny Watson, patiently transcribed taped interviews with the surviving pilots. Our three sons, Julian (whose helicopter provided an excellent camera ship), Clive and Brian have been more than supportive. Finally, none of it would have been possible without the encouragement and patience of my dear wife, Polly, to whom goes a very, very special hug.

Peter Vacher 2005

Revised Edition

I wish to thank Bob Goodwin for telling the story of, and providing the sketches by, his father, Fred Goodwin. Peter Freeman-Pannett at 91 years old has told his own story of his time as 605 Squadron ground crew. The menus from the dinners of the Hawker Drawing Office, preserved by Oliver Wareham, have been supplied by his son, John. The painting of Peter Simpson's Hurricane on Woodcote golf course is reproduced by kind permission of the artist, Mark Postlethwaite and the Royal Automobile Club. The artist, David Shepherd, has graciously allowed me to reproduce the painting of the moment that John Milne destroyed a Me 110 over Dorking. Keith Foster has supplied the pictures of the LMS Derby works.

Thanks are due to those who provided photographs including John Dibbs, Jim Dooley, David Brown, Michael Shreeve, Richard Paver, and Dave Welch.

I was delighted that Keith Dennison wrote so graphically about what it is to fly a Hurricane. His piece is reprinted by permission of the editor of *Flyer*.

I am grateful to Nicolas Livingstone for writing the extraordinary story he unearthed in Chapter 7. All the quotations and most of the information come from a single file in the National Archives, AIR 14/390. Sgt Parrott's record is in file AIR 76/389/149, and the Operations Record Book Appendices for No. 10 OTU are in file AIR 29/640. The photo of the Whitley is from the Imperial War Museum.

Finally I must again thank James Brown for so kindly taking over custody of Hurricane R4118.

PV 2017

A Twinkle in the Eye

HIS Highness the Maharaja of Banaras gave us a charming welcome. From his Ramnagar fort overlooking the holy River Ganges, we could see the ghats from which the ashes of the departed are launched on their final journey.

John Fasal and I were on our travels from Calcutta to Delhi in March 1982. John, an intrepid researcher into the fate of older Rolls-Royce and Bentley motor cars, was continuing to find material for his book *Rolls-Royce and Bentley in Princely India*. For me it was a privilege to travel with him, meeting the princely families who owned the cars in the nineteen tens, twenties and thirties. In the palace garages still lurked such fine, forgotten cars. For myself, a vintage enthusiast, these vehicles represented the epitome of engineering excellence, and of the coachbuilders' art. The fact that many of the cars were covered in layers of grime and sat on rotting tyres only added to their romanticism. Here were the untouched relics of a bygone era, an era of pomp and circumstance, of splendour and majesty.

For the most part, the palaces we visited mirrored the condition of the cars. The chandeliers still hung, but the cobwebs obscured their sparkling beauty. In the libraries, the illiterate termites devoured volume after volume. Our search for early motoring pictures of the Raj was a dirty and hazardous one, perched on top of rickety sets of library steps and surrounded by fleeing cockroaches, beetles and silver fish.

Yet the filth, the decay and discomfort were nothing. The welcome from those families in their faded palaces had not dimmed. The warmth we received wherever we went was to bring us back to India again and again.

On our travels we were also meeting the latter-day maharajas – India's business tycoons. For several of these, recognising India's fine heritage of vintage motor cars had led them to acquire substantial collections of the world's most incredible machinery, all built to the order of their original royal customers with no expense spared. These cars were better preserved, as indeed were their new owners' homes.

Our arrival at the holy city of Banaras, one of the places to which every Hindu should make a pilgrimage once during his life, coincided with the festival of Holi. Although a religious festival, it has a time-honoured tradition for Indians to enjoy themselves. The children are given pots of brightly coloured pigments which, after mixing with water, they throw at each other. You can imagine what fun the kids have. Not so funny is when the riotous behaviour extends to the older teenagers – we were terrified when a crowd of six of them began dancing on the roof of our taxi and then tried to turn it over.

From a visit fifteen years before, John remembered that there were two exceptional Roll-

Royces lurking in the engineering department of Banaras Hindu University. Grabbing an auto-rickshaw, we bumped and weaved our way through Banaras' bubbling bazaars. Arriving we were suddenly hit by the tranquillity and seclusion of the campus. Claimed to be the largest in Asia, the university is set in five square miles of tree-lined glades. The buildings, erected by the British between 1918 and 1936, mirrored the splendour of the palaces of the Raj. At that time, the engineering department had been equipped with the latest machine tools from Britain. Today's students are still taught on the same machinery.

The place was deserted. Could John remember where those two Rolls-Royces were among the huge expanse of grounds and buildings? And being Holi, everything was shut up. A chowkidar wanted to help and disappeared for a couple of hours, emerging triumphant on his bicycle with a set of keys.

To say that I was stunned when the doors opened would be an understatement. Sitting proudly in the middle of the engineering workshop there lay a 1924 Rolls-Royce Silver Ghost, formerly belonging to His Highness the Maharaja of Jodhpur. A polished all-aluminium tourer with coachwork by Barker & Company, it was the most beautiful car I had ever set eyes on. Behind the long bonnet, a V windscreen protected an interior in which everything was exactly as it had been in 1924. Alongside stood an equally fine Rolls-Royce Phantom I of 1928, bodied by Hooper & Company.

After the sheer excitement of finding such exceptional cars, I was ready for a little light relief.

Coming out of the workshop, we saw in an adjacent compound the remains of two aeroplanes. With a bit of clowning around, we took it in turns to sit in the cockpit of one of them and take a photograph. We knew little about aircraft then, but we did recognise one as a British fighter and we could see through the cowling that it was powered by a Rolls-Royce Merlin engine. There were no wings and no covering to the fuselage – just a network of tubes.

Must be a Spitfire we said to each other. When I got home I put the photo in my album.

Rescuing a Hero

CHAPTER 1

That's not a Spit, that's a Hurricane!

I N November 1993 my wife Polly and I went to stay with friends in Canberra, Australia's capital city, for a month. Polly thought it would be fun to skydive, but I made it clear that there was little more boring for a husband than to sit on a draughty airfield waiting for his wife to float down and then fly up again. So we agreed to find an airfield where she could skydive and I could learn to fly.

Finding such a spot near Australia's capital was not easy, so in the end we both learnt to fly a light aircraft. Skydiving was put on hold. We quickly became hooked on flying but did not stay long enough in Australia to get our private pilots' licences. On returning home to the UK, Polly continued her training and soon gained her licence. Talking to one of her instructors, Pete Thorn, I found that he had flown on the Battle of Britain Memorial Flight and spent his early years working on Lancasters. I remembered that photograph I had taken in Banaras eleven years earlier.

When I showed Pete the picture of the 'Spitfire', he laughed. "That's not a Spit, that's a Hurricane," he said. How interesting, I thought. Even I knew that the Hurricane played a major part in the Battle of Britain and today is much rarer than a Spitfire. I began to read up on the Hawker Hurricane. Did this plane really save Britain in its hour of need in 1940? The more I discovered about Hurricanes, the more I was fascinated.

In March 1994 I found myself back in Australia. Not this time on holiday for I had been given an eighteen month contract to start the Australian arm of a close friend's UK publishing company. I went back to the Canberra flying school and this time completed my PPL. Polly and I started flying little Cessnas and Pipers around south-east Australia. "This flying lark is just amazing," I said to myself. Polly was totally hooked and now added 'retractable' to her licence. It wasn't long before she was training for her instrument rating.

In my Canberra office I had a file labelled 'Hurricane'. I found myself continually peeping at the photograph taken in 1982. A Hurricane – what a rebuild project that could be. Rather naively, rebuilding a Second World War fighter from what appeared to be a pile of scrap held no fears. After all, I had totally restored, mainly with my own hands, some ten vintage cars in my time, including four Rolls-Royces. What a challenge it would be to resurrect a flying machine with a Merlin engine conceived by that master of all engineers, Sir Henry Royce.

Australia was an amazing experience for us. The warmth and hospitality of the members of the Rolls-Royce Owners' Club and the 20 Ghost Club were overwhelming. We were even lent a 1911 Silver Ghost and a 1934 Bentley to use for the duration of our stay. We toured with club members through much of eastern Australia. The Aussies think nothing of driving their seventy and eighty-year-old cars flat out across miles of bush, dirt roads and all. Those early products of Rolls-Royce just seem to take the punishment.

In the middle of our Australian stay, John Fasal arrived and we spent a week assembling the text and pictures for his two-volume work *The Edwardian Rolls-Royce*. We spoke to the curator at The Australian War Memorial Museum where they have one of the best remaining Lancaster bombers, but were told that no Hurricanes remained in Australia. In fact only one ever went there (V7476) and it was used in a training role.

For the last six weeks of our time in Australia, Polly and I hired a single-engined Piper Dakota and flew right around the periphery of the sub-continent, over outback and desert – but that is another story!

So this flying thing was beginning to dominate our lives, and, frankly, I was getting a little bored with old motor cars. In addition to spending most of my spare time restoring Rolls-Royces in the 1980s and early 1990s, I had paid several more visits to India. In John's company I continued to track down and even repair Rolls-Royces on behalf of their princely owners, but never went back to Banaras.

By late 1995 I felt I had to do something about this nagging idea. I was determined to see if I could rescue the Banaras Hurricane.

I had begun to acquire a library of Hurricane books and videos. I studied the various marks of plane and engine. I took the 1982 photo to a Hurricane expert. How careful I had to be not to let on where it was. Fortunately the picture showed a rather unexciting building in the background such as one might find in an eastern block country. My expert assumed it was taken in Russia. His eyes lit up. "This is the most complete unrestored Hurricane I have seen in years," he said. I was amazed that such a pile of bits could be regarded as 'complete'. "It is an absolute must for restoration. You have so much of the basic structure and all the fittings." So my excitement rose.

John and I arrived at Varanasi, the modern name for Banaras, on 5 January 1996. Things had deteriorated in the city since our last visit. The roads were rougher, the traffic was solid and the resultant pollution left a haze over the sky, masking out the Indian sunshine. Two hundred thousand pilgrims a day are said to visit Banaras. Pedestrians, pigs, cows, donkeys, goats and chickens competed for road space with ox carts, cycle rickshaws, auto-rickshaws, motor bikes, jeeps, cars and overladen trucks. Amongst this lot, the women still managed to look beautiful in their saris. And most of the men, if not wearing dhotis, wore smartly pressed trousers. The school children bubbled with energy. Everyone was going somewhere, as only they do in India.

But would the aircraft still be there? We had had one report that it had disappeared. Again we were momentarily lost in the vastness of the university. Then, rounding a wall, there it was

The aircraft pictured on the first of our 1996 visits to Banaras. Comparison with the picture taken in 1982 shows substantial further deterioration with the canopy now just visible on the ground under the front of the centre section.

just as it had been fourteen years earlier. By now a jungle had grown around it. A tree, which in our original photograph had been a small shrub, now towered 18 feet into the air, its 10-inch trunk almost touching the nose of the Hurricane.

At our cursory visit in 1982 we saw only a fuselage with engine and cowlings. Now to our great excitement we found the wings lying a few feet away, and beyond them the propeller. Indeed the remains of the entire aircraft seemed scattered around the compound. The wings were fairly complete, but the tailplane pretty well rotted away. The fuselage stood on its undercarriage, although by now the ground had risen over wheel axle height. The tailwheel was similarly disappearing. Although the instruments were all smashed, the cockpit area looked to have most of its fixtures and fittings. Even the flare tube for night landings was in place.

The Director of the Institute of Technology gave us permission to view the two Rolls-Royces which we had seen on our previous visit, and also to look at the aircraft. The hunt was on to identify which model of Hurricane it was. The Mark III plate on the Merlin engine showed it to be a Hurricane I. A call to a splendid chap in England, who tracks the minutiae of aircraft, told us that the markings on a plate attached to the remnants of the tailplane – 'DRG D73531 RAS/41H/94903' – indicated that the tailplane was built by Hawker, but that the number 'DRLM

G-5-92301' affixed to the diagonal structural tube in the cockpit meant that the aeroplane had been built at the Gloster Aircraft factory. No other identification could be found.

We wandered through the engineering department, lined with lathes and milling machines which had been the latest technology in the 1930s. We came upon a number of radial aero engines still in their original crates and then, lying neglected in a corner, a Rolls-Royce Griffon 66. Griffon 66s were only fitted to Mark XIX photo-reconnaissance Spitfires, but the engine could be usefully rescued with the Hurricane.

Before leaving England I had checked on the whereabouts of all known surviving Hurricanes. Thankfully the Banaras Hurricane was not on the list. But there were said to be two other Hurricanes in India, one at the Indian Air Force Museum at Palam adjacent to New Delhi airport, the other at Patna. We got chatting to the restaurant manager at our hotel in Banaras who turned out to be a graduate of Patna Business School. There being little further we could do in Banaras, we set off for Patna, 235 kilometres away. In the evening we called on His Highness the Maharaja of Hathwa, whose family had owned a Rolls-Royce Phantom II.

In the morning we leapt aboard a cycle rickshaw in search of the Director of the Patna Business School, to whom we had been given an introduction by his former pupil, our hotel restaurant manager. After pedalling furiously around the city we found the Director about to chair a conference entitled 'Women in Computing'. We explained that we were trying to find an old aircraft reputedly stored at the Indian Air Force in Patna. He made some phone calls, finally tracking down an army general who knew the head of the local air force station.

In conversation with the Director, I had indicated that I had been a publisher in Oxford. Before we could take our leave, I found myself swept along by the Director and his entourage and ushered onto the stage at one end of a long conference hall and asked to take a seat next to him. The sight which greeted me I shall never forget. Here in front gazing up at us were several hundred young ladies in their saris creating the most glorious carpet of colour. It quite took my breath away.

Along with the other eight members of the conference table, I was garlanded by three attractive young girls. The Director asked the first VIP to make a speech of welcome which lasted twenty minutes. Another worthy spoke for fifteen minutes. Then a lecturer read out a speech of welcome from the State Minister which took half an hour. The Director himself stood up and welcomed the delegates for a further fifteen minutes.

While all this was going on, John was not being very helpful. He had slipped away to the rear of the hall from where he was pulling faces. I wanted to laugh. He kept pointing to his watch, showing that we would never get to the air force base if I did not leave. But I was trapped on the stage. Then, oh horror, I heard the Director say, "I would now like to ask my very old friend, Peter Vacher from Oxford University, to bless this conference."

What could I do? I was not a professor, I was not from Oxford University. But I could hardly make the appropriate denials without the Director losing face. I stumbled to my feet, mumbled something about bringing greetings from Oxford, spouted some nonsense about how the Internet was opening up opportunities for women in computing, and sat down. Within twenty seconds I had made my apologies and fled. Needless to say, correspondence from John to myself has ever since been addressed to 'Professor Peter Vacher'!

We were most warmly welcomed by Wing Commander Joseph Sekhar at the Bihta Air Force Base near Patna. He introduced us to his charming family and we stayed to lunch. There was great excitement as we were driven down the massive runway to greet two microlights whose pilots were flying from Delhi to Calcutta. We had singularly failed to find any trace of a Hurricane at the air base, but one of the microlight pilots told us of three Spitfires he had personally seen in the jungle adjacent to Burma. He suggested that we might like to contact the 8th Assam Rifles Regiment in Shillong from where we could lead an expedition of recovery. O adventurous reader, the Spitfires are certainly still there! However, for your protection you might also like to take the 12th and the 15th Assam Rifles with you.

Upon our return to Delhi we arranged to visit the Hurricane in the Indian Air Force Museum at Palam. This turned out to be a totally complete Mark I, one of the first batch of forty Canadian-built Hurricanes and almost certainly the only surviving Hurricane Mark I built by the Canadian Car and Foundry Corporation. Ultimately CCF were to build a total of 1,451 Hurricanes of various marks. The RAF numbers painted on the fuselage, AB832, are totally bogus, so we vowed on our next visit to establish its true identity, helped by a plate in the cockpit which showed the manufacturer's number CCF/41H/4026. Could it be the twenty-sixth Canadian Hurricane?

We subsequently confirmed the museum aircraft to be P5202.

CHAPTER 2 Negotiations Start

FEBRUARY to June 1996 was a period of inactivity. How should we approach Banaras Hindu University? Stories are legion of the pitfalls of western commercial companies doing business with India. What would be involved for a UK individual trying to purchase a piece of RAF hardware abandoned in India from a group of academics?

Over the years John Fasal had built up good relationships among major industrialists in India, as well as his earlier contacts with the maharajas. Although still revered by their local populations, the maharajas are today not necessarily much respected outside their immediate states. So we talked to a shipping magnate in Bombay. His advice was not encouraging. He said that the university would never be allowed to sell the pile of scrap without permission from the Indian Institute of Technology, the Civil Aviation Authority, the Indian Air Force and any number of other government bodies. Additionally, tenders for the scrap would have to be sought. He knew it would take much time.

I thought I knew better.

In July 1996 John set off on one of his frequent Indian travels. I asked him to call at Banaras and make an offer directly to the university. We had not got a clue as to where to pitch the offer. Should it be 30,000 rupees (about £500) which might be its maximum scrap value in India, or should it be a figure towards what one might have to offer for an historic fighter, albeit in scrap condition, in the UK? In the end we decided on the latter, which meant a very high price in rupees. Although this was the most honest course, the high figure we placed on these remains was to lead to all sorts of problems.

When John arrived at BHU he was warmly welcomed by the Director of the university's Institute of Technology, but was promptly advised that any approval for sale would have to go before the Vice-Chancellor. This was a bit of a shock. One could hardly imagine the Vice-Chancellor of Oxford University, BHU's equivalent in England, being concerned about a pile of old scrap. Anyway, John managed to fix an appointment with him. Getting to his office resembled breaking into Fort Knox. A team of soldier-looking types guarded the wrought iron gates carrying their Lee Enfield rifles from the Great War. John was a little puzzled as to how the 12-bore cartridges in the belts around their waists would fit the rifles, but perhaps the

John Fasal uses his best toothbrush to reveal a barely readable 'R4118' on the fuselage tail door, the first clue to the aircraft's identity. There was a degree of confusion when 'L2039' was found stamped into the reverse side of the panel. Subsequently 'R4118' was found on a number of components.

average visitor is not aware of such niceties.

The Vice-Chancellor was charming. "Of course you can take the plane away. If it was down to me you could remove the scrap here and now. But . . . . ." And then it started. The whole matter would have to be discussed with other members of the university. This would take some time. "In the meantime, ask Mr Peter to confirm his offer in writing." This I did, to include the spare Griffon 66 engine, pointing out that payment to the university would be made in full before removal. I faxed a copy of my offer to BHU to John in his Banaras hotel. Unfortunately, faxes are very public. I might just as well have taken the front page of the *Times of India*. In fact, later this was to hit the headlines, causing huge difficulties.

You will remember that at this stage we had not established the identity of the Hurricane, beyond knowing that it was a Mk I. In the modern day warbird world, identification of a British military aircraft hinges around its RAF number. With the help of the staff of the engineering department John got down to trying to find its number. The team helped to lift each wing, searching for a number as had been painted on the underside of early Hurricanes. Not a trace could be found, only faded RAF roundels and bits of paint in a tropical livery. We wished afterwards that some timbers had been placed underneath the wings to keep them above the waterline when the monsoon rains came.

John did manage to read the full Merlin engine number, 24927, which was later to prove the final piece in the identification jigsaw. To read it he removed the port engine cowling in the hope that the aircraft's RAF number would be painted inside the cowling. It was common practice for removable panels, such as cowlings, to have the number stencilled on the reverse to aid re-installation on the correct airframe. Alas there was no trace in this case. This episode nearly cost John dear. A huge swarm of wasps flew out of the engine compartment. Operations were suspended while they were smoked out.

This visit, John's fourth to the Hurricane, had produced an engine number and opened negotiations. He left on 22 July. It sounded as if we should have the aircraft in the UK well before the end of 1996. But that was western thinking.

The Vice-Chancellor and his team of secretaries and PAs liked to work late into the evenings. So started a regular stream of telephone calls from England to India at 10 o'clock at night. I rang on 28 July and sent a fax on the 31st. I rang on 7 August to be told that it would take another three weeks to settle the matter. I telephoned again on 23 August to be told that a committee of six senior members of the university had been appointed to look into the matter of selling the aircraft. When I phoned on 30 September no-one would talk to me!

We were getting nowhere, so I sent a fax message that John and I would be arriving at BHU on 12 November to meet the committee with a view to reaching a final agreement. Surely, if we were on the spot, the whole thing could be cleared up.

It was hard to understand why such important pieces of history like the Hurricane, and some of the cars, had been left to rot. Further, on reflection, one seems to do little in India except wonder to behold, and wander to see, faded relics of a glorious past. Does the basic Hindu belief in re-incarnation make one look forward only to attaining perfection and an end in eternal rebirth? If so, maybe we can begin to understand the irrelevance of the past. Why preserve it?

On this visit we had two clear objectives, to establish the Hurricane's identity and to get it back home. From our hotel room we tried to telephone the Vice-Chancellor, but he was in a meeting. After a night spent half awake both from buzzing mosquitoes and snoring from the room next door (understandable as the partition between us and the next occupant did not reach to the ceiling), a further call to the Vice-Chancellor was greeted with 'Not available'. Obviously our persistence over the past eleven months was not producing much effect. We tried another tack. We got our trusty driver, Nasir Ahmed, to take us to the home of the Director of the Institute of Technology at the university (not to be confused with the Indian Institute of Technology which controls much of education throughout India). In the intervening months the Director had retired, but gave us a warm welcome. He said that we would have to talk to his successor. We went off to see the Hurricane.

Penetrating oil is not easy to find in India, but brake fluid does just as well. We knew from our previous trips that getting the cowlings off the aeroplane would be difficult, with dozens of rusty fasteners to be freed off. We went armed with an oil can and poured liberal quantities of brake fluid into the fasteners and anything else we thought we might have to loosen now or in the future. The RAF number just had to be stencilled inside one of those engine covers. Beyond that which John had removed on his last visit, we had one further one free after an hour. Not a trace of a number. So now we would have to get that large top cowling off. So far the fastenings had loosened without too much trouble. But now one refused to budge. Perched on top it was not easy to get a good purchase on the screwdriver. "Leave it for a bit," said John. We turned our attention to the tailwheel which had all but disappeared beneath the mud. We managed to lift the whole of the rear end and settle the wheel on a stone. That would keep it in the dry.

Our attention reverted to the top cowl. At last it was free and we could see its underside. Still no number! Where could we look now? John went around the back to have a look, and his foot landed on something hard. Bending down, he lifted from the mud a piece of metal of a size about twelve by eighteen inches. As one side bore the remains of similar colouring to the wings, it must be from the Hurricane. Everywhere in India there is a stream running close by. In most cases it doubles as a sewer, but John was so excited that he was soon washing the mud off the piece of aluminium – and there was a number, though difficult to read at this stage.

We packed up our things and rushed back to the hotel. Under the tap in the bathroom we used a toothbrush to carefully brush away the mud and a little paint. It was somewhat crudely painted, but here was a number R4113 or was it R4118? I had Frank Mason's book on the Hurricane with me. Both numbers came from Mk I aircraft from the second batch built by the Gloster Aircraft Company during 1940. From a kiosk in the bazaar I put through a call to my friend in the UK. He said it would only take a moment to look up his list and determine which number it must be. He pointed out that very few Mk Is went to India, so one of the numbers could be eliminated. But wait, the list showed that both R4113 and R4118 had gone to India. Indeed the only Hurricanes of the hundred in the 'R' series to go to India were R4113 and R4118. R4113 was 'struck off charge' in July 1944. R4118 was 'converted to Ground Instructional' in October 1944 and 'struck off charge' on 1 January 1947. If it was a ground instructional aircraft and now lying at a university, perhaps it was more likely to be R4118. The more we scrubbed with the toothbrush, the more it looked like an 8. Then we saw another number. Stamped onto the front of the panel was L2039. Well, we were not going to resolve the fighter's identity sitting in northern India, so we slipped the panel into my suitcase for further research.

CHAPTER 3 Unwelcome Publicity

I COULD hardly wait to return to England to establish the Hurricane's identity. We had a choice of L2039, R4113, R4118 or none of these. I began by examining the records of L2039. This was an early Mk I converted to a Sea Hurricane Mk IA for the Fleet Air Arm in the latter part of 1941. In 1939, during the 'phoney war', it had crashed at Tangmere whilst flown by 501 Squadron. After repair it went, in July 1940, to 242 Squadron commanded by Douglas Bader and served in the Duxford Wing during the Battle of Britain. It moved in September 1940 to 73 Squadron, being used for the night defence of London. The aircraft was severely damaged on 27 September. After repairs at Austins, it moved to 27 MU (maintenance unit), then to 48 MU and finally to 52 MU before passing to the Fleet Air Arm. It travelled with 804 Squadron to Gibraltar on HMS *Ariguani* in October 1941 but was back at David Rosenfield Ltd, a part of the Civilian Repair Organisation, by June 1942. It was last mentioned as being at Crail on the Firth of Forth in October 1943. One thing is for certain, L2039 never went to India. Further research would establish how the panel, which we had now identified as the tailwheel inspection door, clearly stamped L2039, came to be fitted to our Indian aircraft.

Having eliminated L2039, I turned my attention to R4113 as being the next least likely identity. This had arrived in India in June 1943 and was struck off charge in July 1944. Aircraft in India recorded as being 'struck off charge' from mid-1944 were invariably scrapped locally, with some parts such as engines retained for possible further use. It was unlikely that R4113 survived, but there was no conclusive proof of its demise.

The roughly painted number on the door was still hard to read. Then we had a stroke of luck. My mother-in-law was a near neighbour of Air Commodore Hugh Probert, formerly head of Air Historical Branch at the Ministry of Defence. The history of each military aircraft is recorded on a Form 78. These are stored at the defence ministry, but microfilm copies are kept for general access at the Public Record Office at Kew. On prints from the microfilm it was not possible to read the Air Ministry engine number. Hugh kindly went to the Air Historical Branch and had sight of the original Form 78. He was able to clearly read the engine number A167621, written in pencil. As aircraft had frequent engine changes, the practice had been adopted of writing the numbers in pencil.

I then asked Mike Evans and Peter Kirk at Rolls-Royce at Derby to delve into their Merlin archives. From John Fasal's earlier visit to Banaras we knew that the engine fitted to the aircraft was Rolls-Royce number 24927. Fortunately Rolls-Royce had always tried, although frequently in vain, to correlate their own engine numbers with the Air Ministry engine numbers. They told me, to my great excitement, that 24927 and A167621 were one and the same engine. As A167621 was recorded on the Form 78 of R4118 and 24927 was on the engine of the Hurricane at Banaras, we had conclusively confirmed its identity. Later cleaning of the engine data plate revealed the AM number A167621 in addition to the RR number 24927.

It was now possible to establish much of the aircraft's history. More of that anon. I began to suspect that there would be plenty of time for detailed research whilst trying to prise the aeroplane out of India.

Apart from gathering enough clues to find the Hurricane's identity, our visit of March 1996 yielded few results. Everything went quiet. Then suddenly out of the blue there appeared, on 11 March 1997, an advertisement in the *Times of India*, Bombay and Delhi editions; and in *The Hindu*, Madras edition. Banaras Hindu University were offering for sale by tender a Hawker aircraft and cylinder engine in scrap condition. Of course I was immediately apprehensive that the advertisement would be seen by enthusiasts in India, and worse, around the world. Anyway, I sent off my tender post-haste.

When Hurricanes were sent for major overhaul, the front port side of the fuselage frame was stamped with the RAF serial number. Upon stripping the airframe, discovery of this number was the final confirmation of the aircraft's identity.

BANARAS HINDU UNIVERSITY

Following items are available for sale on "as is where is" basis.
Item (1) Hawker Aircraft Sr. No. D57 580 G5-92301 V-12 Cylinder Engine Type - One no.
Item (2) V-12 Cylinder Engine Block No. HHB-9355-16A 66, 27-15 AM Block No. GN 8012/3 GSJ - 710 Head No. GN 10633/1 GHL 630 - One No.
Interested parties may inspect the items in the Department of Mechanical Engineering, I.T., B.H.U., Varanasi, on any working day and quote their prices in sealed cover. The quotations be addressed to "The Head, Department of Mechanical Engineering, Institute of Technology, Banaras Hindu University, Varanasi - 221 005" so as to reach latest by 31st March, 1997.

The original advertisement which appeared in three national Indian newspapers offering the aircraft for sale by tender.

Fortunately I had been able to open up another line of communication. The Director of the Department of Mechanical Engineering, in whose charge the aircraft resided, was keen on technology and had himself hooked up to the Internet. He sent me an e-mail on 20 March:

"Thank you for responding to our advertisement regarding the sale of the Hawker Aircraft and cylinder engine. We will wait for bids from other parties, if any, till 31 March 1997. I have talked to the Vice-Chancellor in this regard. I hope that we shall be able to finalise the matter by the first week of April 1997."

A further e-mail of 4 April led us to believe that we had secured the aircraft: "I am pleased to inform you that your quotation for the aircraft and engine has been accepted by the committee in its meeting held on 1 April 1997. You will be receiving detailed information shortly."

Fired up by the news, I dashed to Bombay on 7 April and checked with the shippers as to customs' requirements. I was told I would have to produce the following:

1. Permission from the Directorate of Civil Aviation allowing the export.
2. Registration book of the aircraft.
3. Certificate from an aeronautical engineer showing the airworthiness or otherwise of the aircraft, together with a fair value in its present state.
4. Evidence of payment of foreign exchange.
5. Invoices, packing lists etc.

From Bombay I flew to Delhi to the northern offices of the shipping company. I was rapidly learning that one does not get anywhere in India without knowing someone that knows someone. In this case the manager at the shippers knew the Director of Airworthiness at the Civil Aviation Authority. Parting with five rupees, I took an auto-rickshaw through New Delhi's wide streets to the CAA. On the third floor, hidden behind mountains of files, I met Mr Singh. "No problem," he said. "The aircraft appears never to have been on the Indian civil aviation register, so we can have no objection to the export."

The shipping agent then introduced me to a friend who knew an engineer who would give the necessary technical evaluation and valuation. Things seemed to be going well.

I flew home to organise the team to come to India to dismantle and pack the fighter in a container.

My hopes were soon dashed. I tried to find out from the university to which department the payment should be sent. I needed to make the collection arrangements. I could get no response to my faxes and e-mails. I subsequently learned that allegations had been made against the Vice-Chancellor that he was receiving baksheesh. Nothing could have been further from the truth. All correspondence had been on the very public fax in his busy office. He was a man of great integrity and was sorely hurt by the suggestions being made.

A scurrilous article appeared in the *Hindustan Times* of 11 September 1997, implying, without actually saying so, that shoddy dealings had been going on. I was described as a 'vintage car dealer' which I was not. The piece stated: "The process of the deal, in which a foreign national is involved, has created an atmosphere of suspicion in the campus. Moreover, the selling of the aircraft which has antique value, has also raised many an eyebrow."

Old warplane becomes apple of British dealer's eye

Binay Kumar Singh
Varanasi

A British dealer in vintage motor cars has offered 25,000 pund sterling to purchase the old aircraft and spare engine lying in the premises of the Institute of Technology (IT), Banaras Hindu University (BHU).

In his urgent message to the BHU Vice-Chancellor, Dr Hari Gautam, the dealer, Mr Peter Vacher expressed his keenness to buy this aircraft of the Second World War period.

The letter, which was faxed on July 20, 1996, was forwarded to the director of IT, registrar and finance officer (FO) by the V-C for comments.

As told by many others that the aircraft was donated by the Royal Indian Air Force to the BHU after the Second World War for study purpose. It is said that BHU obtained the aircraft with the help of the initiatives taken by the then Prof Charles King and Prof Phil Pott of Benaras Engineering College (IT was not established at that time) in 1944.

However, the vice-chancellor of BHU, Prof Hari Gautam is ignorant about the source from where the aircraft was obtained. Prof. Gautam, when contacted, said that he did not know from where the aircraft had come.

He, mentioning that it was use-less, said that all the rules and regulations would be followed in selling of the aircraft. The final decision is yet to be taken in this regard, he added.

The member of the executive council of BHU, Prof HN Tripathi categorically denied that the aircraft of Royal Indian Air Force was being sold. According to him, the scrap of another plane, which crashed during the World War II, is being auctioned.

He also mentioned that the executive council of the university had given the right to the V-C to sell the aircraft.

On the other hand the finance officer (FO) of the university, Mr Prabhat Chandra was not certain about the fact that the aircraft was donated to the BHU. He is of the opinion that it was purchased by the university for its flying club. The head of the department of mechanical engineering Mr BB Bansal also accepts that the aircraft is being sold because it is use-less and cannot be repaired.

He also mentioned that tenders were invited from different parties about three months ago which had been sent to the V-C for final decision. He refused to reveal the total number of tenders and the name of the parties describing it as confidential.

According to the information received from the public relation office of the university, an adver-tisement was published in March 11, 1997 issue of the Mumbai edition of 'The Times of India' for the purpose.

Interestingly, the advertisement for the sale of the aircraft was published in March 1997 whereas the negotiation of the deal had already started before July 20, 1996.

Mr John Fasal, the friend of the vintage motor cars dealer, Peter Vacher met the V-C, Dr Gautam through Dr Talukdar before July 20 to discuss with him for the possible purchase of the aircraft alongwith the spare engine which he (Peter) had already seen during his visit to the city eight months ago.

On his friend's suggestion, as the letter reads, Peter Vacher contacted Dr Gautam to confirm that he (Peter) was very keen to bring this pile of scrap back to life. He, in his letter, clearly mentioned that he would bear the shipping costs and carrying out the necessary export formalities.

He would also make payment to the university in full from his bank in the UK to the university's bank in India before the delivery of the aircraft.

The process of deal, in which a foreign national is involved, has created an atmosphere of suspicion on the campus.

Moreover, the selling of the aircraft which also has antique value, has also raised many an eyebrow.

The article which appeared in the Hindustan Times *on September 11 1997.*

The problem was that most deals involving government bodies in India seem to have become so corrupt that no one is prepared to believe that a transaction can be completed without bribery.

The Vice-Chancellor dealt with the situation by refusing to communicate on the matter at all. He left it to his secretaries and PAs, of which there were many, to speak to me when I telephoned.

By October 1997 it was clear that the hopes raised by acceptance of my tender in April had heralded a false dawn. As a westerner I was not equipped to deal with this situation in an Asian culture. I had a cousin in Bombay and sought his advice. For the last thirty years he had been well served by a lawyer.

I decided to take the lawyer into my confidence. I poured out my frustrations. He agreed to try to bring the deal to a conclusion. He was well connected, including knowing one of the Council members at Banaras Hindu University. He was soon getting the University Council to confirm approval of the sale. He also found that permission had to be granted by the Human Resources Development Ministry and set about obtaining it.

Then another spanner was thrown in the works. In December the Vice-Chancellor received a letter from Headquarters, Central Air Command, Indian Air Force which read: "Your university is requested not to dispose off *(sic)* Government property without obtaining clearance from the Ministry of Defence/Air Headquarters. You are requested to forward photographs.......and serial numbers....." At this point the Vice-Chancellor clearly thought that as the aircraft had lain in the compound for the last fifty years, it would be less hassle if it remained there for the next fifty. He did not reply to the letter from the Air Force, so no one did anything to unblock the Ministry of Defence embargo. My lawyer was at least able to have a quiet chat with the Vice-Chancellor and so discovered how upset he had been over the newspaper article and why he was taking no further part in the sale process.

The frustration was getting unbearable. We had to get movement somehow. So John and I took off again for Bombay. We met our lawyer who confirmed that no-one had communicated with the Air Headquarters. In his opinion, the only solution was for Air Force staff to be persuaded to see the aircraft for themselves and take whatever details they might need. Our lawyer's contacts worked again. He had a nephew whose father was an air vice-marshal. He arranged for him to instruct the staff at Air Headquarters in Allahabad to carry out the inspection. This could take for ever, so John and I decided to go to the headquarters and see if we could get things moving. Of course no-one had given us any contact number in Allahabad so we dropped in on the Indian Air Force offices in Bombay and spent an hour with an air commodore who, after the customary cup of tea, produced the Allahabad telephone number.

On our way in the taxi we passed a slogan painted on a sign. Pithy sayings are plastered all over Indian cities. This one read: "Politicians either do not speak, or those that speak speak rubbish." My favourite is over the station master's office at Jodhpur: "It is nice to be important, but it is more important to be nice."

After a couple of days in Bombay we flew on to Banaras via Delhi. On our plane John recognised the Vice-Chancellor. We greeted him, but he was clearly uneasy in case anyone saw us together – harking back to that wretched newspaper article. He nevertheless seemed happy for us to talk to the Director of the Department of Mechanical Engineering in whose charge was the aircraft. Our by now established driver, Nasir, met us at the airport and propelled his Maruti at breakneck speed towards the university, scattering bullock carts, pigs, bicycles and rickshaws to left and right. We outlined our programme to the head of mechanical engineering, who could not have been more helpful. We bit the bullet and put a call through to Air Headquarters at Allahabad which is 110 km from Banaras.

In India, either you beat the system, or the system beats you. That day it was the latter.

The local MP had got into an argument with a member of the staff of the telecommunications company, the equivalent of our BT. Not only were words bandied, but punches thrown. The entire telephone network was silenced by a strike of its employees. There was no way we could get through to the squadron leader to whom we had to speak. I was pretty fired up by now and said to John that if we could not get him on the telephone we would drive to Allahabad to see him the next morning. The following day was a Sunday, so I presumed that all would be quiet at the air base and that the squadron leader would have time to spend with us.

Our three and a half hour trip was not exactly relaxing. Indian trucks conventionally 'play chicken' down the single lane tarmac strip in the middle of the road. If you are not as big as them you very quickly veer off the tarmac

Squadron Leader Rajender and his team were sent by the Air Ministry to inspect the aircraft, to confirm its services were not needed by them.

onto the dirt, leaving it as late as possible to show how brave you are. Trucks usually hold off overtaking each other until a blind bend, going through with all horns blaring. Trucks upside down, trucks on their sides, trucks head on with others litter the road. I drove for a few miles but my nerves were on edge. I did not have the guts to overtake in the face of oncoming traffic. If we were going to reach Allahabad that day I had to hand back to Nasir.

At last we arrived at the guard room. Passes were elaborately written out. We were about to call the squadron leader on the internal telephone when all hell broke loose. White-gloved military policemen appeared from nowhere, everyone, except us, stood to attention and saluted. A motorcade swept through the gates of the base. In the jeeps were commandos, guns at the ready. We just could not believe it – we had timed our arrival to coincide with the annual headquarters inspection by the air chief marshal! What was more, the man we had come to see was in charge of the banqueting arrangements.

Not surprisingly we had to hang around, but by early afternoon the charming squadron leader had asked us home to tea. Things worked out quite well as the air commodore commanding the IAF Selection Board at Banaras was at that moment in Allahabad for the air chief marshal's visit. The squadron leader introduced us to his CO, a group captain who arranged for us to be in touch with the air commodore upon his return to Banaras.

That night we borrowed an old Remington typewriter from the hotel reception. We drafted letters from BHU to the IAF confirming the university's willingness to part with the aircraft, and from the IAF in Banaras to Air Headquarters in Allahabad giving relevant frame and engine numbers. True to their word, two days later we collected two young squadron leaders from the Selection Board offices and drove in their Jeep, complete with blue flashing light, to the campus. We picked our way between the two wings on one side, the propeller on the other and the remains of the canopy trapped by a tree growing through the middle of it. They examined what was left of the airframe, confirmed the details and such numbers as were visible, and said that they would make their report to Air Headquarters. They left us in no doubt that we were completely nuts to imagine that we could restore this pile of bits to airworthy condition.

There was not much more we could achieve in Banaras until the IAF officers had made their report to Allahabad and Allahabad had advised the Ministry of Defence in Delhi. We knew from bitter experience that this would take time. We decided to visit old friends in Jodhpur, including His Highness, the Maharaja. There we uncovered a remarkable archive relating to the Jodhpur Flying Club and the RAF in India from 1931 to 1954 – but that is another story.

CHAPTER 4 Monsoon

THINGS seemed to be hotting up. On 16 July 1998 my lawyer wrote: "To my belief even the approval of the Ministry is ready." It was time to plan another visit to tie up the purchase and pay over the money to the university. There was one snag looming on the horizon. The Vice-Chancellor's term of office was three years and that was up on 2 August. This meant he might or might not be elected for an extension for another three years. The Director of the Department of Mechanical Engineering sent me an e-mail: "If the Vice-Chancellor stays back, then your visit will be worth. If a new V/C is coming, then you may have to delay your visit until he settles. Let us hope for the best." I could see two years of negotiation going up in a puff of smoke. It was vital that we conclude the deal before the Vice-Chancellor's departure.

John and I arrived to a hot, humid Bombay and got soaked on the way from the airport. Goodness knows where the water came from, but there was not a dry spot in the back of that PAL. Bombay teems with its PAL taxis built around an early 60s Fiat design. Riding in them is always exhilarating. One tends to judge one example from another by the degree of play in the steering, usually between six and twenty inches.

The following morning the lawyer assured us that everything in Banaras was in order. We called on the shipping company. Yes, they could send an open-top container to the university. It could be packed and sealed there so that there would be no further customs' involvement as it came back through Bombay.

On arrival at Banaras our usually trusty driver, Nasir, was nowhere to be seen. From a call to his boss we discovered that our airmail announcing our arrival had only just reached the office. Nasir was in Agra, but a car would pick us up in thirty minutes. We drove directly to the university only to find that our friend, the Director of the Department of Mechanical Engineering, had just left. Undaunted, we found his house and were given a great welcome. We discussed our plans for the following day.

By the time we left, it was nearly 9 pm but, knowing the hours that the Vice-Chancellor kept, I thought it worth a try to see him. However he was being elusive again. The situation with him was not looking too good. Another newspaper article had appeared on 24 April 1998 in the Hindi language newspaper *Rashtrya Sahara*. My Hindi is non-existent but the Director's

FROM HINDI NEWSPAPER "RASHTRYA SAHARA" by Brijesh Kumar Singh on or about 24 April 1998.

Two gentlemen came from England to purchase aircraft which is of historical importance and was used in the Second World War.

From reliable sources we have come to know that Peter Vacher of Britain has a hobby of collecting antiques and that particular hobby has brought him to Varanasi. Benaras Hindu University administration sometime back wanted to sell the aforesaid aircraft. The deal was almost final when the press and others raised their voice against it. In the moth of September last year Defence Ministry and Ministry of Information and Broadcasting (Human Resources Development Ministry) raised objections against it and the matter subsided for a time.

The reliable sources said that on 18 April Peter Vacher and John Fasal reached Varanasi. They went to hotel Taj at 1.20 p.m. and hired room no. 128. They were supposed to reach there on 20 April and they already had this booking. They stayed a day longer up to 21 April in Varanasi. They then extended it for a further day, the 22nd. On 22 April they flew to Jodhpur.

According to reliable sources Peter Vacher and John Fasal went to BHU to finalise the deal for the aircraft. For this they used Nepal Tours car. According to the sources they generally use Nepal Tours car and driver Nasir for visiting Varanasi. Nasir is regarded as trustworthy by Fasal. According to the sources Peter Vacher and John Fasal are driven by Nasir in car No. UP65H 1467 and went to BHU twice or three times.

According to the sources Peter Vacher and John Fasal went to the Department of Mechanical Engineering to get the required information and for inspecting the aircraft. The matter came to light when some people saw them inside the boundary examining the aircraft and taking photos. A peon of the Department of Mechanical Engineering, who had taken them to the compound, was also with them.

Sources say that when people wanted to get information from the peon, he said that the Head of Department had instructed him to show the aircraft to these persons. He showed his ignorance about the whole matter. According to sources Peter Vacher contacted Prof. M Battacharya, Director of the Institute of Technology on 21 April by telephone and showed his desire to meet. After talking on the telephone, 10 a.m. on 22 April was fixed for their meeting but Peter Vacher could not reach in time and therefore the two could not meet each other.

According to reliable sources Peter Vacher and John Fasal went to meet ex Director of Faculty, Prof. Vikram Singh along with Prof. K. K. Bansal. They also obtained information about the Rolls-Royce cars received by Malviaji (founder of BHU) as a donation, as well as information on the aircraft.

According to sources Peter Vacher is also preparing a catalogue of Rolls-Royce cars. According to reliable sources, after obtaining the necessary information about the aircraft, Peter Vacher and John Fasal went to the Hotel Pallavi situated in the Hathwa Market on 22 April during their stay in Varanasi. This is the hotel where John Fasal and Peter Vacher stayed in July 1996 and were finalising the deal on the aircraft. According to sources they possibly changed their hotel because their last stay at the Hotel Pallavi became known.

According to sources the deal for the aircraft started in the last month of 1995/ At that time discussion on the sale was held between John Fasal and the then Director of the Institute of Technology. Prof. M. K. D. Thalukdar. The source says that Peter Vacher had sent a fax to the Vice-Chancellor, Prof. Hari Gautam, on 20 July 1996 (fax no. 0123 55366 74) for finalising the deal. In the fax message it was informed that John Fasal was staying at the Hotel Pallavi until 22 July and that the Vice-Chancellor should finalise the deal by contacting him. It was proposed that a donation of £25,000 should be given towards the cost of the aircraft. It was also mentioned in the fax message that he will bear the expenses himself for other formalities and export permission. According to sources it was mentioned in the fax message that the full amount would be deposited in the University account before removing the aircraft. In case required permissions were not received, the deposited money had to be returned back. According to sources, The Vice-Chancellor, referring to the fax message from Peter Vacher, forwarded the letter to the Registrar, Finance Officer and Director of the Institute of Technology for their comments.

The executive council has passed a resolution authorising the Vice-Chancellor to finalise the sale of the aircraft. According to sources the tender was advertised in the newspapers to avoid any controversy after the deal for the sale of the aircraft is finalised.

wife had kindly translated it for me. 'Reliable sources' quoted our movements in the previous April step by step, even giving the registration number of the car in which we were driven. The accuracy was disconcerting. Again no accusations were made, but there was plenty of innuendo. With the Vice-Chancellor awaiting re-appointment, his sensitivity to the issue was understandable.

The following day was something new for me. Although I had now visited India seven times, I had never arrived in the monsoon. It poured and it poured. The streets of Banaras became running rivers – and water was not the only thing that swept down the roads! Banaras in the rush hour is something else. I could not believe the good-natured way in which humanity waded before us. The cars threw great waves into the tiny shops in the bazaar. The auto-rickshaw drivers came to a grinding halt with water all over their ignition. The cycle rickshaw wallahs were the best off – they just kept pedalling. For them the trade was brisk, especially among the ladies of wealthier husbands who did not like spoiling their brilliantly coloured saris. The school kids were equally determined that the monsoon

A depressing experience to see how the aircraft, and especially the wings, were submerged every monsoon.

rains would not stop them getting to school, even though the smaller ones were up to their waists in brown water.

Following the adverse publicity, the Director of Mechanical Engineering called the correspondent, Brijesh Kumar Singh from *Rashtrya Sahara,* to set the record straight. He was sent to see the plane to evaluate it for himself. The Director said, "The Institute of Technology is neither a charity nor a museum. If this scrap is thought to be of national historic interest, please take it away to a museum. However," he went on to point out, "as the aircraft was built in a foreign country it could hardly be part of India's heritage." The initially hostile reporter started to write in a more conciliatory vein.

The Director outlined the procedure which had so far been adopted. A committee of six members of the Institute of Technology had been appointed to decide whether the aircraft was in a repairable condition (all things are possible, but since it had been lying outside since 1947 or earlier, repair at the university was unlikely!). If not repairable and no longer required, then the committee had to declare it condemned. A new committee was subsequently formed to approve the decision of the first committee. It was this latter committee that had placed the advertisement in the newspapers. Tenders were opened in the presence of the committee, each of whom signed each tender. In fact only one tender was received (from the author) plus two offers to sell the scrap on behalf of the university. The committee recommended that the aircraft be sold to the author. This recommendation was placed before the Executive Committee of Banaras Hindu University, consisting of three members from BHU, three previous vice-chancellors of other universities and three VIPs. The entire committee drove in two cars to see the pile of scrap. They appointed a sub-committee of two to look into the matter. Subsequently the Vice-Chancellor was authorised to proceed with the sale. One member objected on the grounds that the university could not dispose of something which had been donated, but was overruled.

At BHU our first visit was to the Registrar. He had the usual outer office with six people sitting at an assortment of desks, awaiting instructions from on high. His own office was large, with a huge empty desk. We were motioned into the next room. Here was an even larger desk, six chairs and nothing else. After five minutes the Registrar appeared with his peon carrying his brief case. It would not be acceptable for the Registrar to move it from one office to another.

The Director of Mechanical Engineering explained the purpose of our visit, as it would be the Registrar who would receive the payment. The Registrar nodded, but then said that the matter would have to go before a committee. "But it has already been before three committees!," I wanted to scream. He suggested that we see the Chief Financial Officer as his approval would be required. We took tea and left.

The Chief Financial Officer asked if we would like tea. The last cup had been excellent, so we said yes, please. The officer pointed out that he was not employed by the university, but by the Government of India, to ensure that the finances of the university were run properly. He then told us that the approval of the Internal Audit Officer would be needed, so he was wheeled in. He turned out to be most positive until we explained that the university would have to fill out the export documents. "We are not exporters, that is not possible," he said. Oh well, we thought, we will sort that one out when the time comes.

To see these gentlemen, we had come to the Central Office Building, the main administration block. There were two staircases, one labelled 'FOR GOING UP', the other 'FOR GOING DOWN'. We saw more activity here than elsewhere in the university. Hundreds of secretaries, nearly all male, were moving files from office to office. Files were piled floor to ceiling in almost every office. The Chief Financial Officer had been signing his files when we arrived. His secretary would open one, point to the place where a signature was required, and the officer would sign. This ritual continued whilst the pile of signed files on the floor grew ever larger. I began to wonder if the 'Hawker Aircraft and Cylinder Engine' file would ever emerge from a system in which everyone signs but no-one decides.

In all this to-ing and fro-ing nobody seemed to have heard of the permission from the Ministry of Defence which we had been assured would have reached the university. So we had to get to the Vice-Chancellor. Fortunately it was now dark. We were in an Ambassador, the Indian version of the 1955 Morris Oxford. At one time ubiquitous in India, now new ones are only bought for government officials. Our driver flashed his lights at the gates to the Vice-Chancellor's fortress and miraculously they opened. We swept through and entered the inner sanctum. We were not in the least surprised to be told that he was in a meeting and unavailable. One of his PAs was left to deal the body-blow – no permission had been received.

Panic struck. Was this trip going to be another waste of money, time and effort? I made a frantic call to the lawyer in Bombay. "Where is the permission?" I demanded. He promised to find out. Without the permission from the Ministry of Defence, no-one would progress anything. It also looked increasingly likely that the Vice-Chancellor would be out of a job in a couple of days. Gloom and despondency.

John and I had to cool our heels over the weekend, only to find on the Monday that the permission still had not been sent from Delhi. We were told it would be issued in two days time but that regulations prevented faxing it to BHU. It would have to be delivered via the Indian Air Force internal mail.

By this time we had been re-united with our regular driver, Nasir. He had, of course, been in Banaras all the time. He had changed companies and his old employer was not going to tell us how to find him. We got down to serious motoring through the bazaars with Nasir driving flat out as only he knew how. We saw the Director of the Department of Mechanical Engineering. He shared our view that the permission would be more likely to take two months than two days to arrive.

So that was that, a thoroughly wasted trip in a beastly monsoon season. We returned home, both with a liberal helping of 'Delhi belly'.

CHAPTER 5 Frustration

Permission from the Ministry of Defence, or rather the lack of it, had become a major problem. The arrival on the scene of a new Vice-Chancellor on 27 August 1998 had been expected to delay things even further. But in fact his appointment raised my hopes that here might be a man of action who would get things moving.

Pressure was kept up on our Bombay lawyer to chase said permission. The obstacles were well outlined in his fax of 28 September: "Staff in the Secretariat do not oblige any one in friendship. There are Dussera holidays in Delhi which will be followed by Diwali from 16 October.........." This meant another month's delay.

It was not until mid-November that I realised how naive I had been. Nothing happens in India unless you find the people who know the right person to influence the situation. A client of my lawyer telephoned to say that his brother-in-law was Joint Secretary (General) in the Ministry of Defence and that he could seek the permission if I were to meet him in Bombay and explain what was needed. A promise was given that the permission would arrive in fourteen days. In the event, approval was issued on 22 December but did not reach me until 9 January.

Tele: 3377277

Air Headquarters
Vayu Bhawan
New Delhi-110011

Air HQ/60294/383/MC-2

22 Dec 98

The Vice-Chancellor
Banaras Hindu University
Varanasi - 221 005

SALE OF VINTAGE AIRCRAFT

Sir,

1.   Reference is made to your letter No.VCL/REGR/1739 dated 7 Mar 98 regarding the Sale of Vintage Aircraft.

2.   Your case has been considered at appropriate level at Ministry of Defence and this Headquarters. You are hereby given clearance for the sale of the vintage aircraft.

3.   Kindly acknowledge.

(PV Karapurkar)
Air Cmde
DMA
for ACAS(Lgs)

Among the seven permissions deemed necessary to purchase what was effectively a pile of scrap, this letter came from the Air Force headquarters.

FRUSTRATION

Getting this Hurricane out of India was proving to be a real-life game of snakes and ladders. Armed with permission from the Ministry of Defence, I felt that at last we were at the top of a long ladder and surely there could be few snakes still in our path. Another trip was planned to reach Banaras on 19 January. My fax to the new Vice-Chancellor was replied to by the Registrar: "In this connection I am directed by the Vice-Chancellor to inform you that the University is yet to receive the opinion of the Accountant General, U.P., Allahabad in this connection and the final clearance of the Ministry of Civil Aviation, New Delhi. After the necessary formalities are completed the matter shall be placed before the Executive Council for a final decision in this regard. Therefore, you are requested to kindly bear with us and wait for some more time till the official formalities are completed."

So here were two new snakes to slide down. The university now wanted permissions from the Accountant General and from the Directorate of Civil Aviation. No doubt when we had those permissions, they would think up some others it might be handy to obtain. Anyway, undeterred by the fax, I asked Roy Noble (a friend and expert video photographer) to accompany me to India. Our pleasure at being upgraded to business class on Air India was short-lived when we had to spend nine hours in Bombay Airport awaiting our onward flight to fog-bound Delhi.

Arriving late the following day in Delhi, an acquaintance at an airfreight company, owned by a Parsee family in Bombay, was unbelievably helpful in taking us to the Deputy Director of Airworthiness at the Civil Aviation Authority. To our amazement, the permission was faxed to us in Banaras two days later – the fastest thing to have happened in the entire saga!

Our trusty driver was not at the airport to meet us, but we soon found his dwelling in a Banaras back street. He took us to the university campus where we arrived just in time to see the Vice-Chancellor leaving the central office for his residence half a kilometre away. He sat in an Ambassador with a large red light on the roof and flag fluttering on the bonnet. Heading the procession was a Jeep with five armed police. Bringing up the rear was another Jeep with a further five policemen. Everyone saluted. Perhaps the Vice-Chancellor of Oxford University should be accorded such a display?

The next day we met with the Vice-Chancellor, the Registrar, The Director of the Institute of Technology and the Financial Officer. I outlined to the Vice-Chancellor the history of our negotiations with his predecessor. All was going well until one of the others mentioned the scurrilous articles in the newspapers, whereupon the Vice-Chancellor started looking for excuses. He said that nothing could be done without the approval of the Executive Council. But, I explained, we already had permission from the Executive Council. "Ah," he said, "but now we have a new Executive Council so we must be seeking their permission." "And then," he went on, "we must get the approval of the University Grants Commission." Another snake. I exploded. "This bureaucracy in India is quite ridiculous." "Ah," retorted the Vice-Chancellor, "but who taught us?" "But you have elaborated upon it," I replied. Roy, sitting beside me, could hardly contain himself! We took our leave, vowing to find the names of the Executive Council members and do some quiet lobbying. So, although on this trip we had obtained permission from the CAA, the new Vice-Chancellor had managed to throw up more obstacles.

Of course we never did manage to find out who was on the Executive Council. A strong plea for them to decide on the matter at its meeting on 20 March 1999 produced no result, although we were subsequently given to understand that two of its members were appointed as a sub-committee to look into the matter. Yes, another committee! Still undaunted (could we keep this up?) I pressed our lawyer to try other avenues. It turned out that he knew someone who knew an ex-chief minister in Vishakapatnam who knew the Vice-Chancellor.

Both my lawyer and the chief minister telephoned the Vice-Chancellor.

Hoping that these two might have brought some influence to bear, John Fasal and I planned yet another visit. The university was about to close for the summer vacation so we had to get there before everyone was 'out of station'. A meeting with our lawyer in Bombay elucidated the fact that the Vice-Chancellor wanted to become either chairman of the University Grants Commission or India's ambassador to Japan – his heart hardly lay in his role as Vice-Chancellor of the largest university in Asia.

We had arrived in Banaras at the height of the summer heat with temperatures between 44 and 50°C. As we entered our hotel, John spotted His Highness the Maharaja of Banaras who was Chancellor of Banaras Hindu University. We were soon ushered up to his suite. In conversation it appeared that he knew much of the goings-on at BHU, so he was evidently more than a titular head. He promised to speak to the Vice-Chancellor on our behalf. We then visited the Registrar, presenting to him a banker's draft (made out in favour of the university) for the tendered amount for the aircraft which had been agreed in 1997. Not surprisingly he was not prepared to accept it. Pleadings for us to be allowed to rescue the aircraft before it rotted completely away fell on a smiling face but deaf ears. We did discover, to our surprise, that the Executive Council was meeting that weekend and that the Registrar was secretary to the Council. We asked him to ensure that the aircraft was on the agenda. We again met with a smiling face.

Meanwhile John had heard of another Rolls-Royce Silver Ghost rotting away in a remote village 400 kilometres away. With nothing we could usefully do in Banaras until after the Council meeting, we decided to go and investigate the car. Just as we were driving out of the city, we called on the cousin of the chap who owned the car. It was just as well that we did. The owner was now 'out of station' and had gone to Katmandu. No one else had a key.

Another change of plan and we headed for Patna, in pursuit of Hurricane V6846. This time we were expecting to find it in the Patna Aeronautical College which we were led to believe was in the engineering department of Patna University.

What a perfectly preserved museum the engineering department turned out to be. Rows of shafts and belts were driven by huge stationary engines powered by steam boilers. Row upon row of British machine tools lay under thick dust. We found six students aimlessly practising cutting bits of steel plate with blunt hacksaws. They were the only signs of life across five huge workshops. No sign of a Hurricane here, but there in the corner, partly dismantled, was a Merlin XX engine such as used in a Hurricane II. We recorded the engine number.

There was indeed an Indian Institute of Aeronautics at Patna Airport, but still no Hurricane. A Rolls-Royce Avon engine, and an ex-Indian Air Force Canberra were on display, but otherwise students were being taught solely on light aircraft. The drive back to Banaras took eight hours, mostly in the dark – highly dangerous with our Tata Sumo continually forced off the road by oncoming trucks.

We should have guessed! The Executive Council had been cancelled. We did get to see the Vice-Chancellor again however, surrounded by his staff. The meeting was somewhat acrimonious as I had written a letter saying that we would have to go through the courts if they did not honour the contract made in 1997. He again repeated that nothing could be decided except by the Executive Council. "What a fine man you are, Mr Peter," he smiled, "and how nice to have you here with us." But the pressure applied by the chief minister from Vishakapatnam and our lawyer was clearly getting to him. He asked me to back off! Showing him the banker's draft only produced the retort, "Do you think we need your money?" The meeting did cool down and we left on reasonable terms. But we had achieved precisely nothing.

No matter how impossible things seemed to be, I just could not get R4118 out of my head. No matter that my hair had turned from black, to grey to white. A fax sent to my lawyer in May produced a telephone call early one Sunday morning. He had telephoned the Vice-Chancellor who told him that nothing would be done until he and the chief minister came to see him at Banaras. This they immediately did, to be told that the committee would approve the sale in July," always providing that India and Pakistan are not at war"! Presumably the Hurricane might be needed.

As I later discovered, the Executive Council did indeed approve the sale of the aircraft to me at their July meeting, but that did not mean I could pay for it and take it away. Apparently, under the rules of the university, a decision taken at one meeting had to be ratified by confirming the minutes at the next. So our lawyer wrote that "now there is no impediment in", I would collect after the August meeting, and "I shall be grateful if the university will keep ready the required invoices in triplicate and other documents required by the Government authorities to complete the deal."

Whether or not an Executive Council meeting took place in August as had been indicated to the lawyer, I never did discover. Why was no meeting held in September? Well, you see, the students at the university went on strike. Then the lecturers went on strike. By the time all that was resolved, it was October.

In anticipation of the meeting arranged for 20 October, our lawyer and the chief minister turned up at Banaras (at my expense, of course) on the 21st, to be told that there had regrettably been no meeting held as insufficient members had arrived to form a quorum. Now this was a new excuse. I had expected one, of course, but I thought it to be that in early October the military had staged a coup in Pakistan. I was sure the Hurricane would again be needed.

By now I was convinced that I was being taken for a ride. I sought assurances from the lawyer." The meeting stands adjourned until the beginning of December, but do not worry, everything is in order. I have seen with my own eyes the resolution to sell the aircraft to you."

I swore to myself that either I pulled out of the whole deal, or I went along with it all. I decided to keep everything crossed and keep going.

At the end of January 2000 I heard that the last attempt to hold an Executive Council meeting had ended in a fight. Naturally the minutes of the previous July meeting were not ratified. John Fasal and I set out to Bombay on 1 February in the vain hope that our presence might speed things along. We met with our lawyer who informed us that the problem all along had been that the Vice-Chancellor does not speak Hindi and can only communicate with his staff in English for which, as Head of the Banaras Hindu University, he is not much respected. However I was assured (again) that all would be in place by the end of February and we should expect to be in Varanasi by 6 March to take delivery. We were advised not to go to Varanasi on this trip, so instead we set off to see the British High Commissioner in Delhi to test the waters to see if he could bring pressure to bear on the university if necessary. The Deputy High Commissioner saw us and said he would help with letters as necessary and also use contacts within the British Council. I was loathe to take up these offers as I could see that such intervention could slow down rather than speed up matters.

The Executive Council meetings scheduled for February, March and April did not take place, so it was just as well that I did not bother to prepare to be in Varanasi for 6 March.

Then I heard the good news. The Executive Council met on 18 June and ratified the minutes of the previous July. It had taken nearly a year. I was told to be in Varanasi by 15 July. Not believing that the 15 July would materialise, I set off for India on 26 June. I hung around in Bombay for a week. I agreed my lawyer's fee. I felt very poor. Then the next bombshell was dropped. My lawyer showed me an article which had appeared in the news magazine *India Today*. On the back of a story about one of his lecturers, the Vice-Chancellor was criticised by staff and pupils, and riots were threatened for the start of the new term. There was not likely to be much progress on the sale of a heap of scrap.

On 18 July I rang the Registrar in whose hands the matter had now been placed. He said "There is no problem. All matters have been agreed. We are just waiting for a meeting of the Executive Council." "B-b-but," I answered, "you have ratified the minutes of the July 1999 meeting (at which you agreed the sale) at your meeting on 18 June 2000." "That is correct," he replied, "but now we have to wait for a meeting to ratify the minutes of the meeting at which the minutes of the first meeting were ratified." Instead of crying, I laughed.

Then on 12 August my lawyer advised that the Registrar had just told him that the official acceptance letter from the university had been sent by post to me on 8 August. They could not fax it as it was important. My cousin in Bombay rang to tell us to get out the champagne. I, on the other hand, was quite sceptical. Of course by the end of August no letter had arrived. A further call from my lawyer established that no letter had been sent. Why do they tell you only what you want to hear?

The next message said, "There has been a bit of agitation. But do not worry, your business has been done. You have waited so long another week or so will not make any difference."

CHAPTER 6

Home at Last

W ITH little prospect of success, I nonetheless decided to cite to the Vice-Chancellor his promise that it may be possible to collect the aircraft in May or June that same year, 2001. Several phone calls to him at the beginning of June met with the usual "he is out of station", but ultimately I had a message from him to speak to the Registrar. I had little hope that this would get me very far. Imagine my amazement when the Registrar told me that I had to collect the aircraft the following week!

I could hardly believe my ears, but had to gamble that this might really be the realisation of all I had worked for. I telephoned the shippers in Bombay and organised them to get a forty foot open-topped container on its way to Banaras. They promised that it would arrive by Tuesday 5 June latest. I caught a flight to Bombay on 1 June, met with my lawyer the following day and was in Banaras by Sunday 3 June. I met with the Vice-Chancellor and the Registrar early the following afternoon.

They asked me when the container was arriving. I said that it was due the following day. "Right," said the Vice-Chancellor, "the aircraft has to be out of the campus by tomorrow night." I could not believe I was hearing this. For the last six years I had been begging and cajoling them to release the aircraft and every possible delay had been put in the way – and here they were giving me twenty-four hours to crate a complete aircraft and get it out of the university. I said nothing, although I knew their demand was impossible. They did however have good cause to encourage the early removal of the aeroplane. They explained that it would be impossible to hide from the press that this pile of scrap was moving and that 'one hell of a hullabaloo' would happen. I passed over a banker's draft for the tendered price.

Tuesday I spent freeing off the joints of the undercarriage as I knew this had to be folded to fit R4118 into the container. By that evening there was no sign of the container. Wednesday morning a call to the shippers elucidated the reply that the truck driver had been attacked by dacoits and left injured. I was naturally very sorry to hear this but wanted to be assured that the container was still on its way. "Yes, it will be with you tomorrow," came the reply.

I sped to the airport to collect John Fasal who had dashed from the UK together with Al Watts, an engineer from Retro Track and Air at Dursley in Gloucestershire. We all worked for the rest of the day preparing the Hurricane for its move.

Thursday came with still no sign of the container. A further phone call was greeted with, "It is very sad but we have all been at the driver's funeral." I was shocked. And by now we had another fly in the ointment. The university's bankers declared that the draft I had brought with me was not a banker's draft but a banker's cheque which would take at least two weeks to clear. I was not to remove the aircraft until the money had actually reached the university's account, regardless of the assurances faxed to their bank from my UK bank. So here I was with no money to complete the deal and no container in which to pack the aircraft.

And from there matters seemed to get worse. We could see the aircraft slipping from our grasp. I had a phone call from the *Times of India*, then one from the Press Association of India, then from the *Hindustan Times*. All had heard we were removing an aircraft from Banaras Hindu University and would I give them an interview? I remembered that in 1997 I had turned down a similar request soon after I had opened negotiations with the previous Vice-Chancellor. This had resulted in that scurrilous article suggesting that there were some underhand dealings going on. So on this occasion I agreed to talk to them. Imagine my horror when the next couple of days saw reports in all the English and Hindi language national papers. The front page of the *Times of India* carried the headline "Tony Blair sweeps to second term" followed by "Antiques buff buys World War II aircraft". In a box in the middle of this report was a piece saying that the teaching staff of the university had met to protest the sale of the aircraft and that this 'prized treasure' should not leave the university. The *Hindustan Times* carried a picture of the Hurricane under the headline, "He's out to rebuild a plane from junk at BHU yard!"

R4118 about to be lifted to the skies for the first time since 1943.

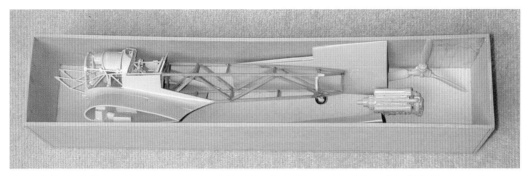

A model was built so that a structure could be developed to support the aircraft in the container, but pressure from media interest meant we virtually had to throw R4118 into the container as quickly as possible and hope it would survive reasonably intact.

Frantic phone calls to our UK bank produced a promise to wire the funds immediately. Meantime Friday arrived with still no sign of the truck and container. On Saturday morning, having heard that the truck was only a few kilometres from Banaras we went in search with our trusty taxi driver up the Grand Trunk Road. No sign. But on our return there was the truck, but the driver had disappeared. His assistant volunteered the information that the driver had safely driven all the way from Bombay, had not been attacked by dacoits but had, in fact, just got married and had been 'lying on his wife'!

Although it was made clear that the truck could not leave the campus until the money had arrived, we were allowed to pack the aircraft. So, with our nerves on edge that at any moment someone might appear to stop its removal, we spent Sunday stuffing R4118 into the container. Gone were the careful plans to remove the Merlin engine and to build structures inside the container to support the fuselage and wings properly. We just had to get the job done before an official, maybe from Delhi, decided that, despite the aircraft never having even been assembled in India, it should not leave, but rather be left to continue to rot.

We worked in a temperature of 104 degrees fahrenheit with a humidity of 95%. I drank four litres of water and never had a pee. We had a crude crane whose driver was more used to picking up rolled trucks from Indian roads than handling a delicate object. At one ghastly moment the fuselage was dropped into the container. We got it out again. Sadly it had suffered quite some damage, but now was not the time to worry about it. We just had to get every part into that container and secure it. The fuselage was too wide to fit flat so had to perch in the container at 45 degrees. By late afternoon everything was inside except the spare Rolls-Royce Griffon engine which came as part of the deal.

The plan for Monday morning was to strap everything well, and add the Griffon. That was not to prove easy. The professor in whose laboratory the engine had been lying since the Second World War decided that he did not wish to release it. A letter authorising the release was drawn up and several hours passed whilst the signatures of the Registrar, The Director of the Institute of Technology, the Head of the Department of Mechanical Engineering and the laboratory head were obtained. Reluctantly we were allowed to move it, albeit with great difficulty as no lifting equipment seemed to be around.

Peter and Polly Vacher celebrate the safe return of R4118 to the UK after fifty seven years.

So now it was Tuesday, one week later than we had been allowed to take. The aircraft was sealed in its container, but the truck was locked up in the compound and not allowed to leave. With my nerves now driving me to panic, I chased the Banaras bank but no, the funds by wire had not arrived, nor had the banker's cheque cleared. Another day went by. In desperation I rang home and got my nephew to rush to London, get an Indian visa, book an airline ticket, dash back to my bank and draw out the necessary funds in cash. By Thursday he was all set to leave for India. After strong words with the bank in Banaras, it transpired that the funds had been received at their branch in Calcutta some two days before but they had not bothered to inform Banaras. Anyway by 5 pm the funds had arrived, I was able to cancel my nephew's flight. With great help from the Registrar final formalities were completed and, to my huge relief, the truck left the campus at 8 pm on Thursday. We followed it through the back streets of Banaras. A forty-foot container is pretty exceptional on the roads of India – hitting trees and tearing down electric wires as it went, scattering all before it. At last it was on its way.

My fear was that the aircraft would next be stuck in customs in Bombay, but the shippers were highly efficient. The truck was five days on the road and within a further week the container was on the high seas in the MV *Safmarine Cerebos*.

To great acclamation R4118 arrived safely at Abingdon, almost sixty-one years since F/O Bunny Currant refuelled at Abingdon en route from Drem to Croydon when this great aeroplane first entered service in the Battle of Britain.

Looking back, most of the Indian people with whom I had had dealings were very much on my side, not least the two Vice-Chancellors at Banaras Hindu University on whose shoulders the final decision to release the aircraft rested. Many of the staff were also supportive. It was just that things move so slowly in India and decisions are exceptionally hard to come by. At the end of the day, I am grateful for all the help I received.

An Extraordinary Tale

This chapter has been kindly contributed by Nicolas Livingstone
who specialises in research into the Special Operations Executive.

A FEW years ago, when I lived near RAF Benson, the occasional appearance of a Hurricane overhead used to puzzle me. I knew the history of the blue Spitfires and Mosquitos there – my father had flown Mosquitos with 540 Squadron – but a Hurricane? All became clear soon after I moved a few miles to North Moreton: one afternoon I heard the unmistakeable growl of a Merlin, close and low. I ran to the front garden. Only then did I realise that an airstrip lay a few fields away. Our village hosted a Hurricane! It got better: before any weekend engagement, R4118's pilots would finish each test-flight with several passes over Peter's airstrip, in full view from our home on the hill.

For several years I had been researching and writing about the RAF's early clandestine operations to parachute agents into Nazi-occupied Europe. In the spring of 2015 I was searching online when a forum discussion caught my eye. It referred to an incident in August 1940, when a Whitley had been shot down by a Hurricane. One post quoted from the subsequent Court of Inquiry, and I noticed the Hurricane's number. I already knew about the incident: the Whitley's pilot had been Flying Officer Jack Oettle, who had flown many of the early clandestine sorties.

When Peter researched the history of Hurricane R4118 he had no reason to suspect that anything worth recording might have taken place between 23 July, when it arrived at 22 Maintenance Unit (MU) at RAF Silloth, and 17 August 1940, when it was delivered to 605 Squadron. In normal times R4118 would have spent most of these twenty-five days in limbo, stored ready for dispatch to a squadron.

But these particular times were far from normal, for this was the Battle of Britain. The events of one afternoon in August came close to marring the history of this aircraft. Of course an aircraft does not wage war; its pilots do. A fighter pilot may shoot down other aircraft, and even kill, but the aircraft itself is merely an instrument designed and fashioned to express the pilot's will. It cannot be guilty of its pilot's actions any more than John Wilkes Booth's Deringer is guilty of killing Lincoln. But if we venerate this aircraft for its provenance as a participant in the Battle of Britain, then we must temper that veneration by acknowledging the near-tragedy that occurred on 5 August 1940.

We are apt to regard the Battle of Britain as a done deal; a battle fought mainly over southern England, with a beginning, an end, and a known outcome. On 5 August 1940 the main battle had yet to be joined. It was still an extended skirmish: the Luftwaffe was reserving its attacks for the Channel convoys, and had yet to attack the mainland in force. An attack might be made anywhere. Invasion scares were universal: even in western Scotland fields were spiked with poles against enemy landings. Fear of 'fifth-columnists' made any stranger suspect.

RAF Silloth, an airfield on the coast of the Solway Firth west of Carlisle, was home to No. 1 (Coastal) Operational Training Unit (OTU). It trained Coastal Command aircrew on long-range patrol types such as the Anson, Blenheim, and Hudson. Silloth might be far from the front line, but it was still prepared. Of the OTU's aircraft only the Blenheim could – by 1940, charitably – have been described as a fighter, so Silloth's standing orders required 22 Maintenance Unit to provide four Hurricanes for defence. The pilots were to be provided from the OTU's instructors, under the orders of the Station Commander or Duty Officer.

Rumours of German ruses-de-guerre were common, and some acquired a mantle of apparent evidence. On 25 July Coastal Command issued a signal:

Following information received from Air Ministry there is evidence that enemy have used British type of aircraft. According to his own recognition and other difficulties it is unlikely enemy will adopt these tactics to any great extent. His intention may well be in part to create uncertainty amongst our pilots as to which aircraft are friendly and which hostile. Air Ministry consider it preferable that an occasional British aircraft flown by the enemy should escape destruction rather than instructions should be given which might lead to the destruction of our own aircraft in error. Therefore no British type of aircraft should be regarded as hostile unless it carries some additional authorized markings of a kind which might be useful to the enemy for recognition by his own forces or unless it acts in an unmistakably hostile manner. As code letters are not standard recognition markings their absence is no indication that aircraft are hostile.

The signal was received by the headquarters of No. 17 (Training) Group, Coastal Command. The Duty Staff Officer immediately passed a truncated version to all its stations, consisting of just the first sentence and the last two. In this form it was copied into the Silloth Pilots' Order Book on 29 July.

On the late morning of August 5, Flying Officer Jack Oettle was captain of a Whitley V on a navigation exercise from RAF Abingdon. Oettle had recently completed a full operational bombing tour with No. 51 Squadron. He was now being 'rested' as an instructor with No. 10 Operational Training Unit (OTU), which gave new aircrew their final training for night-bomber operations over Germany. The exercise simulated a bomber operation across the North Sea to Germany, only in daylight. Flying an outward route via Worcester and Holyhead, they crossed the Irish Sea via the Isle of Man to pinpoint near Stranraer. Turning east towards Silloth, the Whitley crew would then head south-west to make a dummy bombing run over Workington before dropping practice bombs on a sea range. Pinpointing on St Bees Head, they would re-

A similar aircraft to R4118's victim, Whitley Mark V, N1503 M, of No. 19 Operational Training Unit based at Kinloss, Morayshire, parked at Abingdon, Berkshire, while visiting No. 10 OTU.

cross the Irish Sea to Llandudno before heading home to Abingdon.

Oettle's crew consisted of three trainees who would form the nucleus of a new Whitley crew – pilot, navigator and W/T operator – and one W/T instructor. There was no rear gunner, surely unnecessary in friendly skies outside German fighter range. As they approached Workington Oettle was in the pilot's seat. The trainee navigator, Sergeant Hather, was behind his right shoulder at the navigator's table, with a view out over the port side. Pilot Officer Stevens, the trainee pilot, was either in the aircraft's nose or in the well leading there. The two wireless operators could have seen little through the square porthole in their cubby-hole aft of the navigator's table. No-one would have had a good view to the rear, or much reason to look. Their Whitley had British markings and a large letter 'X' on the fuselage, but no unit letters; this uninformative marking was common for OTUs of the period. It was carrying eight practice bombs, visible in the racks between each engine and the fuselage.

At 12.30 the Duty Officer at Silloth, Flight Lieutenant Cleugh-Fair, an instructor with the OTU, went to lunch, and Flight Lieutenant Moody took his place. F/Lt Moody was a Regional Control Officer, a forerunner of modern air traffic controllers. Five days earlier, when a Whitley had been seen in the area, the Station Commander had instructed F/Lt Moody that, if a British aircraft was established as hostile, or committed a hostile act, it should be shot down. Moody had then instructed Sergeant J C W Parrott, a pilot instructor with the OTU, to the same effect, but it appears that on this occasion no interception was made.

In August 1940 Sergeant John Charles William Parrott was 34. He had joined the RAF in 1928, qualifying as a sergeant pilot the following year. He flew the Westland Wapiti and the Hawker Hart before his transfer to the Reserve in 1934, and he was discharged in 1937. His record states that he was "discharged on termination of engagement having declined offer of re-engagement". While trying to nail his joining-date I happened upon the nugget that inter-war sergeant-pilots were limited to five years flying duties after which, while keeping their rank, they reverted permanently to ground duties; which might explain his departure. By 1939 he was too old for front-line fighter service, but after the Hart the Hurricane's cockpit would have been comparatively familiar.

At approximately 13.10 Moody ordered two pilots to investigate a Whitley which had been seen to the south-west. Moody relayed to both pilots the Station Commander's instructions. Flying Officer Tyler, a pupil pilot with the OTU, was despatched in a Blenheim crewed by a navigator (with Aldis lamp) and an air gunner. The other was a Hurricane flown by Sergeant Sibbert, the duty pilot.

At 13.30 Cleugh-Fair returned from lunch. A few minutes later a lookout reported a Whitley over Criffel Mountain, a prominent hill to the north-west, in Scotland. Cleugh-Fair ordered the standby Anson up to check it out. Either this was a tardy report about Oettle's Whitley or it was a different aircraft, for there is no further mention of either it or the Anson. At about 13.50 – timings given at the Court of Inquiry were inconsistent – Cleugh-Fair saw a Whitley over the airfield, descending from about 5,500 feet to 3,000 feet. He ordered up two more Blenheims, one flown solo by Flight Lieutenant Lewis, and he also phoned for Sergeant Parrott, who arrived at the Watch Office on the run. Cleugh-Fair briefed him in a matter of moments, and Parrott took off shortly in Hurricane R4118. Cleugh-Fair also believed that the pilots were authorised to open fire, but instructed Parrott only to investigate and report back.

All the Silloth pilots questioned at the subsequent Court of Inquiry believed they had been authorised to fire on a British-marked aircraft if it acted in a hostile manner. There was no local air defence control system, and no discernible radio communication, either between the scrambled aircraft or between them and the ground. It might have been 1918.

To Jack Oettle in the Whitley, the first Silloth aircraft arrived at about 14.00. Lewis's Blenheim and Sibbert's Hurricane found the Whitley first, near Workington. Without signalling equipment they could only buzz around the Whitley, flashing their identification lights. Oettle thought they were making practice attacks, and played along. They were soon joined by Tyler's Blenheim, whose navigator signalled the Whitley with an Aldis lamp up to five times before it responded with two yellow flares. Lewis and Sibbert were satisfied and left the area, but Tyler hung around briefly as he remained suspicious of the Whitley's actions over Workington.

Sergeant Parrott came upon the Whitley either shortly before or after the others had left. (Lewis claimed to have seen two Hurricanes.) Parrott considered the Whitley's actions suspicious, and manoeuvred in front of it and to the side, gesturing with hand signals for it to descend. Getting no response, he moved R4118 to a position above and behind the Whitley.

Oettle became aware of R4118 only when it crossed in front of the Whitley, and didn't know that this Hurricane was a new arrival. He then lost sight of it. Oettle's view to the front and sides would have been fine, but he had no view to the rear. His crew would have been busy with their tasks.

In the Hurricane, Parrott had received no acknowledgment to what he believed were his clear instructions for the Whitley to land. He fired two bursts from his guns, and the Whitley turned away seawards. Parrott then opened fire twice, this time on to the Whitley itself, damaging both engines in turn, and saw it descend to the south-west. In the Whitley, Oettle had felt: "a severe vibration through the aircraft, and heard a loud hammering noise, and also saw a number of holes appearing in both main planes. I sent the wireless operator back to ascertain the damage. He reported punctured tanks, and other damage, and so I turned towards land, and made a landing at Squire's Gate, at about 1450 hours."

Parrott then broke away and returned to Silloth, also landing at about 1450. Oettle's Whitley was found to have been severely damaged, having been hit by about 400 rounds. No-one in his crew was injured.

The Court of Inquiry was held at Silloth on August 12. On August 26 the Court issued its judgement: it found Sgt Parrott to blame, directly for shooting down a friendly aircraft without orders with insufficient reason for assuming it was hostile, and indirectly for failing to obtain explicit orders and for not reading the Pilots' Order Book. F/O Oettle was considered directly to

EVIDENCE.

1st Witness   359233 Sgt. J.C.W. Parrott states:-

"I am a pilot of the instructional staff of No. 1 (C) O.T.U. Silloth. At about 1350 hours on the 5th August 1940 I was given orders to report to the Watch Hut. On arrival there I saw the Duty Station Officer, F/Lt. Cleugh-Pair, who ordered me to take Hurricane No. R.4118 and intercept a Whitley aircraft reported over Maryport, and establish its identity. He told me that if I could not establish its identity I was to try and force it down. I took off at about 1355 hours and intercepted the Whitley at about 1425 hours, flying at about 6000 ft. above the clouds, flying South. I dived across the bows of the Whitley, once from each side to draw attention and then flew up close in on the port side and a little ahead of the Whitley and endeavoured by means of hand signals to indicate that the Whitley was to go down. I received no signals of any description, and the Whitley continued on its course at the same height. I next flew above the Whitley, and by flying close tried to force it down. This had no effect and so I then flew across its bows from both directions, and fired two bursts with my guns. The Whitley then turned slowly west to seawards, still maintaining height. As I considered the Whitley was acting in a very suspicious manner, I decided to disable it by firing into its engines.

I did this and my first burst produced a large puff of smoke from the starboard engine. I fired again into he port engine, and after this I noticed the Whitley was descending slowly, still flying in a south westerly direction.

Sgd. J.C.W. Parrott,

Sgt. 359233

A portion of Sgt. John Parrott's evidence to the Court of Enquiry.

blame for assuming that R4118 was one of the earlier aircraft he had signalled. The Duty Officer, Flight Lieutenant Cleugh-Fair, was held indirectly to blame for not issuing explicit orders, and the Station Commander for not issuing orders to cover the situation. The Court also noted that a crucial portion of the Coastal Command signal had been omitted:

> Air Ministry consider it preferable that an occasional British aircraft flown by the enemy should escape destruction rather than instructions should be given which might lead to the destruction of our own aircraft in error.

Silloth's ad-hoc fighter force was disbanded almost immediately, on August 15th. A copy of the proceedings was sent to Air Commodore Howe, AOC No. 17 Training Group, Coastal Command, who wrote his own comments on 13 September. He agreed with the findings against Sergeant Parrott, but considered Jack Oettle guilty only of assuming the other aircraft were making practice attacks, for these were forbidden without prior arrangement. Air Cdre Howe also accepted that a Duty Staff Officer from 17 Group was to blame for omitting a crucial part of the 25 July signal when relaying it to Silloth.

The episode did little harm to Sergeant Parrott's revived air force career: from Warrant Officer he was commissioned in 1942, and two years later he was promoted to Flight Lieutenant.

Coastal Command sent a copy of the Court of Inquiry proceedings to Bomber Command, but it refused to forward a copy of Air Commodore Howe's remarks; he apparently considered the whole affair an internal matter. It clearly was not: in October a staff officer at Bomber Command, Schneider Trophy winner W/Cdr John Boothman, AFC, took a jaundiced view of the affair:

> A coastal station away from the normal war zone was maintaining a private fighter force of aircraft filched from an MU and operating without any reasonable control or without any of the normal aids which are considered essential. This force must have been a menace to any law-abiding pilot for miles around. That a local fighter force should be operating is at least interesting in these days of organised defences and if the idea spreads we will no doubt shortly be having the Ministry of Aircraft Production operating his own protective group. The whole scheme appears to have been organised and conducted in a most haphazard fashion.
>
> The Proceedings of the Court are also interesting. How any responsible officer could have put his signature to the findings defeats me. Paragraph 2 is an instance in question. A pilot giving instruction over the west coast in broad daylight with a correctly marked aeroplane is not expected to assume that every British aeroplane is going to attack him and, in consequence, fly along firing off the colours of the day.

Jack Oettle's Flight Commander had served on the Court of Inquiry which had judged him partly, but directly, to blame. Fortunately, help soon arrived in the shape of Squadron Leader Teddy Knowles, the Air Ministry officer responsible for organising clandestine flights to Europe. He could not recruit aircrew through the normal channels – secrecy was paramount – so his approach was personal. In mid-September Oettle was posted to No. 419 (Special Duties) Flight, formed in late August specifically to carry out agent insertion and recovery operations by air. Oettle may have been relieved to get back to the relative safety of operations.

On 21 September Oettle piloted Whitley P5029, with Flight Lieutenant Walter Farley as his second pilot, in the third attempt to parachute SIS agent Philip Schneidau into the Forest of Fontainebleau. It was the first of Jack Oettle's twenty-two operational sorties of this kind; he had dropped twelve agents, one twice. In April 1941, returning from an aborted attempt to deliver a team of six Polish agents to sabotage a Bordeaux power-station, Flight Lieutenant Oettle, DFC, stalled his still-loaded Whitley while attempting to land at Tangmere: two crew were killed and Oettle was seriously injured. Returning to duty in September, on his first flight he stalled another Whitley. This time no-one survived.

CHAPTER 8 The Battle of Britain

F OR the six years I was trying to get R4118 out of India, I could think of little else. Many people advised me to give up the pursuit, sure in the knowledge that I would not be able to beat the bureaucracy. But I was determined and, besides, there was plenty of research to do in the meantime.

When I initially set out to acquire the aircraft, I had little clue as to what an exciting find I had stumbled upon. As has been seen, the first breakthrough was when we found its RAF number on that rear fuselage panel, and tied it up with the number of the Merlin III engine still under the cowlings.

The Air Historical Branch of the Ministry of Defence is remarkable in collating documentation relating to aircraft and personnel. The results of its labours are placed at the Public Record Office at Kew in London. I was to spend many weeks there.

I started with the Air Ministry Form 78, the movement card for R4118 which detailed each

During 605 Squadron's time at Drem, together with other squadrons, a Sunday service included a blessing of the Hurricane and Spitfire.

unit to which it was allotted. The aircraft was built by the Gloster Aircraft Company at Gloucester. Glosters had been taken over by the Hawker Aircraft Company in 1934. R4118 was one from the second batch of 500 Hurricanes ordered from Glosters and was delivered to 22 Maintenance Unit at Silloth on 23 July 1940. On 17 August it joined 605 County of Warwick Squadron at Drem near Edinburgh. 605 was one of the select band of Royal Auxiliary squadrons which had been formed well before the war from volunteers who undertook part-time flying training. The Auxiliaries were largely formed of public school chaps, an elite bunch with busy social lives. Pomposity and formal discipline were frowned upon. An Auxiliary enjoyed membership of a gentlemen's club where family and status were essential.

So from the Form 78, I was led to the Form 540, the Operations Record Book for RAF Station, Drem. 605 Squadron was resting and re-equipping after being heavily engaged with its Hurricanes in the Battle of France. The squadron was under the command of Squadron Leader (later Group Captain) Walter Churchill DSO DFC.

Referring then to the Operations Record Book of 605 Squadron, the squadron left Drem for Croydon on Saturday 7 September at the height of the Battle of Britain, to join 11 Group. The day was significant, for it was on that morning that the Luftwaffe switched its tactics from attacking airfields in the south of England to an all-out blitz on London and major cities. Thirty-one British fighters went down that day whilst the enemy lost thirty-nine aircraft.

R4118 was flown south by Pilot Officer (later Wing Commander DSO DFC and Bar) Christopher Frederick 'Bunny' Currant DFC (RAF no. 43367). With the Hurricane's limited range, Bunny had to refuel at Abingdon where he was ordered to 'get the hell out' as German bombers attacked the airfield.

Bunny is a fund of stories, a favourite being of leading the squadron in November 1940 "at some dizzy height". It was very cold and Bunny's bladder began to complain bitterly. He goes on: "I did a quick appraisal. Should I turn round, dash back to Croydon and run like hell? I knew I'd never make it. So I got into a position where I could perform. I struggled with my flying clothes but at last succeeded. The relief was so great, I couldn't have cared if the whole of the German air force was behind me. However I saw to my amazement that the pee built up a huge pile of ice on my compass!"

Wing Commander Christopher Frederick 'Bunny' Currant on 23 June 1942 at RAF Ibsley, on the award of the DSO in addition to his DFC and Bar. He was awarded the Croix de Guerre (Belgium) in April 1943. On 7 September 1940 he flew Hurricane R4118 from Drem to Croydon ready for its first sortie in the Battle of Britain.

After that, Bunny was known as a pretty good pilot but a lousy navigator – he could never read his compass properly! At the age of 93 (2005), Bunny retains a razor-sharp memory although he claims that he "cannot quite catch the Bunny girls any more".

Once at Croydon, R4118 was soon in action. Squadron Leader Churchill flew it to Kenley and back on 8 September. I was fortunate, through the ubiquitous Internet, to trace Walter Churchill's son, James. He kindly allowed me to copy his father's log book which disagrees with the ORB in that the flight to Kenley was recorded as being in P3583. The ORB and Churchill's log agree that the following day Walter's first combat flight in the Battle of Britain was in R4118. It was also our Hurricane's first taste of conflict. By the time Walter Churchill led his squadron into battle on that September day, he already had 1173 flying hours under his belt and been awarded a Distinguished Service Order and a Distinguished Flying Cross simultaneously. His citations read:

DSO: Flight Lieutenant Walter Myers CHURCHILL (90241)

This officer assumed command of a squadron shortly after its arrival in France and led it with marked success, inspiring his pilots and maintenance crews magnificently. He undertook the tactical instruction of new pilots, led many patrols successfully and organised his ground defences and crews in an exemplary manner. While under his command, the squadron destroyed 62 enemy aircraft and he was throughout the mainspring of their offensive spirit, their excellent tactics and their adequate maintenance results. Only four pilots of the squadron were lost. Flight Lieutenant Churchill destroyed four enemy aircraft, bringing his total to seven.

DFC: Flight Lieutenant Walter Myers CHURCHILL (90241)

This officer has shot down three enemy aircraft since his arrival in France on 10 May and has led many patrols with courage and wisdom.

As such, and with time in the Battle of France, Churchill was one of the most experienced pilots. When he flew R4118 into battle on 9 September, he witnessed an extraordinary feat by Flight Lieutenant Archie McKellar, commander of B Flight, destined to be one of 605's aces. The story was well told in David Masters' *So Few* published in 1943:

It was a beautiful day, with some cloud at 4,000 feet and a clear sky above. Heading south the Hurricanes climbed steadily to intercept at 20,000 feet. They had reached 15,000 feet when the voice of Archie McKellar came to his leader over the radio-telephone. "Enemy ahead, sir," shouted the Scotsman as he caught sight of a cloud of thirty Heinkel 111s with an escort of fifty Messerschmitt 109s about 4,000 feet above them and twenty Messerschmitt 110s to guard the flank.

At that distance Wing Commander Churchill could see no more than six Messerschmitt 109s and at once went in to draw them off with his section in order to give the other fighters a chance to get at the bombers which Archie McKellar told him were present. Directly he had drawn off the first batch of Messerschmitts and seen them go flashing past, he saw six more and as he was forcing them away a bullet grazed his leg and sent him spinning down out of the formation.

By the time he recovered, he had lost the bombers and his squadron, but he headed after them all out on the course they were following. To his amazement, he soon observed the Heinkels still flying in the same direction as though unaware of the British fighters who were stalking them.

As he flew to overtake them, he saw Archie McKellar's section of three turn up sun and swing round to the attack. At that very moment the Heinkels turned into the sun straight toward the Hurricanes which were concealed by the glare. The Germans were, in the parlance of the fighters, 'a piece of cake'. No deflection was necessary at all. Archie McKellar, seeing the leading Heinkel in front of him, just pressed the button on his control column and squirted at it, and Wing Commander Churchill watched it blow up in the air and knock the wing off the port Heinkel, which immediately went down just as the starboard Heinkel turned straight into Archie McKellar's stream of bullets and got what is known in the service as a 'gutser'. Black smoke began to pour from the engines, the nose of the bomber reared up for a moment, then the third Heinkel went down on its back.

"It was the most marvellous show," commented Walter Churchill.

Churchill's time with 605 Squadron was to be short-lived when on 11 September he received a bullet in his arm. He remained with the squadron until he was posted to command 71 Eagle (American) Squadron at Church Fenton. The ORB stated, "He will be much missed by the squadron; he was a fine CO both on the ground and in the air during training days at Drem. His eyesight unfortunately made him unfit for operational flying down here." Notwithstanding eyesight problems, Walter Churchill flew a Spitfire off HMS *Furious* onto Malta in August 1942 but was killed later that month over Sicily.

Battle of Britain Day is celebrated on 15 September, marking the daylight hours when Hitler sent wave after wave of bombers and fighters to knock out London. There were severe losses on both sides that day, but for some reason it was one of the few days that month on which R4118 did not fly. Perhaps it was under repair from its combat two days earlier. In any event, remaining grounded that day fortunately increased its chances of survival.

At this point one should explain the structure of the squadron, which comprised twelve aircraft, divided into two flights. A Flight consisted of three aircraft each in Yellow and Red sections. Similarly B Flight had three aircraft each in Blue and Green sections.

For the next fourteen operational sorties, Pilot Officer Jock Muirhead adopted R4118 as 'his' aircraft. On 24 September, at the controls of R4118, Yellow 1, he shared the kill of a Dornier 215 with Pilot Officer Glowacki who sadly did not survive the mission. The engagement was recorded in the Intelligence Patrol Report:

Two Hurricanes (Yellow Section) 605 Squadron left Croydon at 1541 hours on 24 September 1940 with orders to patrol Beachy Head, angels 10 [10,000 feet]. While flying east near Beachy Head at angels 12, they saw a Do. 215 at angels 14, in cloud, also flying east. These clouds were more in the nature of mist down to 12,000 feet with visibility of about 1,000 yards. Yellow 1 and Yellow 2 climbed and overhauled the Do. 215 rapidly, Yellow 1 attacking with a 3 second burst from starboard ¼ astern from underneath, but observed no result. Yellow 2 then attacked from the port quarter with a similar attack. The enemy aircraft then jettisoned 10 bombs from the rear compartment and 6 from the front, which probably fell into the sea. Yellow 1 then made an astern attack from 250 yards closing to 100 yards, with a 6 second burst, setting fire to its port engine and wing. The enemy aircraft then turned left and Yellow 2 made a beam attack after which both of its engines were on fire; it lost height, and Yellow 2 made a further attack while the enemy aircraft was losing height. Yellow 1 and Yellow 2 followed it down just below cloudbase, which in mid-channel was 1,000 feet, and saw it crash into the sea 5 miles SW of Cap Gris Nez. At this moment 4 Me 109s appeared overhead, so Yellow 1 and Yellow 2 dropped down to sea level and crossed the French coast at Albemeuse. After this, Yellow 1 did not see Yellow 2. The Me 109s attacked Yellow 1 over land, so he hedge-hopped east for 15-20 miles, then turned south-west, shook off the Me 109s and crossed the coast again between Boulogne and Le Touquet, climbing into cloud at 12,000 feet, and returned to Croydon 1725 hours.

While low flying, Yellow 1 was fired at by only a few ground defences, the fire consisting of red cannon.

Yellow 1 saw five ambulances along the Boulogne-Le Touquet road, painted grey with a white circle and red cross in the middle, very similar to RAF ambulances. Along the same road there were only a few scattered troops. Yellow 1 saw six lines of two boats abreast moving very fast northwards 3 miles off the coast between Boulogne and Le Touquet, practically no boats inside the mile at Boulogne, and only a few offshore from Le Touquet, which he thought were barges. It appeared that there was no serious attempt at immediate invasion from this quarter.

1 – Do. 215 destroyed
Yellow 1   P/O Muirhead [R4118]
Yellow 2   P/O Glowacki (missing)

Signed: D H Price F/O Intelligence Officer, 605 Squadron, Croydon.
As Leader of Yellow Section I wish this Dornier to be credited equally between myself and P/O Glowacki.

Signed: P/O Muirhead

From the last paragraph it is fascinating to discover that the RAF pilots were expected to observe troop and marine movements during their sorties and to report back to the intelligence officer. This report shows just how aware the British were of a possible imminent invasion.

It is worth relating that Jock Muirhead had earlier been with 605 Squadron in the Battle of France and had subsequently been confined to a hospital bed from 20 May until mid July, as the following letter to the Irving Parachute Company tells his story:

Royal Air Force
Officers' Hospital
Torquay
8/7/40
Dear Sirs

I am writing this short account which may interest you of the extremely efficient operation of one of your seat type parachutes.

I was patrolling Dunkirk on 20 May in a Hurricane when I encountered a Me 110 which I subsequently engaged and disposed of. Shortly after this operation which took place at 3,000 ft out to sea I found a bullet had lodged in the cockpit and cut a glycol pipe. As fumes and boiling glycol were entering the cockpit rapidly I made for the shore and endeavoured to land at Steene, then in Belgian hands. Unfortunately the cockpit had become untenable and I was unable to see the instruments.

I then decided to jump and with that end in view disconnected my oxygen and microphone leads. I left the aircraft at 1,000 ft over Nieuport by rolling it onto its back at an airspeed of about 150 and pushing the stick forward as I became inverted. I was immediately thrown out of the machine and when some 300 ft clear pulled the rip cord.

The parachute opened so rapidly that I can only assume I had unconsciously eased the ring before pulling it as I never even got the ring clear of the pocket.

I was then fired on violently by Belgian troops and civilians and was able to escape by partially collapsing the chute by climbing up one set of rigging lines. I let go at about 200 ft and landed in a tree which I was unable to avoid as there was quite a strong wind. I subsequently was obliged to abandon the parachute as I had great difficulty in preventing the Belgians from shooting me by mistake as a German.

I eventually got back to this country two days later after being torpedoed and am still in hospital but I am grateful to you for the extremely efficient manner in which your parachute behaved at low altitude.

Yours sincerely
P/O J. Muirhead D.F.C.

Muirhead was killed on 15 October in a major fight over southern England. The Intelligence Patrol Report on 605 squadron for 15 October 1940 makes formidable reading:

11 Hurricanes of 605 Squadron left Croydon at 0825 hours on 15 October 1940 with orders to scramble Kenley angels 25. The squadron (A Flight leading) climbed to 28,500ft and were flying south-west in sections vic line astern in the neighbourhood of Maidstone, when Controller informed Red 1 that enemy aircraft were approaching from the south-east at 18-20,000ft. Eight Me 109s were seen about four miles away flying north-west, at 23,000ft with a wide vic of five leading and the remainder straggling in no particular formation. He therefore turned the squadron through south round to the left. The squadron then dived straight out of the sun on to the Me 109s, the two leading sections diving upon the leaders of the enemy formation. Just before the squadron got within range, the Me 109s turned left and split up fanwise, some diving away left, others climbing and circling. Red 1 made a diving beam attack on the leader of the leading vic with full deflection, giving a 5 sec burst from 200 yards. Bits were seen to fly off the enemy aircraft, it rolled over and dived south, disappearing into the clouds, which were 10/10ths at 2,000ft. Another Me 109 came into Red 1's sights and he gave a full deflection beam attack at this enemy aircraft from 200 yards. Bits fell off and it, too, rolled over and dived into the clouds. Red 1 then had to take violent evasive action as other Me 109s were behind and above him. Yellow 1 meanwhile dived upon the left-hand aircraft of the leading vic, opening fire from 400 yards in a 9-10 second burst, using two rings deflection from ¾ astern, finishing dead astern. The enemy aircraft emitting glycol smoke from its radiator, pulled right up in front of Yellow 1, stood on its tail, fell over on to its back, and went spinning down in the neighbourhood of Detling. Yellow 2 following Yellow 1, made a diving beam attack, developing into a quarter attack on another enemy aircraft, but no results were observed. The Me 109s were now split up, and Yellow 2 found another one upon which he made an astern attack from 200 yards, closing to 100 yards, with an 8 sec burst. This enemy aircraft stalled, fell on to its back, and went spinning down – also in the neighbourhood of Detling. Blue 3 opened fire upon an Me 109 which was diving away left giving it a long burst in beam attack, developing into ¾ astern from 100 yards. Bits flew off one wing root, oil and glycol streaming from it, and it went steeply down to the south of Eastchurch. Blue 2 meanwhile chased another Me 109 eastwards, giving it two consecutive bursts of 5 secs each from quarter astern finishing dead astern from 150 yards, closing to 50 yards. White smoke was coming from it and it dived vertically towards the cloud in the neighbourhood of Manston. Owing to there being 10/10ths cloud at 2,000ft and to the presence of many other Me 109s no pilot was able to see any one machine actually crash.

The only evasive action taken by the Me 109s was that they throttled right back when attacked.

None of the Me 109s at 32,000ft joined in the engagement.

Red 1 reports that one Me 109 which he attacked was turning almost as steeply as he was at 25,000ft, although he was using full boost, and 2,800 revs – nor was he able to catch it on the dive.

Nine Hurricanes returned to Croydon 0925-0935 hours, one returning 1020 hours, having refuelled at Gravesend. F/Lt Muirhead was killed.

Red 1	F/Lt Currant	2 Me 109s damaged
Red 2	P/O Rothwell	
Red 3	Sgt Sones	
Yellow 1	Sgt Wright	1 Me 109 probably destroyed
Yellow 2	P/O Foster	1 Me 109 probably destroyed
Yellow 3	P/O Milne	
Blue 1	F/Lt Muirhead	
Blue 2	P/O Hayter	1 Me 109 damaged
Blue 3	P/O Passy	1 Me 109 destroyed
Green 1	P/O Ingle	
Green 2	P/O Cooper-Slipper	

(sgd) D H Price
Flying Officer,
Intelligence Officer
605 Squadron RAF Croydon

R4118 must have experienced some mechanical trouble that day, as that morning P/O Alec Scott took it up on an air test. Perhaps that is why the squadron was one aircraft short for its 0825 hours sortie.

Jock Muirhead's loss was a bitter blow to his fellow pilots. Always jovial, he had distinguished himself in the Battle of France where he had been awarded the DFC. His 'Recommendation for Honours and Rewards' was rather more interesting than his brief citation, especially as it was signed by Air Vice-Marshal Keith Park, Commanding 11 Group and countersigned by Air Chief Marshal Hugh Dowding, Head of Fighter Command:

For his cool daring and sound knowledge of tactics resulting in consistently successful work while operating from England over NW France and Belgium where in five days he carried out eight patrols, shooting down one He 111; one Henschel 126; two Junkers 87s and one Messerschmitt 110. During his last patrol he was forced to bail out and landed on Allied territory whereupon he took immediate steps to rejoin his unit. The boat he caught was constantly being bombed so he overhauled and manned its Lewis gun. The boat was eventually torpedoed and by his cool resourcefulness during four hours in the water and ultimately by signalling to other craft he was able to save not only his own life but the lives of others.

Signed G R Edge, Officer Commanding

REMARKS BY THE AIR OFFICER COMMANDING

This young officer is outstanding in his skill and cool daring. He shot down five enemy aircraft. He 'bailed out' on his return, manned a Lewis gun in the vessel he was in, which was subsequently torpedoed. He assisted in saving the lives of several airmen by his resourcefulness during four hours in the water.

I very strongly recommend him for the Distinguished Flying Cross.

K R Park, Air Vice-Marshal Commanding, 11 Group. 15 June 1940.

REMARKS BY THE AIR OFFICER COMMANDING-IN-CHIEF

Approved.

H C T Dowding, Air Chief Marshal, Fighter Command. 17 June 1940.

Non and Johnny ('Archie') Milne in March 1946 prior to their return to Johnny's home in Saskatchewan, Canada. Non is wearing the uniform of the Queen Alexandra's Royal Army Nursing Corps.

From 26 September R4118 became the mount of Pilot Officer John Archibald 'Archie' Milne. A Canadian with a Scottish father, he had heard that the RAF might be in need of pilots. So he jumped on a ship and reported in May 1939 to Adastral House in Kingsway, London. Already a competent pilot, he was summoned for training at Gatwick on 8 August. Until he joined 605 a year later, he variously flew Tiger Moths, Harts, Audaxes, Miles Manchesters, Harvards and Spitfires. Archie tells his story:

I would go over to 10 Group from Aston Down. They used to throw parties and get me to go over to St Mary's on the Scilly Isles to pick up lobsters and fresh vegetables. One day I was detailed to collect lobsters and crabs in a Proctor. I'm a lad from the prairies, so not familiar with lobsters and so on. They set a bucket of lobsters on the seat beside me. Halfway home the lobsters came out of the bucket and these damn things crawled around. I guess it wouldn't bother a fisherman, but it sure did me! I landed as fast as I could and got someone to tie them up and give them out.

Milne was involved in several combats in R4118, with the kill of a Messerschmitt 110 on 27 September. The combat report was quite brief:

0925 hours. The squadron climbed to 18,000 feet circling around some Me 110s which were being engaged by fighters. The section went into line astern. As we closed with the Me 110s one of them broke left away from his formation and I delivered a full beam attack at 300 yards with a 5 sec burst. He began to spiral down in left and right hand turns and I delivered two more attacks of 3 sec bursts from astern. Both engines were smoking after my first attack, and his port engine burst into flames at 3,000 feet just east of Dorking (approximately). I then returned to base.
Signed J A Milne P/O.

On 22 October Archie, in another Hurricane, was in a dogfight with an Me 109 over Dorking. They appear to have shot each other down simultaneously. A young nurse was just coming off duty at Dorking hospital and saw two aircraft tumbling from the sky. Saddened to think that two more young lives had been lost, she continued home. When she came on duty the following morning, she found a German pilot and a Canadian pilot in adjacent beds. A year later Miss Non Williams QARANC (Queen Alexandra's Royal Army Nursing Corps) married the Canadian, Archie Milne!

There were other fighter aces who flew R4118 during the Battle. Pilot Officer (later Wing Commander DFC AE) Bob Foster (RAF no. 80815) claimed a damaged Junkers 88 on both 13 September and 28 September (in his fourth sortie of the day) and shared the kill of a Junkers 88 on 1 October, crediting him with the most damage inflicted by any pilot when flying R4118. Bob had learnt to fly Hurricanes at No. 56 Operational Training Unit in 1940 at Sutton Bridge, one of the OTUs to which R4118 would find itself in 1942 being used for air gunnery training. His later career included flying Spitfires in 1942 in defence of Darwin against attacks by Mitsubishi 'Betty' bombers and Japanese Zero fighters. He was the third pilot to claim five successes over Australia, giving him his 'ace' status. After the Normandy landings in 1944, in his new role in the Air Information Unit, Bob was one of the first RAF officers to enter Paris, joining de Gaulle's triumphant procession along the Champs Elysées.

From the time we owned R4118, Bob Foster and his wife, Kaethe, became our close friends. Being one of the longer surviving 'Few', Bob was chairman of the Battle of Britain Fighter Association until his death. We were privileged to fly R4118, 'his' aircraft over his funeral in Hastings on 11 August 2014. Keith Dennison was at the controls and in true Battle of Britain style, undaunted, he battled through minimum visibility to pay the final tribute. Fortunately Bob had been persuaded to write his autobiography *Tally Ho!*, well supplemented by an obituary in the *Daily Telegraph* on 8 August 2014. He died aged 94.

He was particularly interesting on the subject of his time when first with the squadron at Drem. The squadron was closely involved with the development of a night-landing system which became known as 'Drem Lighting'. Because it is probable that R4118 was used in testing the system (it was fitted with night-flying exhaust shields), I am grateful to Graham Crisp for his description of how the early version worked:

The system was developed as a means by which a returning squadron could locate, orbit and then be guided to the runway threshold of their airfield when it was safe for individual aircraft to land. Ideally a high visibility system would prove effective in this

case. Many airfields, realising the need for their aircraft to land and take off in blackout conditions, had already produced their own systems. There was a great deal of variance in the ideas adopted, however certain of the features in use at RAF Drem in October 1940 showed great promise. One aspect of particular interest was the provision of an 'approach' system, this being probably the first time this important feature had ever been used. After analysis and modification by the Air Ministry a standard system of airfield lighting was defined. Commonly known as Drem Mark 1, it consisted of:

1) An 'Outer Circle' of lights, slightly more than one mile in radius from the centre of the airfield.
2) An approach 'Funnel' of six lights in a 'V' shape which directed the pilot towards the runway in use. There was a separate funnel for each runway, and clearly only one was lit at any time.
3) Two pairs of totem poles per runway, delineating the overrun areas at each end.

Pilot Officer Bob Foster damaged two and shared the kill of one Junkers 88 whilst flying R4118. Before the Battle he was involved with 605 Squadron in the development of the Drem Lighting system.

4) A 'Glide Path Indicator', plus a 'Floodlight' at the touch-down point.
5) A 'Flarepath' of electric lights spaced at 100 yard intervals down the left-hand side of each runway.

Two extras were considered essential at fighter stations:

1) Four groups of 'Outer Lights' which effectively increased the radius of the outer circle for faster aircraft.
2) A pair of 'Taxi-ing Post' lights for each flarepath. These marked the holding or marshalling point for the runway in use.

A returning aircraft would orbit the station using either the outer lights, or the circle, until it was given the clear to land. A mobile floodlight external to the airfield could assist the pilot in locating the funnel in use. He would then turn and enter through the funnel. The threshold floodlight would then be switched on and with the aid of the totem poles, the pilot would be able to judge the touch-down point on the runway. As soon as he had touched down, the floodlight would be extinguished, and he would continue down the runway using the flarepath on his left-hand side as a guide.

Within a very short time experienced pilots were suggesting that if the runway had the flarepath on both sides, then it would give a much better appreciation of height and distance, than was obtained at present using the floodlight and totems. This was tried and proved to be a substantial improvement, such that it was then suggested that the totems and floodlight were possibly superfluous!

Alec Ingle in 1943. After the Battle of Britain he was heavily involved in the testing of the Mk II Hurricane.

Drem Lighting came to be extensively used at RAF stations throughout Britain. Ian Piper in his book on 605, *We Never Slept*, claims the whole system was designed by the members of 605 and suggested to the Station Commander, 'Batchy' Atcherley. Piper claims it should have been described as '605 Lighting'.

Pilot Officer (later Wing Commander DFC) Alec Ingle (RAF no. 83980) flew R4118 only once. He had a very distinguished career. He was shot down three times in six weeks during the Battle, recovering sufficiently by December 1940 to undertake the high altitude testing of the Hurricane II for which he received a special mention in April 1941. He took over command of 609 Squadron from Roland Beaumont only to be shot down and captured shortly thereafter in France. He held various senior posts in the RAF and was one of the thirteen Battle of Britain pilots who marched at the head of the procession for Winston Churchill's funeral.

Alec recalls his side of Bunny Currant's story:

We'd been sent up on patrol, we were about 22,000 feet or something over Kent, and we'd been there for quite some time, and we were very cold, very cold indeed, because we'd throttled right back, just waiting, and suddenly old Bunny was taken short. Well, we didn't know this at the time, but the first we knew, we'd descended into cloud, and the entire squadron was in a steep turn, and we came out of this cloud, we couldn't understand what the bloody hell was going on, but the entire squadron went into an even steeper turn. Eventually we came out of the bottom of this cloud and straightened ourselves out, and learnt about it afterwards, that old Bunny had been taken short and peed on his compass, and had cleaned it away with his thumbnail!

Alec Ingle was shot down by a Me 109. His escape with only a minor injury was so remarkable it is worth hearing Alec tell the story:

On October 27 1940 I was returning to base from an engagement in Hurricane V7599. Whilst flying at about 12,000ft I was hit from an unexpected quarter by heavy fire.

Immediately I took evasive action by diving into cloud beneath me, whereupon my engine seized and black oil covered the windscreen. When I emerged from the cloud, I looked for a suitable field in which to land, but most were heavily obstructed. However I sighted a field within which I estimated that a wheels-up landing could be made, so I headed towards it. It was only possible to see by craning my neck around the windscreen, and to do this I had to release the shoulder lock on my Sutton Harness.

At about 800ft I decided to turn into the field but there was no response to the ailerons, so I had to proceed straight ahead. On looking at the starboard wing, I noticed a large hole with two jagged ends of wire protruding from it. I then saw a row of trees ahead of me and, by jinking, saw that there appeared to be a gap between them, dead ahead. I was low, had no airspeed indicator, and could not turn. I tried the flaps without result when suddenly a railway cutting appeared and I just managed to jump the aircraft over it and arrived somewhat heavily on t'other side, amongst the trees.

My head had obviously impinged on the gunsight because I could not lock my harness. Somewhat dazed, therefore, I was surprised to see a number of people around me, including a district nurse. She stuck a plaster on my head and the next thing I knew I was back at Croydon. I vaguely remembered that I should recover the radio crystals, as they were in short supply, but whether I did stop I cannot now recall.

The aircraft had been hit by cannon shell and machine-gun bullets from below. The aileron controls were severed, the air speed indicator damaged, the oil and hydraulic pipe lines fractured, and, of course, the engine seized.

During two visits to Alec Ingle in 1999, the author was able to go through his log books. And there was the solution to a mystery. Although the serial number, R4118, was known, and that the aircraft must have carried 605 Squadron's letters UP during the Battle of Britain, it had not been possible to discover the identification letter. The Operational Record Book only showed the serial number. In Alec's log he had meticulously recorded both the serial number and identification letter. There it was – UP-W! So now R4118 could be rebuilt bearing its original identification. Alec also reminded the author that a squadron was made up of A Flight with Red and Yellow sections, and B Flight with Blue and Green sections. Each section comprised three aircraft. Alec told me that flying during the Battle was not a precise science:

If you were attacking bombers, ok you had a quick crack at a bomber and then you came round and saw what was going on, but if there were 109s above you, you had to watch your step pretty damn carefully. I mean, you could be tangling around the place and at some stage, you've got to dive out of it, and try and come back in again, and of course, almost invariably, when you did that, by the time you wanted to come back in again, there wasn't a bloody aircraft to be seen! There could be everything in the sky one minute, two minutes later there wasn't a damn thing.

Mike ('Tom') Cooper-Slipper was particularly remembered for smashing his Hurricane into a Dornier.

A fellow pilot was Mike Cooper-Slipper. He flew alongside R4118 on several sorties, however not on one occasion when he rammed another aircraft. Mike's aircraft had been hit by fire from a German bomber. He lost control and smashed into a Do17, losing his port wing. He bailed out but sustained only light injuries. His Hurricane was L2012, one of the few still fighting fitted with a two position De Havilland propeller. On a visit to Croydon by Winston Churchill, Mike got chatting to him and managed to get him to sign his log book. On another occasion, Mike was chasing an enemy bomber racing for the Channel. In an attempt to increase its speed the bomber jettisoned its bomb load on the houses and fields in the local area. A few days later Mike attended a social event where he overheard a beautiful young lady telling friends about being nearly killed by bombs dropped from a bomber being chased by a Hurricane. Mike introduced himself as the pilot of the Hurricane. The girl was Rita, who later became his wife.

Bunny Currant has vivid memories of Mike and his encounter with the German bomber:

I have very warm positive memories of that young nineteen-year-old man at Croydon during the Battle of Britain. As a flight commander, he was my No. 2 in the flight and was a brilliant pilot. Always smiling, enthusiastic and cheerful, he was a delight to have around. I was an old fogey of twenty-nine with well over two years flying the magnificent war-horse, the Hurricane. I remember so well the day (15 September) we took off from Croydon to attack a large formation of about fifty German bombers flying at 18,000 feet and escorted by Me 109s. At that time, I was leading the squadron of twelve Hurricanes – we dived into that gaggle of bombers. I chose my target, fired and then broke away down below the bombers. I looked up and above me was a bomber with a wing gone, spinning round slowly and alongside was a Hurricane, also with one wing gone, spinning rapidly! I then saw six parachutes, five Germans and Michael Cooper-Slipper, the result of the collision. Later in the day Michael turned up cheerfully at Croydon and gave me a trophy – a German Mae West! He was full of eager beaver enthusiasm as always – a great lad.

Another ace to fly R4118 just once during the Battle was Pilot Officer (later Group Captain DFC) Peter Douglas Thompson (RAF no. 84697). His introduction to 605 Squadron was an interview with Squadron Leader Archie McKellar, the Commanding Officer who had taken over from Walter Churchill. "We were wheeled in to see Archie McKellar, we saluted very smartly, and saw this worn-out little half-pint. He was about five foot six, he was the No. 1 ace at that time, he was the top scorer in Fighter Command, and he said, 'Well, sit down, you're in A Flight, you're in B Flight. Oh, yes, when it comes time to fly, put on clean underwear! This is a very practical situation. If you got shot, you might end up in your underwear!' Anyway, he was a very tired man at the time." Despite having his propeller shot away during the Battle, Peter Thompson survived relatively unscathed. He went on to be one of the twenty-four volunteer pilots who flew Hurricanes off HMS *Ark Royal* for the defence of Malta in 1941. He related a fascinating story to the author in 1998:

Peter Thompson who was largely responsible for assembling the Historic Aircraft Flight, which later became the Battle of Britain Memorial Flight.

I'll tell you what we did. In order to get more lift for take-off, we lowered the flaps, we'd got wooden blocks, and the airmen put in the wooden blocks, and we put the flaps up again. Well, we wanted half-flap for take-off, so we put the wooden blocks in, once you got airborne, you put the flaps down, and the blocks fell off, and you'd put the flaps up again! It worked, it worked very well! Anyway, twenty-three of us got there, never did know what happened to the other one.

In 1957, whilst commanding RAF Biggin Hill, Peter Thompson was largely responsible for establishing the Battle of Britain Memorial Flight, then known as the Historic Aircraft Flight. Three Spitfire PR XIXs joined the then only surviving flying Hurricane to form the initial core of the collection.

Among R4118's sorties during the Battle of Britain, it was also flown by Sgt L C 'Charles' Sones, Pilot Officer A M W 'Alec' Scott (his first flight with 605 was in R4118), Pilot Officer Derek Forde and Pilot Officer Charles English. English last flew R4118 on 5 October and was killed in combat two days later in another Hurricane, his parachute being caught in the tail of the aircraft as he bailed out. Charles Sones recalled the terrifying plight of Charles English as his aircraft took him down to the ground. Alec Scott was killed on 2 January 1941, his Scottish wit being sorely missed on the squadron. Both Sgt Sones and P/O Forde safely survived the war.

I asked Bunny Currant about the flying training he had received:

I wanted to fly when I was three-years-old. I had said to my mother, 'When I'm five, I'll take you up in my own aeroplane'. In 1914, I was outside our home in Luton and I heard a great noise of aircraft, and I looked up and there were all these formations of bi-planes

George R.I.

George VI, *by the Grace of God,* OF GREAT BRITAIN, IRELAND

AND THE BRITISH DOMINIONS BEYOND THE SEAS, KING, DEFENDER OF THE FAITH, EMPEROR OF INDIA, *&c.*

To Our Trusty and well beloved **Christopher Frederick Currant** Greeting:

WE, *reposing especial Trust and Confidence in your Loyalty, Courage, and good Conduct, do by these Presents Constitute and Appoint you to be an Officer in Our* Royal Air Force *from the* First *day of* April *1940. You are therefore carefully and diligently to discharge your Duty as such in the Rank of* Pilot Officer *or in such higher Rank as We may from time to time hereafter be pleased to promote or appoint you to and you are at all times to exercise and well discipline in their Duties both the inferior Officers and Airmen serving under you and use your best endeavours to keep them in good Order and Discipline. And We do hereby Command them to Obey you as their superior Officer and you to observe and follow such Orders and Directions as from time to time you shall receive from Us, or any your superior Officer, according to the Rules and Discipline of War, in pursuance of the Trust hereby reposed in you.*

GIVEN at Our Court, at Saint James's

the Twenty first day of May 1940 in the Fourth Year of Our Reign

By His Majesty's Command

Bunny Currant's commission, signed by HM The King.

from Hendon and something went 'boing' through me, never left me. I had to fly, I had to fly, I just had to fly, and all I wanted to do was to fly, and eventually got accepted in 1935 to become a pilot, direct entry, straight in.

We started flying in Tiger Moths in January '36. I consider that we all have something essential in us that we must, or want, or long to do. Every human being, I think, gets this or, if they don't, they're unfortunate. It can be anything. It can be an engineer, it can be a preacher, it can be anything, it could be a burglar, but you get this thing in you, right in the core of your very being, this is what you want to do. That's what I had. Lots of people get it for lots of reasons. So you've got millions of people in the world who are square pegs in round holes because they're not doing the job they really want to do, and then you've got many, many, many more who are round pegs in round holes, and I considered myself to be a round peg in a round hole, because when I started to fly it was so easy, I had no difficulty at all, never have had. They used to give you assessments, and they were Exceptional, Above Average, Average, Below Average and NBG. Right through into my squadron service, I was still getting 'Exceptional'. Well, I didn't have to work for it, as many of them did, I found it so normal and natural to fly. I could do it from the moment I sat down. I had eight hours of dual and then Mr Jerdan, who was my instructor, got out of the front cockpit of the Tiger Moth, much to my relief, and patted me on the head and

A merry group of pilots of 151 Squadron at North Weald in 1937. A jovial Bunny Currant is on the right next to Sir Samuel Hoare, Minister for Air and Kingsley-Smith, Secretary of State for Air. Note the early two-bladed Hurricane behind the Secretary of State.

said, "OK, Currant, one circuit and landing" and I did it, and came down and I thought 'this is bliss'. I had no thought whatsoever of war or fighting in an aeroplane. It hadn't ever entered my head. I wanted to fly, and I enjoyed every second of it, until suddenly we were in a situation where one had got to fight for one's existence.

Then they sent us to Egypt, for FTS (Flying Training School), on the canal near Abu Suier where we did nine months flying Hawker Harts and Hawker aircraft, the forerunners of the Hawker Hurricane. And then the Royal Air Force, in its wisdom, said to us all at the end of our time of training and after we'd got our wings and we were then going to go into the world, into the RAF somewhere, "Where would you like to be posted?" I was young and single, and said, "Overseas, overseas, overseas." Where did I end up? RAF Kenley, next door! And there they had a squadron of Bulldogs and a squadron of Gauntlets, and I was in the Gauntlet squadron. I started my fighter training with 46 Squadron at Kenley in December '36.

There has been much discussion on the relative merits of the Hurricane and its fiercesome opponent, the Messerschmitt 109. Both were still under development by the opening hostilities in 1939, and even by May 1940 not all Hurricanes had the benefit of Constant Speed airscrews without which they were no match for the Me 109. Fortunately, our Hurricane emerged from the factory in July 1940 with such a propeller, the need for which was highlighted in a report from the Squadron Leader, Officer Commanding, 67 Wing, RAF:

REPORT ON TRIAL OF HURRICANE versus MESSERSCHMITT 109

1. On 2 May, 1940, a trial took place to discover the fighting qualities of the Me 109 as compared with the Hurricane.
2. Owing to the absence of oxygen apparatus in the Me 109 the trial was carried out between 10,000 and 15,000 feet.
3. The comparison consisted of (a) take-off and climb to 15,000 feet, (b) a dogfight, and (c) line astern formation.
4. Both aircraft took off together. Both the take-off and initial climb of the Me 109 was better than that of the Hurricane, in spite of the fact that the Hurricane was fitted with a Constant Speed airscrew, and full throttle and full revs were used.
5. At 15,000 feet the aircraft separated and approached on another head-on for the dogfight. The Hurricane did a quick stall turn followed by a quick vertical turn and found himself on the 109's tail. The pilot of the 109 was unable to prevent this manoeuvre succeeding. From that point the Hurricane pilot had no difficulty remaining on the tail of the Me 109. The pilot of the 109 tried all possible manoeuvres and finally the one most usually employed by German pilots, namely a half-roll and vertical dive. The Hurricane followed this manoeuvre, but the Me drew away at the commencement of the dive, and it is felt that had the pilot

ROLLS-ROYCE AERO ENGINES FOR SPEED AND RELIABILITY

An advertisement from Rolls-Royce showing how to hand start a Hurricane. It hardly matches its claim for 'speed and reliability'. The pilot seems to be scratching his head. One hopes those are not enemy overhead!

continued this dive he might have got away. However, in the pull-out the pilot of the Me 109 found that it was all that he could do to pull the machine out of the dive at all, as fore and aft it had become very heavy. In fact, the pilot was of the opinion that had he not used the tail adjusting gear, which itself was extremely heavy, he would not have got out of the dive at all. The pilot of the Hurricane found that he had no difficulty in pulling out of his dive inside the 109, but that he had a tendency to black-out, which was not experienced by the pilot of the 109. This tendency to black-out in the Hurricane when pulling out of high speed dives is in my opinion largely due to the rather vertical position in which the pilot sits. It is very noticeable that in the 109 the position of the pilot is reclining, with his legs well up in front of him. It has also been noticed that German pilots do pull their aircraft out of dives at very high speeds, and as I think the position in which the pilot sits is the main reason that black-out is avoided, I feel that this is a point which should be duly considered when in the future a fighter is designed to meet other fighters.

6. After the dogfight the 109 took position in line astern on the Hurricane and the Hurricane carried out a series of climbing turns and diving turns at high speeds. In the ordinary turns the Hurricane lapped the 109 after four complete circuits,

The only known photograph of a 605 Squadron Hurricane taken during the Battle of Britain. It is being refuelled before being flown by Mike Cooper-Slipper. Note the repair to the starboard wing which shows as a patch on the leading edge.

and at no time was the pilot of the 109 able to get his sights on the Hurricane. In the climbing turns, though the 109 could climb faster he could not turn as fast, which enabled the Hurricane again to get round on his tail. In climbing turns after diving, the weight on the elevators and ailerons of the 109 was so great that the pilot was unable to complete the manoeuvre, and in the diving turns he was unable to follow the Hurricane for the same reason.

7. During these tests one point became abundantly clear, namely that the 109, owing to its better under camouflage, was very much more difficult to spot from underneath than the Hurricane. This difference gives the 109 a definite tactical advantage, namely when they are below us they can spot us at long distances, which we when below them find most difficult. As in all our combats at the moment initial surprise is the ideal at which we aim, I strongly recommend that the underside of Hurricanes should be painted a duck-egg blue, the roundels remaining the same, as it is the contrast between black and white only which is so noticeable from below.

Conclusion

8. The Me 109 is faster than the Hurricane by some 30 to 40 miles an hour on the straight and level. It can out-climb and initially out-dive the Hurricane. On the other hand it has not the manoeuvrability of the Hurricane, which can turn inside without difficulty. After this clear-cut demonstration of superior manoeuvrability there is no doubt in my mind that provided Hurricanes are not surprised by 109s, that the odds are not more than two to one, and that pilots use their heads, the balance will always be in favour of our aircraft, once the 109s have committed themselves to combat.

9. In this connection, judging from the tactics at present being employed by the 109s, namely sitting above us and only coming down when they can surprise a straggler, and then only completing one dive attack and climb away, I am fairly certain that the conclusion of the German pilots is the same as our own, and I cannot help feeling that until all Hurricane aircraft have Constant Speed airscrews to enable them to get up to the height at present adopted by the 109s we shall have few further chances of combat with this particular type of German aircraft.

What was not covered in the above report was a comparison of the armament of the two aircraft at the time. The relative merits of the fire power of the cannon-equipped Me 109 versus the Browning machine gun-equipped Hurricane at the time of the Battle has never been resolved. What is interesting is the mix of bullets fitted to the Brownings in the Hurricane. The most advanced was the 'de Wilde' bullet. Belgian inventor, de Wilde, produced an incendiary bullet. Incendiary bullets were less effective at puncturing enemy aircraft than armour-piercing ones, but they could ignite fuel in tanks. In fact the 'de Wilde' bullet in the Hurricane was an improvement, by Major Aubrey Dixon from the Royal Arsenal at Woolwich, on the original, but the 'de Wilde' name was retained to prevent the enemy discovering Dixon's formula. There was an acute shortage of Dixon's bullet, so a typical loading of the eight guns was one with 'de Wilde', two with armour-piercing, with tracer in two and ball in the remaining three. At the outset of the Battle of France, the eight guns were harmonised at 650 yards with minimal effect, but in the Battle most squadrons had their guns harmonised at 250 yards or less, giving, as Bunny Currant said to the author, 'a good pattern of lead'.

The following letter from an Old Etonian appears as an appendix to the 605 Squadron Operations Record Book for 28 September:

Extract from a letter written by F/O Ralph Hope to his family, relative to his parachute descent on Saturday 28 September 1940, and forwarded with the request that it may be inserted as Appendix to this Unit Summary of even date – 'F/O Hope was shot down, bailing out on top of an oak tree near Ticehurst – unhurt.'

...Saturday was not quite such a success from my point of view, as on our third patrol I lost my aircraft. We were at about 21,000ft when we got involved with a squadron of Me 109s. They got me before I even saw them, which is very annoying. I first felt a kind of funny bump, and as I turned to see what was up, my controls suddenly felt funny, a lot of red sparks and black smoke appeared round my feet and a cloud of white smoke, probably glycol, began streaming back from the engine. The aircraft began going downhill fast. I slid back the hood and began to get out, my goggles were shipped off and my helmet began to lift up in the slipstream; I realised I hadn't undone my straps so I pulled out the retaining pin and stood up, standing on anything which came handy (the seat, the instrument panel or the stick; I don't know really). The air seized hold of me and there was a wrench as my oxygen tube snapped off (I had forgotten to undo it) and I shot out into the sky. The aeroplane disappeared. It was nice and cool falling. I was head down of course, but found the position quite comfortable; there was no sense of speed or feeling of falling. I had a look at the clouds below (they were about 4,000-5,000ft) and then collected the odd bits of my helmet and had a look round. My parachute was still on my seat, both my boots were on, and I did not seem to have lost anything except my goggles, and a handkerchief and map which must have fallen out of the pockets in my knees when I first went upside down. After a while I thought about pulling the rip cord. "What about giving the old 'brolly' a try out?" I thought. I seemed to have fallen a goodish way, so I pulled. The canopy streamed out, there was a hard jerk, and there I was right side up, quite comfortable and floating slowly, Oh! so slowly, earthwards. I was about 9 to 10,000ft so I had fallen free for about 8 or 9,000ft (from about 18,000ft) and might have fallen further with advantage. When I looked up I could see a shining white canopy above me, and little silver specks having no end of a dogfight in the clear blue above me. A Spitfire dived down past me with a high pitched whine, but that was the only disturbance. The parachute began to swing me about and it wasn't long before I felt sick, very sick in fact by the time I landed. It was fun going into the clouds as the sun played a sort of 'spectre of the Brocken' effect on my shadow as I approached them. When I emerged the countryside looked pleasantly open, and after drifting quite a way I thought I saw where I should land. Two farm hands had the same idea. We were all wrong as in spite of attempts on my part to avoid it I came down in a spinney of young oak trees, pulling up short about twenty feet from the ground, hanging in my harness. I managed to get hold of a trunk, pull myself over to it, get out of the parachute harness and climb to the ground, where I remained quite still until I was found. The Army soon took charge of me, gave me a drink and some lunch, and drove me back to Croydon. The only damage I sustained was a hefty bruise on my right shoulder from hitting the tail as I jumped, and a bruise on my leg, and a torn trouser from the somewhat unceremonious descent through the upper branches of the oak tree. Now I go about with my arm in a sling, feeling particularly good as I have been given a week's sick leave.

Hope's experience was mentioned in the ORB 'Summary of Events' for 28 September which highlights problems facing the fighter squadrons:

The squadron was up in the air four times today, twice encountering Me 109s above them and each time being jumped on from a superior height. Feeling is growing rather strong about being sent up against the Me 109s without bombers at an inferior height, and complaints continue to be made to Control. It is realised, however, that Group Controllers are faced with a difficult task when twin engine fighters are sent over with single engine fighters, thus making it difficult for the Observer Corps accurately to report the presence of bombers amongst single engine fighters. F/Lt Currant destroyed one Me 109, F/O Hope was shot down, bailing out on top of an oak tree near Ticehurst – unhurt, and F/O Crofts being killed. P/O Madle posted to the squadron. In the evening P/O Foster [in R4118] and Sgt Wright damaged a Ju 88 off Beachy Head while attempting to bomb shipping.

Ralph Hope was killed on 14 October. The ORB recorded, "Apart from being the only original 605 Squadron auxiliary still in the squadron, his charming personality and quiet sense of humour and stability will be much missed by everyone in the squadron."

This combat report, written by the squadron's intelligence officer, for 22 October signalled the end of R4118's role in the Battle:

12 Hurricanes of 605 Squadron left Croydon at 1411 hours on 22 October 1940 with orders to patrol KENLEY – BIGGIN HILL at angels 20. The squadron were flying in flights abreast pairs astern with one aircraft weaving in front and above and another weaving behind and slightly below the squadron. Then the squadron were flying approximately

Hurricane Combat by David Shepherd: John 'Archie' Milne, flying R4118 UP-W, destroys an Me 110 over Dorking at 0945 hours on 27 September 1940.

east in the neighbourhood of TONBRIDGE at 22,000ft, 7 Me 109s were seen ahead of them at 24,000ft flying south-east. No other enemy aircraft being seen in the air at the time, the squadron followed the enemy formation, attempting to catch it up, but were unable to do so. Shortly afterwards five Me 109s were seen at about the same height as the other Me 109s, but approaching from the north-east. These enemy aircraft flew round behind the squadron into the sun, and two of them commenced to dive upon A Flight, who were flying to the right-hand side of B Flight. As soon as the 5 Me 109s were sighted, the squadron began to make a defensive circle to the right. Before however, this could be completed, 2 of the Me 109s dived upon the rear pair of A Flight (nearest to them). Yellow 2, weaving behind the squadron, endeavoured to climb up to the enemy aircraft, who were by then attacking the next pair of A Flight. One of the Me 109s saw Yellow 2 and broke away right and climbed. Yellow 2 gave it a 3 second burst from 200 yards, using 1½ rings deflection. The perspex hood appeared to come off, it turned on its back, and went into a vertical dive. Yellow 2 followed it down to 5,000ft, firing two 4 second bursts from astern from 200 yards, increasing to 400 to 500 yards. Pieces came off the tail of the enemy aircraft, which was eventually lost in haze at 3,000ft towards DUNGENESS.

It is thought probable that these two formations of 7 and 5 Me 109s respectively were originally one formation (or part of some larger formation) and that, having sighted 605 Squadron before the squadron sighted them, the seven aircraft went on ahead as a decoy so as to enable the 5 Me 109s to carry out the attack described above.

After this attack, the squadron reformed over Gatwick and orbited at 30,000ft but nothing further was encountered.

COMBAT REPORT.

Sector Serial No. ....(A) —

Serial No. of Order detailing Flight or Squadron to
Patrol ....(B) —

Date ....(C) 22nd October 1940.
                                                                                            Yellow 2.
Flight, Squadron ....(D) Flight : A. Sqdn. : 605.

Number of Enemy Aircraft ....(E) 5.

Type of Enemy Aircraft ....(F) Me.109.'s.

Time Attack was delivered..(G) 14.45hours.

Place Attack was delivered ....(H) TONBRIDGE — DUNGENESS.

Height of Enemy ....(J) 24 — 25,000ft.

Enemy Casualties ....(K) 1 Me.109 damaged.

Our Casualties....................Aircraft...............................(L) —

                                Personnel ....(M) —

GENERAL REPORT ....(R) Yellow Section airborne

14.10 hours. When patrolling in pairs by Flights at 22,000ft.(I was weaving

underneath the rear of the Squadron) two Me.109's, followed by 3 more, passed

us on the port side going the opposite way, and flew round behind us into the

sun. As the Squadron turned right towards them the three made a feint attack

while the other two came out of the sun into the last pair of "A" Flight. I

endeavoured to climb up towards the two Me.109's which had broken up our last

pair and were now attacking the next two of "A" Flight. One of them saw me

coming and broke away right, and climbed. I gave him a 1½-ring deflection from

200 yards, 3-sec. burst. His perspex hood seemed to come off, he turned on to

his back and went into a vertical dive. I followed him down to 5,000ft. firing

at 200 yards range from astern, but increasing to 4 - 500 yards (2 - 4sec. bursts).

Pieces came off the tail end of the aircraft, but did not affect his flying ability.
He continued in a shallow dive, going S.E., and I lost him in haze at 3,000ft.
towards DUNGENESS.

Signature *E W Wright*
                                                                Sgt.
                                                        ⎧ Section Yellow.
                                        O.C.   ⎨ Flight A.
                                                        ⎩ Squadron 605 Squadron No.

OC off Re .

(3567—1611) Wt. 27885—2533 850 Pads 9/39 T.S. 700 FORM 1151

Eric ('Ricky') Wright, flying as Yellow 2, filed his personal combat report for 22 October. In this engagement, R4118, flown by Derek Forde as Yellow 1, was badly damaged marking the end of its participation in the Battle of Britain.

A reunion of 605 Squadron pilots in 1990, all of whom flew in the Battle of Britain.
Back row: Bunny Currant, Ken Jones, Bob Foster, Mike Cooper-Slipper.
Front row: Archie Milne, Alec Ingle, Gerry Edge, Jack Fleming, Peter Parrott.

11 Hurricanes returned to Croydon 1515 to 1600 hours.

Red 1	F/Lt Currant
Red 2	Sgt Howes
Red 3	P/O Foster
Yellow 1	P/O Forde [in R4118]
Yellow 2	Sgt Wright
Yellow 3	P/O Milne

Our losses – (1 aircraft Cat III, 1 aircraft Cat II [R4118]. P/O Milne wounded).

R4118, mentioned in this report as Yellow 1, staggered back to Croydon with Derek Forde but was found to be Cat II (damage beyond repair at site). This was the same engagement in which Archie Milne's aircraft (Cat III) was destroyed but which happily led him to marry his nurse. The ORB records, "P/O Milne force-landed near Dorking, slightly wounded in his back. He put up a very fine show in managing to land his machine beyond the town, but in doing so fractured his hip bone, which will take a long time to mend."

Apart from being a distinguished fighter ace, Bunny Currant in his quieter moments writes poetry and paints. 'I wanted to paint an air battle scene from above.'

These brave young fighter pilots would not be left unscarred by their experiences. Bunny Currant has left us with several flavours of what it was really like to serve his country in the air in those days of 1940. His comments, his poetry and his letters need to be treasured, not as a dull record, but for those of us who follow to appreciate the quiet uncomplaining sacrifice those young men were prepared to face, day after day. Here Bunny starts by summarizing his thoughts on the Battle:

I am going to try and share my feelings and sensations during the five years and eight months of World War 2. But more specifically of the period known as the Battle of Britain, which was officially declared as between 10 July and 31 October 1940, three months and twenty days.

In that particular period of 112 days I took off to engage the German Air Force 72 times. During that time I attacked and either shot down or damaged 28 German aircraft. Those are the known facts at the time as it happened to myself.

Now to try and share the emotions in those 72 events is quite a different matter entirely. I can only explain my emotions and sensations, no-one else's. Of course there was fear but always BEFORE the event, whether on the ground or airborne towards the event. Please remember that every single moment of every event is unknown before it happens, and may or may not occur exactly the same as in any other event, highly unlikely in fact! In my case it was first of all fear, but in spite of the fear of the prospect one never hesitated to DO IT. Something drove the inner being of oneself to jolly well get stuck in – as they say. I was never aware of any other pilot who appeared to hesitate to do his stuff. ALL, I repeat, ALL got stuck in. Once you were inside the cockpit the bulk of the fear vanished. Why, you may ask? Simple! One was very, very busy with controlling one's aircraft especially when in tight formations. One was one hundred percent focussed on that task: hence a lot (not all) of the fear vanished. Then to be told by the controller of a raid of one hundred plus ahead of you made me feel sharply aggressive. And then to see them I became incensed with a cool determined anger. How dare they come over here and drop their bombs all over the place, murdering deliberately, murdering human beings they would never know or see? These ugly grey metal monsters with black and white Swastikas on their aircraft – get rid of these invading swine!!! I must destroy these hideous metal machines, every man jack of them supporting Hitler and his hideous cruel war machine. No single thought about ME it was all about THEM. NO, no thought at all about me but I must destroy these ugly machines! So one dived into them and exhausted one's ammunition, then one belted back to base to refuel, rearm and up again and again. Sometimes on five occasions in one day. It was most extraordinary how one's thoughts were always on MUST GET STUCK IN TO BLAST THEM AWAY. Never ever worried of oneself of the danger or that I might get hurt: it didn't exist as far as I was concerned. That was my only permanent and persistent AIM and DESIRE. Fear? Yes, but in spite of that one just got on with it. It had to be done – end of story!

Looking back upon it at almost 91 years of age I would have altered nothing whatsoever except to try and do better next time. No regrets. No judging. Allowing totally, accepting totally with an inner feeling that it was O.K. And ALL RIGHT, NO REGRETS. Yes, I would do it all again, exactly as it happened. Some fears – but same resolve always!

Lesson – never ever regret anything. Feel very sad? Yes, of course. Don't stop yourself weeping with grief and sorrow, but allow every event to be just exactly as it IS. It can only ever be as it IS."

Two of Bunny's letters to his parents, both written from hospital beds, show a quiet determination, tinged with not a little humour.

Officers Ward,
Military Hospital, Shorncliffe, Kent
23.5.40

Dear Mother & Father & All
Heigh ho; heigh ho; we do get about these days don't we? My little story is long but amusing. You must excuse the writing I can only just see what I'm doing because of a black eye and what a beauty and a busted nose, apart from that I'm as fit as can be. I hope to be out again in a couple of days.

Yesterday morning we did an early morning before breakfast patrol over Northern France and the Channel, we saw plenty of activity in various forms and then all returned intact. At 11a.m. we took off again, twelve of us and we made for Arras. Unfortunately before we got there we rather lost each other in cloud layers and only five of us arrived together over Arras. Here we were subjected to very accurate A.A.Fire – pretty to watch but too close for a quiet snooze so I and another lad nipped into some cloud for protection. When we came out the other three had disappeared so had the A.A.bursts much to our relief. Then I met three Heinkel bombers or they met me, anyhow they were in the process of bombing – funnily all the bombs fell in a field in open country but it annoyed me to see them and so I waded into them and knocked one down in five seconds and then played catch me hit me with the other two. I hit the oil tank of one brute but he had the last laugh as his oil smothered my aircraft. I couldn't see a thing and my aircraft was rather shot about now and in due course the engine refused to play any more. Most irritating – no blue-pencil engine – no vision forward and 6000 feet over the German lines. I headed north gliding down, turning the clouds black and blue with curses. By now streams of steam from a burst glycol tank and volumes of black smoke from my oil tank were belching out and I must have looked a pretty sight. I hit the ground on my tummy – the aircraft's belly is more precise and then either my face hit the gun-sights or the gun-sights hit me and there I was all alone by my little self in the middle of a ploughed field, somewhere in France. Such a nice new Hurricane, and with great glee I took out a box of matches got at the petrol tank, sprinkled liberally and then lit same and retired immediately. A beautiful blaze and the dear old thing had gone.

I gathered up my gear and walked across the fields to a cottage where I met a number of French peasants. They were terribly kind and patched me up and poured large quantities of rum and wine down me. After about an hour in this cottage I set off determined to get to the Coast and England if it took me years. Before leaving I asked for a dictionary which they kindly gave me and with this and my gear I was on my way. I was carrying my helmet, sidcot, life-jacket and parachute and thus burdened and bloody I walked five miles into a small hamlet, stopped here for ten minutes for another sup of rum, then I proceeded to stop every refugee car I could and eventually got a lift as far as St Omer. Thousands of refugees thronged all the roads some going north and some south. All stared at me and crowded round and jabbered continually. They were all emphatic that the Germans were just over the hedge a few fields away, full of rumour and unfounded facts, all absolutely untrue.

The French people lose all dignity and reserve in an emergency, panic easily and whine continually. I have no time for them at all they've no guts, excellent when their troops are advancing but abject cowards in retreat. It was most depressing. I have transgressed from my narrative. At St. Omer I scrounged another lift, town empty and recently bombed, and so on to Calais, buildings here still burning from bombing that morning. My luck was in as a boat was just leaving for Dover at 9p.m. I walked into the Mess at Hawkinge after ten hours of varied fortunes, very tired but with tail up.

I have had an anaesthetic and the operation on my fractured nose, it should be nearly straight now. I shall be out of here this Saturday and hope to get some leave and shall see you all then.

My love to all
Christopher.

And back in hospital again:

Royal Victoria Hospital, Folkestone
Tuesday March 10 1942

Dear Mother and Father

Shades of [that] day [in] 1940 waft by with the breeze from my window, only this time it's the back of my face and not the front. Folkestone seems to have an attraction for me, but not I for Folkestone (I don't think that's sense).

History does repeat itself but not in all details or I wouldn't be lying in bed writing this to you. Again I got mixed up with the filthy Hun only this time it was four to one in their favour and they were fighters and not unfortunately fat-lazy bombers. I was roughly over the same spot as before – Fruges near St Pol, and where angels fear to tread I stepped in and leaped out again with three very angry Germans after my blood, they nearly got it too but just not quite, and I'll bet they're cursing themselves now. They certainly hit me and the aircraft. Funny what an awful row metal makes when it goes into all the wrong places, but my skull was tougher than their metal and although it went in the back of my head it met my skull and bounced off and came out again.

I pushed everything forward and spent the next five minutes hurling myself down to the French fields in the craziest way I knew with those three persistent Huns pouring lead at me the whole time. I shot over the French sand-dunes near Berck at 0 feet and some fantastic speed and those three little Huns gave it up as a bad job and flew away. The first time I've ever said a little prayer at 450 miles per hour but speed doesn't have anything to do with it really. I throttled back and flew across the calm bluish sea and took careful stock. Surprising how wet I was and it wasn't all sweat I found. I turned my oxygen full on in the hopes that at least I'd remain conscious until I'd crossed that water, at last Rye loomed up and another little prayer whispered its way up the Heavens. I was beginning to feel fairly groggy by now so searched quickly for Lympne which I found at the second attempt.

I put my wheels down, flaps down, seat down, tightened my straps hard back and motored gently in to land. I touched down quite safely and then the thing I was half-expecting and half-dreading occurred, the aircraft was so shot-up that the undercarriage collapsed, down went the nose and Spitfire and self did a perfect somersault, I ducked instinctively and found myself upside down on the cool grass of England, all very pleasant but I couldn't get out and again a prayer whispered its way out but a much bigger one this time with not a little fear that the wretched thing would catch fire. After what seemed ages some exhausted airmen got me out and I think we all said "thank God". I know I said "good show chaps" and collapsed onto a stretcher. They humped me into sick bay and a young F/O doctor made me comfortable with bags of rugs and hot tea. I lay there about 40 minutes wondering how bad my wound was and hoping like hell that I was all right. Doc kept taking my pulse and told me I was fine and of course I didn't believe him and of course I was all right really as it happened. Another ambulance drove me to hospital and they whisked me into the theatre, gave me a local anaesthetic and then really got down to brass-tacks. The surgeon spent an hour mucking about, I didn't pass out, felt perfectly lousy, but it's wonderful what a nurse's hand can do, bless them.

And here I am as large as life half sitting up and feeling fit except for a bit of a throb. I don't know how long I shall remain here, not long I hope.

My love and thoughts to all,
Christopher.

Bunny summed it all up in his poem written when 605 Squadron faced daily scrambles from its airfield at Croydon:

> *Croydon – September 1940*
> Once again he took to the air, and Croydon was the base
> To fight it out in fear and sweat so many times each day
> To smell the burn of cordite flash, to see the flames of war
> High up above the fields of Kent the dive, the zoom, the soar.
> Returning from a clash of foes one day he came across
> A sight which burnt deep in his soul and never can be lost.
> A pilot dangling from his chute towards the earth did drift
> He circled round this friend or foe so hopelessly alone
> To keep away whoever dared to fire on such a gift.
> It was a useless gesture though, as round and round he flew
> He saw as in an awful dream first smoke then flames spew
> Curl up his back as arms he waved and burn the cords of life
> Snapping the body from the chute, snatching him from war's strife.
> With sickening horror in his heart, he landed back at base.
> He cried himself to sleep that night in thanks to God's good grace
> That he was spared yet once again to live and fight this fight
> Against the things he saw as black, for things he believed were right.

In less than two months R4118 had been flown on forty-nine sorties by eleven different pilots, had been responsible or partly responsible for the destruction of five enemy aircraft, and had itself been severely damaged. The life of the great survivor had truly begun.

Details of the day-to-day sorties of R4118 during the Battle of Britain are to be found in Appendix III.

CHAPTER 9

The Men Behind the Few

H OW often have we heard that the men and women on the ground played just as much a part in the Battle as those in the air? Yet relatively few of their stories have survived. I was fortunate therefore to find Peter Freeman-Pannett who worked on R4118 during the Battle, and Bob Goodwin whose father, Fred, also was a member of 605's groundcrew.

605 Squadron groundcrew at Wick January 1940. Fred Goodwin is third from the left. Next to him is his shorter great pal, Ted Tombs. Amazingly they were both captured in 1942 and remained together in Japanese prisoner of war camps until liberated in 1945.

In November 2005 I interviewed Peter. He was born in 1920 and joined 605 Squadron in 1937 "purely weekends – I was a weekend soldier or airman. I used to go to work on a Saturday morning dressed half in uniform, half in civvies, get on a bus to Castle Bromwich, change, and start my instruction in whatever happened to come along." At the outbreak of war Peter was called up, still with 605 as an engine fitter. The Squadron was posted to Wick. Peter was moved to Leuchars of all places in the middle of winter.

There were around 200 groundcrew of us, with kitbags, and there were bagpipes and we had 200 British airmen trying to march to bagpipes up to the cairns. We only stayed there about a fortnight, then we were posted right up to Wick. It was ghastly. The billets we got there weren't finished, the old potboiler stoves we had in those days, bitterly cold, winds like mad. We had a storm one day. In the old days, we used to tie down these aeroplanes with great big hooks, and the CO kept the last of the Hinds as his own personal aeroplane. We had that tied down all round with these stakes. It ripped that aeroplane out of the ground, complete with the steel tie-downs and smashed it to bits against the hangar wall. That was terrible.

As the Battle of France started, 605 moved again. In many ways times were tougher for the groundcrews than the pilots. Peter was particularly upset by returning soldiers from Dunkirk who felt the RAF had not protected them on the beaches.

We came down from Wick to Hawkinge by train. We stopped about twice on the way at some stations, I can never remember, for a meal and toilets, got down there in the dark and, of course, the bombing of London started, so we spent the night in the train in a tunnel somewhere around London. Came out of there later in the day into Hawkinge where the aeroplanes had arrived but none of us there. Of course, we didn't see much of the aircrews at Hawkinge because they'd all gone. All shot down, like Currant, many lost in action. In seven days, we'd lost the lot, we were off out again, packed up – we never even got our beds, we slept on palliasses in the gym, four of us in turn, because we had to do shifts then, with so much going on, Hurricanes coming in from all sorts of MUs, with Australian, American, South African pilots, you never knew who you'd got. They'd come in, top them up, ammunition, fuel, and you'd never see them again. It was as bad as that. You had to harden yourself to it, because you knew it was going to come. The worst of it was for us, they packed us up, took us down to the Folkestone railway station, put us on the blacktop waiting for a special train to take us.

LAC Peter Freeman-Pannett writes a letter home. Wick, April 1940.

While we were there, there were trains coming up from the coast, Dover and Folkestone, with all the people they had rescued out of the water in Dunkirk, trains full of them. They didn't half treat us rough, threw everything at us – Where were you when we needed you? It wasn't gunfire, but it was bottles, anything. There we were with our kit, standing on the station. We couldn't do a thing. We couldn't answer them. We hadn't been there. That was really the worst thing that ever happened to me. We were deflated, we really were. Anyway, they packed us off on the train eventually, thank God, and we had that long journey and finished up at Drem.

From May 1940 605 Squadron was re-forming and recovering at Drem in Scotland from its battering in the Battle of France. Somewhat rested and with mostly new Hurricanes, including R4118, the Squadron flew down to Croydon on 7 September, but Peter had arrived on 27 August. He was not impressed but determined.

There were no hangars in Croydon. We didn't think anything of it, we just got on with it. We had a job to do. It was our life, because we knew that if we didn't do it, we were going to go under, and that was an even worse fate. That was typical of what we all thought. The job had to be done, and we were going to win somehow. We were going to go down fighting.

Fred Goodwin's watercolour painted from memory when in Changi jail. He swapped his cap badge with the guard for paints.

Peter Freeman-Pannett moved to a number of different Squadrons after September 1940 but amazingly was able to re-join 605 in 1943 on Mosquitos after the remnant of the Squadron had returned from the devastation of Singapore and Java. At 97 (in 2017) Peter is the oldest surviving 605 member from the Second World War.

In much the same way as Peter Freeman-Pannett, Fred Goodwin joined 605 Squadron in 1938.

His artistic gifts have left us, in a 200-page notebook, a unique record of the ground school which the crews undertook. Fred was a rigger, the complimentary skill to Peter as an engine fitter. During the Battle, each fighter had a rigger and engine fitter dedicated to it. Bob Goodwin, fortunately talked at length with his father about his wartime experiences. In July 1938 Fred had cycled across Germany, managing to get a close look at a fighter base and felt that the Germans were better prepared for war than the British. On one occasion at Drem Fred hitched a ride to the other end of the field with a pilot friend, John 'Dumbo' Deanesly on the wing of a Hurricane. Fred had not reckoned on Deanesly accelerating with the tail up to take-off speed. Fortunately they did not leave the ground.

It is worth recording Fred's wartime service, representative of so many who suffered under the Japanese. After the Battle of Britain he continued with 605 which remained exclusively a Hurricane squadron through to the end of 1941. In February 1942 he was en route to Malta with a cargo of Hurricanes when they were diverted to Indonesia. The Hurricanes, being equipped for desert warfare, proved no match for the Japanese Zero fighters. Before they were overrun, Fred and other British personnel destroyed the Hurricanes and fled to the caves. They were captured and sent to Changi prison on Singapore. From there the prisoners were moved on a month-long journey to Hokkaido Island in the hold of the Japanese vessel *Dai Nichi Maru*. More than 50 died in a notorious event under the most appalling conditions, their bodies being simply dumped overboard. Fred was forced down the mines. Throughout his time in enemy hands, Fred drew pictures, many from memory, of the Battle of Britain and the terrible scenes he witnessed at the

AC2 Fred Goodwin, 605 Squadron, rigger.

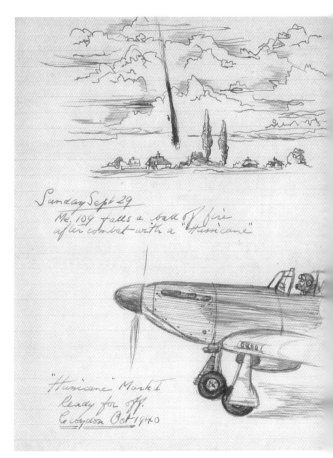

Fred Goodwin's view of a typical day during the Battle of Britain.

JUST ONE MORE.
MESSERSCHMIDT 109
ALMOST INTACT
PASSES THROUGH
REDHILL, SURREY
OCTOBER 9.

Fred Goodwin captured this view of an Me 109 enroute for evaluation by the RAF.

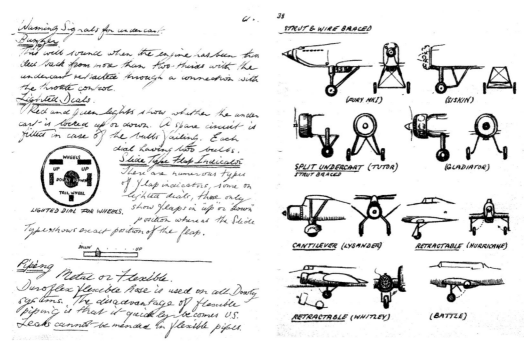

Above: *In his notebook, Fred Goodwin here illustrates a very early undercarriage indicator with the original Hurricane retractable tailwheel, subsequently made a permanent fixture.*

Above right: *At 18 years old, Fred Goodwin was destined to be a fine draughtsman.*

hands of the Japanese. He was liberated by the Americans on the day in 1945 when the bomb was dropped on Nagasaki. The Commandant of the Japanese camp sent Fred off with the words "Emperor give you holiday". Fred was flown out in a Grumman Goose over the sight of the US navy in Tokyo harbour.

The foregoing is a small sample from those who worked behind the scenes to keep R4118 and 605 Squadron in the air. But I cannot resist also adding a little humour from the team of the men who designed the Hurricane. Oliver Wareham worked under Sydney Camm in the Design Office (DO) at Hawkers in Kingston for 37 years. His son, John, worked from 1950 on the production side, proud of his inspection stamp 'HA522'. He carefully preserved much of the ephemera from his father's time including a collection of delightful menus from the Design Office annual dinners.

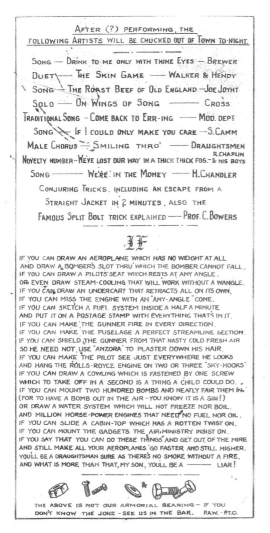

Opposite page: *A page from the 1936 Hawker Design Office Dinner and the signatures found on the reverse. Notable names include Sydney Camm (Chief Designer), P.W.S. 'George' Bulman (Director and Chief Test Pilot), Roy Chaplin (Camm's stress man and in 1939 Assistant Chief Designer), Robert McIntyre (Chief Draughtsman), Harry Viney (Works Manager) and Oliver Wareham.*

Top: *From the Hawker Design Office Dinner menu for 1937.*

Bottom: *From the Hawker Design Office Dinner menu for 1940.*

CHAPTER 10 Accident Prone

O N 23 October 1940, only one day after Derek Forde had nursed the aircraft back to Croydon, R4118 found itself in the workshops of the Service Aircraft Section of the Austin Motor Company at Longbridge. Austins were one of several Civilian Repair Organisations (CROs) established by Lord Beaverbrook in his role as the head of the Ministry of Aircraft Production. This was the first of R4118's four visits to a CRO – was any other fighter aircraft rebuilt (as opposed to being repaired at base) so many times during the war? The CROs, privately run companies, did a remarkable job. Out of the 14,500 Hurricanes built, over 4,000 were returned to operational condition by these organisations, making a huge saving in time and materials.

By 17 December the rebuilt aeroplane was at 18 Maintenance Unit at Dumfries from where it left for 111 Squadron on 18 January 1941. At the time, Treble One Squadron was resting after the Battle of Britain and at the same time acting as a training unit for new pilots destined for the south. It was split into two units, with the HQ based at Dyce, Aberdeen, and a detachment nearby at Montrose to which R4118 was assigned with A Flight.

Upon arrival, R4118 was first ferried by the squadron commander, Squadron Leader Arthur J Biggar, from Dyce to Montrose on 3 February. Of the eleven pilots who were to fly it over the next eight weeks, four were commissioned officers, the remainder being sergeant pilots. The aircraft worked hard, flying up to seven trips a day. Each sortie aimed to teach a specific topic, so there were usually several aircraft up at any one time. Pilots flying R4118 practised combat manoeuvres, scramble, camera gun, formation, dusk landings, climb to 25,000 feet, air firing, weaving, dogfighting, dawn and dusk patrol, formation changing, RT and night flying.

My next challenge was to trace some of the pilots who had flown R4118 with Treble One. The Personnel Management Agency at RAF Innsworth was splendidly helpful. Although they could not give out details of the pilots' service records, they were able to tell me if the pilot was thought to be still living, and his nationality.

From their replies I found that Sergeant (later Warrant Officer) Arnold Lester Hanes was transferred to the Royal Canadian Air Force in 1944. It was worth a shot so I asked a Canadian friend to enquire of the RCAF. However he tried the phone book first and within twenty-four hours had found Arnold (known as 'Skid') Hanes' widow. From there I made contact with Skid's son, Larry, and daughter, Carolle. Carolle came to the party on 20 September 2001 which we threw when R4118 arrived in its dilapidated state from India, and Larry visited Hawker Restorations during the rebuild. He was considerably moved when he found himself in the seat in which his father had sat in 1941, quite understandably when he told me what happened to Skid subsequently. Skid Hanes was shot down in the desert in Libya in December 1941. The Germans handed him over to the Italians and Libyans. Thus started nearly three and a half years as a prisoner of war during most of which he was subjected to the most inhumane treatment. He suffered an acute appendicitis followed by peritonitis. In July 1943 he escaped from his Italian captors only to be recaptured by the Germans and moved from camp to camp in Germany. After suffering acute deprivation, Skid was released by the advancing Allies in April 1945.

The Hanes family was responsible for an amazing find. I had discovered, through a protracted process of elimination, from the Operational Record Book of 111 Squadron that R4118 carried the letters JU-J. Mrs Hanes sent me a photograph of three of the squadron aircraft in formation. Lo and behold there was JU-J! How amazing to find a picture of 'our' Hurricane during the war.

Another Treble One pilot appeared to have had an interesting career. Was Pilot Officer (later Flight Lieutenant DFC) Denis Winton still living? Winton was a fairly uncommon name, so I sorted through the UK telephone directory on the computer at the local library. This produced seventy Wintons with addresses. So I sent off seventy letters. Within a week I was in correspondence with Denis' son and daughter. They had his log books with several JU-J entries. His later entries were very interesting. He had been posted to Malta flying Hurricanes. On 30 July 1941 he was on a strafing run on an Italian motor torpedo boat (MTB) when he was

Exhaust glare shields were fitted to R4118, indicating that it fulfilled a night fighter role, probably with 111 Squadron.

R4118 in service with A Flight on detachment at Montrose with 111 Squadron at Dyce. The Mk I Hurricanes still carry the fin markings of the Battle of Britain period, but the duck-egg blue spinner and band around the rear fuselage have been added as per the Air Ministry order of 12 December 1940. R4118 (JU-J), flown by Sergeant John Stein, is seen behind V6606 (JU-F) flown by Pilot Officer Denis Winton, and P3701 (JU-N) flown by Sergeant Arnold 'Skid' Hanes. This is one of three known photographs of R4118 taken at the same time on 9 March 1941 by Flight Lieutenant Peter Simpson DFC from W9179 (JU-B).

While 111 Squadron was based at Croydon, on 18 August 1940 Peter Simpson, who was to take the photograph above, probably damaged a Do 17, receiving such damage to his aircraft as to necessitate a forced-landing on Woodcote Park golf course, Epsom Downs. Two golfers were only re-assured that Simpson was not an enemy pilot when he produced a pack of Players cigarettes. Hence the title of Mark Postlethwaite's painting 'A Packet of Players'.

attacked by an Italian Macchi 200 fighter plane. Winton's Hurricane was damaged and he was forced to bail out at 700ft over the Mediterranean Sea. He swam two miles to the MTB and spent three hours with the eight dead sailors he had shot. Finally rescued, he returned to Malta with a captured Italian ensign.

SINGLE-ENGINE AIRCRAFT				MULTI-ENGINE AIRCRAFT						PASS-ENGER	INSTR/CLOUD FLYING [Incl. in cols. (1) to (10)]	
DAY		NIGHT		DAY			NIGHT					
DUAL	PILOT	DUAL	PILOT	DUAL	1ST PILOT	2ND PILOT	DUAL	1ST PILOT	2ND PILOT		DUAL	PILOT
(1)	(2)	(3)	(4)	(5)	(6)	(7)	(8)	(9)	(10)	(11)	(12)	(13)
69.45	245.10	3.35	11.25							21.35	14.05	10.40
	.45											
	.45											
	.40			Straffed one M.T.B. Shot down by Macchi – bailed out at 700ft								
	.25			Swam two miles to enemy m.T.B. Boarded her and spent								
	.20			three hours with eight dead 'uns. Returned by float plane								
				with captured Italian ensign. One turtle made a beam								
				attack on dinghy!								
3.00												

Pilot Officer Denis Winton's log book entry.

Although primarily a training unit, the Montrose detachment of 111 Squadron did do operational sorties against bomber raids from Norway. R4118 was involved in several such missions, one of which is recorded in the combat report for 24 March. It was flown by Sergeant Seaman, alongside Sergeant Kucera who went on to become a major Czech ace. Kucera's report read:

Yellow Section (2 A/C) Hurricanes of Squadron 111 A Flight (Sgt O Kucera, Czech, Yellow 1 and Sgt W Seaman, Yellow 2) were ordered to patrol Montrose at 20,000 feet at 1049 hours and left ground at 1058.

When over base at 20,000 feet, Yellow 2 was forced to return to base owing to effects of altitude but landed safely.

Weather was fine with cloud at 23,000 feet and visibility 20-30 miles but mist and cloud over sea 30-50 miles out at 2,000 feet.

Yellow 1 continued patrol and at 1120 hours when flying on a northerly course he sighted an A/C 3-4 miles SE of him and about 10 miles SE of Montrose flying east at 15,000 feet. He pursued it and identified it as a Ju 88.

The E/A dived to 3,000 feet at which height the whole combat took place, Sgt Kucera dived following the E/A and when about 300 yards away the E/A opened fire from the rear top machine gun but did not hit Sgt Kucera who made a stern attack at between 250 yards and 150 yards, giving a 3 second burst and breaking away to port. No immediate effect was noticed from this attack but no further return fire was experienced in the subsequent attack.

Sgt Kucera then made a quarter stern attack from the port side and gave a 7 second burst at between 150-100 yards range on the port engine and glasshouse. Black smoke was seen to issue from the port engine but the E/A passed into cloud just before it disappeared. However it was seen to be rocking from side to side at 45 degrees.

Sgt Kucera then circled around for a few minutes but no further sight of the E/A was obtained. Sgt Kucera being then about 50 miles out to sea asked Controller for a homing but owing to a breakdown on landline between transmitter and base was unable to obtain this. He returned safely and landed at Montrose 1150 hours. The usual camouflage was noticed and no unusual armament.

No cine-gun fitted.

R/T communication was poor.

No stoppages.

Details of the day-to-day sorties of R4118 with 111 Squadron are to be found in Appendix III.

After seventy-nine training or operational flights with 111 Squadron, R4118 moved on 26 April 1941 to an entirely training role with No. 59 Operational Training Unit at Crosby on Eden. There were coincidences. John 'Archie' Milne, who had destroyed an Me 110 when flying R4118, was sent as an instructor and Alec Ingle, who had flown two operational sorties in R4118, was posted to command 59 OTU in September 1941. They would have been re-united with their former aircraft had they been aware of it.

Alec recalls his time with 59 OTU:

You had four flights for just ordinary OTU work, and then you had this odd bird, this extra flight, called X Squadron which was for air firing practice. X Squadron had a Dominie for navigation, which was a bit of a joke but it was a very useful communication aircraft, and when that had to be serviced, they gave us an Oxford, which was quite useful. And then, when the Dominie came back, we kept both, because we somehow accumulated more and more aircraft. We started off with about three Battles, but the Battle was a

59 OTU Hurricanes carried the identification 'MF'. The 'X' indicated the Air Firing Squadron.

very unserviceable aeroplane, and there wasn't the inclination to do much about it. I mean, people could have gone away not having shot at a target, because the idea was they went through their own flight in the OTU, but then they did a period with the Air Firing Squadron before they finished.

The last few weeks were spent trying to shoot at targets and things. Well, there was no great organisation there, it was very hit or miss, there was no question of finding out whether people had actually hit the targets or not, so eventually, being a very energetic little so-and-so in those days, when I took command, I said, "This is absolute nonsense, we're just wasting money and time on this." So, there was a very good armament officer at the Group Headquarters called Mickey Dwyer, and he was very supportive. So I then got increasing numbers of Battles and worked out a system that I made these people hit a target eight times before they left the OTU. We had to set up a thing on the coast. We used to fly up the coast because the air firing was over the coast, south of Silloth. We had a little man parked out there and he was given a schedule of when the aircraft were meant to arrive, what times, and we knew what numbers had been given people, and he was to arrange to be climbing his weary way up and down, recording firing successes or otherwise.

We used to take them out firstly in a Master which just had one gun in it just to show them what to do, so they didn't shoot the ruddy Battle down, and then they went out in Hurricanes and practised their beam attacks using two of the eight guns.

And then, just for sort of sport, we used to have two-foot drones towed behind Hurricanes. You know, a little drone, when I say two feet, I mean it was two feet diameter, a drone, and that was quite an entertaining pastime, hitting one of those things! I should think it was about 400 feet from the towing Hurricane, it was quite close. They weren't encouraged to do astern attacks on it, nothing like that. But we got to the stage where, literally, we'd say, "No, you can't finish until you've managed to hit that thing eight times." It was a lot of work, we did a lot of flying, and we in fact wore out all the Brownings and all the aircraft on the station! You see, we'd just pinched the Brownings from the other flights. A Browning doesn't last very long, so at one stage we'd mucked up all the Browning barrels.

As a matter of interest, Birmingham Small Arms Company built 568,100 Browning machine guns during the Second War.

To have survived nearly six months as a trainer was not bad going for those times. But an accident occurred on 7 October. By an amazing stroke of good fortune I was able to find Sergeant (later Flight Lieutenant) F J M Palmer, a New Zealander in Auckland, who told me his story. Having gained his wings just three months earlier, he was nearing the end of his conversion with twenty-three hours on type. R4118 hit a lorry as it came in to land at Longtown.

Sgt Palmer writes:

I do recall air traffic calling to notify that the runway in use had been changed. Maybe they didn't tell the truck driver. My approach must have been normal and the touchdown also. I was looking out of the port side and as I slowed down a little I saw some men running and a second later the starboard wing hit the truck. I don't recall even looking at the truck, although I suppose I did. Maybe the men who were running were out of sight. I was up before the CFI the next day and he assured me that I had nothing to worry about. As he said, "the men should never have any reason to be working on a runway in use." The Officer Commanding recorded on the accident report: "Contractor allowed one of his vehicles on runway during flying – has been repeatedly warned against it."

Two views of the overhaul assembly line at Taylorcraft Aeroplanes at Rearsby where R4118 was rebuilt after hitting a lorry on the runway. Note the Rotol propeller fitted to the first aircraft in the top picture, compared with the De Havilland 'bracket' propeller on the first aircraft in the lower photograph.

So R4118 was off for major repair again, this time to Taylorcraft Aeroplanes Ltd at Rearsby near Leicester, another of the network of CROs. The poor aircraft suffered so many crashes, it is impossible to accurately work out what repairs were done on each occasion. Although Sergeant Palmer recalls damage to the starboard wing, the wing data plates show that the present wings were replaced much later. What we do know is that the rudder was repaired or replaced by Taylorcraft as it now bears a data plate reading 'TAYR/S2/G5/93914'. This indicates an overhaul by Taylorcraft at Rearsby, one by S2 (unidentified shadow factory), built by Glosters at Hucclecote, and the rudder's serial number. Taylorcraft built their own aeroplane, which became the Auster, but during the war their output of repaired fighter aircraft was prodigious. By 12 December 1941 R4118 was deemed 'RAAA' – Repaired Aircraft Awaiting Allocation.

On 22 December it was taken on charge by 44 Maintenance Unit at Edzell. Within two months it had been damaged again, this time stuffed into a pile of

Overhauled Hurricanes being prepared for flight test at Taylorcraft. Note the extensive use of female labour in traditionally male occupations.

snow by the MU pilot whilst testing the aircraft. An unfortunate Flight Lieutenant Alistair B Lennie was at the controls. The accident report reads: "Swung off runway through lack of brake pressure, crashed into snow bank, the serviceability of the aerodrome due to snow necessitating landings being confined to runways." The Officer Commanding commented: "The pilot should have ensured he had sufficient brake pressure before t/o, and further knowing he had insufficient pressure, should have remained in the air until it was built up." Whilst looking up '44 MU' on the Internet, I found the nephew of Flight Lieutenant Lennie, also Alistair Lennie. He filled me in on his uncle's accident record:

On 23 October 1939, as a Pilot Officer, P/O A B Lennie, whilst attached to 207 Sqn from RAF Mildenhall, was involved in a flying accident, flying a Battle 1, L5185, EM-? He crash landed at dusk. On 29 May 1940, by now promoted to F/Lt, Alistair was again involved in a further accident. He took off from RAF Cottesmore in a Hampden 1, P1275 for a night exercise and crashed into trees on approaching RAF Cottesmore at 0030 hours.

On 8 December 1942, whilst serving with 44 MU at RAF Edzell, Scotland, Alistair died whilst flight testing a Whitley Bomber Mk VII, BD686.

To these accidents I now had to add the one involving R4118. This time the damage was repaired at 44 MU although the work was not completed until early April 1942. At last the

Officers and pilots under training at 56 OTU, Tealing in October 1942. Several trained on R4118 in low-level formation flying and air gunnery. Back row: Sgt. Morgan, Sgt. Wheeler, Sgt. Lawson, Sgt. Balls, Sgt. Nisbet, Sgt. Switzer, Sgt. Davage, Sgt. Brown, Sgt. MacKay, Sgt. Samuels, Sgt. Carr. Centre row: F/Sgt. Stark, Sgt. Paterson, Sgt. Davis, Sgt. Mayhew, Sgt. Ray, Sgt. Villa, Sgt. Richards, Sgt. Cossar, Sgt. Pressland, Sgt. Sutherland. Front row: F/Sgt. Dimond, P/O MacDonald, P/O Thorne, P/O Kilpatrick, F/Lt Humphries, P/O Rothwell, P/O Inglis, P/O Salisby, P/O Cullen.

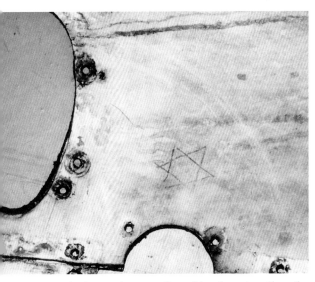

An interesting pencil marking found on the oil tank firewall. Believed to be the 'Star of David', it may have been applied during the aircraft's overhaul by David Rosenfield Ltd at Manchester in 1943.

The aircraft's all-important brass identity plate together with an aluminium one affixed on top after overhaul by David Rosenfield Ltd prior to shipment to India.

The LMS works at Derby manufactured and repaired, including those from R4118, Hurricane wings. The railway company also made parts for Typhoon fighters, and Hampden and Lancaster bombers. Above: *Building a new Hurricane wing.* Below: *A team of ladies make the small Hurricane components.*

A rare photograph of the assembly line at the Canadian Car and Foundry Company at Fort William.

aircraft was back in service, this time with 56 OTU at Tealing. 56 OTU specialised in training pilots in air gunnery. R4118 would have been used both for target towing and for practice firing. The drogue was carried just forty feet behind the towing aircraft. Not surprisingly the attacking aircraft, which carried live ammunition, was only allowed to fire laterally!

To its credit, R4118 survived eleven months at 56 OTU until it was damaged and sent to another CRO, this time David Rosenfield Ltd. They were primarily in the motor engineering business but quickly established themselves as a major aircraft repair organisation. The aircraft was received on 5 April 1943.

When in 2001 we dismantled the wings, we had found from identification plates on the main spars that they had been made by the Canadian Car and Foundry Company in Canada. Whilst the wings were being rebuilt by Bob Cunningham at Bournemouth, of which more later, we uncovered the wing data plates, whereupon I flew into another flurry of research. The plates read:

Wing Port
LMSD/CCF/41H/14136

Wing Starboard
LMSD/CCF/41H/10127

All major components carry data plates showing the part number (same as drawing number), serial number, sometimes the date of manufacture, and inspectors' stamps. In the case of R4118 the starboard aileron was built two years before the rest of the aircraft and is clearly a replacement from another aeroplane.

CCF was easy, but what did LMSD stand for? I started on a round of telephone calls, mostly drawing blanks but always a helpful 'try ringing so-and-so' until I found Barry Abrahams who has studied aircraft manufacturing factories during the last world war. He was pretty certain that LMSD was the London, Midland and Scottish Railway Company at Derby. A search on the web not only confirmed that they specialised in the building and repair of Hurricane wings, but there was a photograph of wings before and after repair!

Whether the wings were fitted to R4118 by Taylorcraft, 44 MU or David Rosenfield remains a mystery yet to be solved. Our Mk I Hurricane is such a kaleidoscope of the history of an aircraft which survived right through the Second World War, I doubt that what part was replaced when will ever be established with certainty.

On arrival back to Britain in July 2001, one of the first tasks was to register R4118 with the United Kingdom Civil Aviation Authority. Although there was absolutely no question of its true identity, it was not until we started detailed stripping of the fuselage that we came across the actual aircraft identification plate. It was attached to the diagonal strut beside the pilot's left leg, obscured underneath another plate which read:

DRG D57580
DRLM-G5-92301

D57580 is the overall general arrangement drawing for the Hurricane. Having previously unscrambled the meaning of LMSD, it was not too difficult to interpret David Rosenfield Ltd Manchester. Their factory for the rebuild of aircraft had been purpose-built on the airfield at

The data stencilling on the port fuel tank includes a list of five modifications. Despite being a Gloster-built aircraft, HA 480 and 511 are marks of the inspectors at Hawker's factory at Langley.

A typical data plate, this one being tucked away inside the centre section.

Barton, Manchester. G5 indicates R4118's origin at Gloster's Hucclecote factory.

Further industrial archaeology into the fragmented remains of the tailplane and elevator revealed that they were built in September 1938 by Rollason Aircraft Services at Croydon and in July 1938 by Parnall Aircraft at Yate near Bristol, respectively. Of further interest, one wing was fitted with an aileron built by Glosters at Hucclecote in May 1938, the other with one built by Glosters at Brockworth in April 1940. Thus we have an aircraft built by Glosters in July 1940, fitted with Canadian wings of 1941 with ailerons, tailplane, fin, rudder, flaps and elevator built or repaired by seven different factories between May 1938 and May 1943.

One has to wonder at the amazing control exercised by Hawkers, the Hurricane Repair Organisation and the Civilian Repair Organisation that parts made at hugely different times in factories across the UK and overseas could easily be swapped between aircraft.

But the Air Ministry had ideas for the future of R4118, well beyond the theatre of the European war.

CHAPTER 11   A Passage to India

READERS will recall that in the early part of 1943, the Japanese had invaded Burma and were advancing towards the north-east of India. To boost reserves of pilots, the decision had been taken in London to provide intensive training of Indian pilots, to be used in a supporting role. Hurricane Is and IIBs were no longer in front line service in Europe but could usefully be used by Air Command, South East Asia (ACSEA) at OTUs in India.

Before despatching aircraft to India, the policy was to totally overhaul the airframes and fit zero-timed engines which were fully inhibited. This work was undertaken at 5 MU at Kemble in Gloucestershire. It is hard today to believe the level of activity at these maintenance units. R4118 was one of a batch of 203 aircraft received by 5 MU in June 1943, and one of 198 aircraft despatched from there in November. It was then forwarded on 11 November to 52 MU at Cardiff, a specialist packing and crating facility for despatch of aircraft overseas. The wings, tailplane, propeller, aerial and exhaust stubs were removed and stacked alongside the fuselage supported on a wooden frame, all in one packing case. That month eighty-six aircraft were shipped from Cardiff to points around the globe. 52 MU was indeed a busy place. Established in early 1940, it packed and shipped a kaleidoscope of aircraft including Harts, Tiger Moths, Hinds, Lysanders, Gladiators, Sea Gladiators, Northrops, Walruses, Vildebeestes and Hurricanes to points as far afield as Takoradi, South Africa, Singapore and India. Cardiff Airfield must have been a small boy's delight as all sorts of aeroplanes were ferried in for dismantling.

Mrs Vera Anderson remembers working there: "We worked an eight hour day, but if a couple of Hurricanes or Spitfires arrived as we were finishing for the day, we were told to go home for our evening meal and report back to strip the planes straight away. It was cold most of the time, it was hard work but we enjoyed it. We had live music as some of the RAF chaps were musicians and there was a piano – we would dance away our lunch breaks. There were only five or six RAF lads working with us on dismantling, handling mainly the undercarriages and guns."

So it was that R4118 found itself on 12 December 1943 aboard the *SS Singkep*. The *Singkep* was a 6,607 ton Dutch merchantman built in 1924. With a speed of 12 knots she would have carried several aircraft but been easily vulnerable to attack from enemy torpedoes. In fact she survived in service until being broken up in Hong Kong in 1958.

The SS Singkep, *aboard which our crated Hurricane R4118 arrived at Bombay on 6 February 1944.*

R4118 was one of eighty Hurricanes of various marks received at the Aircraft Erection Unit, Santa Cruz, Bombay during February 1944. By this time the battle against the Japanese on the Burma front had turned in the Allies' favour. The RAF now needed fewer training aircraft, and certainly it was not worth erecting Mk I Hurricanes. And so R4118 was left in store in its packing case.

The following signal was sent from HQ, ACSEA to the Air Ministry in Kingsway on 11 July:

SECRET

Disposal of redundant aircraft. Prior to receipt your OX.8365. 3 July 1944. This command had decided on necessity for more drastic measures than normal AMO procedure.

PARA. 1. Gives general considerations determining our policy and paras. 3 and 4 particular application to British and American types respectively.

PARA. 2. This command is over-burdened with multiplicity of types of aircraft. Many have become uneconomical to repair through age or spares shortage. Present policy aims at rationalising aircraft establishments. Now vital to concentrate entire repair capacity on later types. Drastic steps necessary to free available space at repair units and aircraft storage units by removing redundant aircraft which deteriorate very rapidly in this climate and absorb valuable man hours if we have to maintain them. Extensive strike-off of older types awaiting repair has therefore already been initiated and is taking effect at present. In some cases aircraft have been parked at storage units pending transfer to repair. These too are being struck off if uneconomical.

For overseas shipping, a complete Hurricane was packed in a single case, the fuselage (with engine installed) standing on a frame, and the propeller, tailplane and wings detached. Once the fuselage had been dragged out to allow sufficient headroom clearance, it was raised on its undercarriage and wheeled out. Although evidently in a warm climate, this Hurricane is not fitted with a tropical filter. Nor was R4118 when despatched to India.

PARA. 3. British Types.

(A) Beaufort 1 and 2. No U.E. commitments. Can offer 30 Mark 1 condition poor and 30 Mark 2 condition fair. Have already instructed strike-off of remainder as uneconomical to repair in this command.

(B) Blenheim 4 and 5. Commitment has ceased. Replacement with fresh types in hand. Condition of aircraft poor. Repair has ceased and policy is entire withdrawal from flying units and total strike-off.

(C) Defiant. Original Defiant target towing commitments now satisfied by Vengeance. Vital need for reduction in number of types. Spares position unstable. Repair uneconomical except by cannibalisation or replacement. Policy is to strike-off and replace with Vengeance at wastage rates. Can offer up to 30 Defiants.

(D) Harlow, Percival, Piper, Miles and Moth variants other than Tiger Moth. Repair has ceased. Six aircraft only in flying units now being replaced. Have instructed total strike-off.

(E) Hurricane 1. All repair and erection has ceased. This mark being replaced by 2C and struck off. Can offer 50 of which 25 still crated. Many untropicalised. Policy to strike-off balance as beyond economical repair.

(F) Hurricane 2B. This mark is being replaced by 2C. Repair is ceasing and intensive strike-off necessary. All Mark 2B are worn out and can offer approximately 60 aircraft mainly in poor condition. Recommend complete strike-off.

(G) Hurricane 2C. This type still current. Policy is to strike off any aircraft which are uneconomical to repair and ensure rapid turnover to prevent deterioration in storage.

(H) Lysander. Commitment has ceased. Aircraft being replaced and struck-off.

(I) Wellington 1C 3 and 8. Commitment is ceased. Repair has ceased. Aircraft are in poor condition and being replaced and struck-off.

(I) or (J) Wellington 10. Commitment for two squadrons ceases shortly. Will then be able to offer approximately 20 aircraft to Middle East. All marks Wellington deteriorate rapidly in storage in this climate. Strike-off of aircraft beyond economical repair has been initiated.

PARA. 4.

(A) Hudson 3 and 6. Policy is to replace with Dakotas and Ansons as available. Aircraft all old and in poor condition. Aircraft being struck off as displaced.

(B) Vengeance 1, 1A and 2. Supply of spares ceasing. See your QX. 225 3 June. Repair of this mark ceased except for target towers. Intensive strike-off un-economical aircraft in hand. We can offer up to 50 Mark 1, 1A and would entail considerable diversion of man hours from more urgent tasks.

PARA. 5. We appreciate implication penultimate sentence your Part 1. When implementing it, request avoidance undue diversion of this commands scarce man hours to preparation despatch aircraft other commands.

PARA. 6. Request that in determining disposal instructions for redundant aircraft you will support the policy given above which is part of bid to streamline maintenance this command and constitutes major contribution to manpower economy.

Undoubtedly R4118 was one of those twenty-five still crated. On 20 July the various units throughout India were issued the following instruction:

From: Headquarters, Air Command, South East Asia.
To: Headquarters, Third Tactical Air Force.
Headquarters, Nos. 221, 222, 223, 224, 225, 226, 227, 229, 230 and 231 Groups.
Headquarters, Air Command, S.E.A.
Director of Repair (DGA),
            234/4 Lower Circular Road, Calcutta
Air Headquarters, India (For attention SENGO)
Date: 20 July, 1944
Ref: CMO/2002/6/4/2/ENG.II

REDUNDANT AIRCRAFT – HURRICANE MARK I

The above type aircraft is now redundant in this Command and action is to be taken for disposal in accordance with the general instructions contained in this Headquarters letter Ref. CMO/2003/4/2/Eng. dated 12 July, 1944. Additional instructions below are to be actioned in conjunction;

AIRCRAFT UNDER ERECTION

All erection is to cease. Tropicalisation work to cease. No further action pending instructions for disposal.

AIRCRAFT IN REPAIR AND OVERHAUL

All repair and overhaul work is to cease immediately.

(a) Aircraft which cannot be completed within seven days, (assuming arrival of spares and full cannibalisation), are to be categorised 'ES' and Serial Nos. forwarded to this Headquarters for 'write-off'.

(b) Aircraft within seven days of completion are not to be worked on pending further instructions.

(c) Future major overhauls or repair arisings are to be categorised 'ES'. (Replacements for these will automatically be Mark IIs)

REMOVAL OF EQUIPMENT

In addition to the items stated in para 3, sub para (iii) of this Headquarter's letter quoted above, the following are also to be removed and returned to the appropriate MU or RED.

Propellers, Air Compressors, Spinners, Hydraulic Pumps, Constant Speed Units, Vacuum Pumps, Fuel Pumps.

ENGINES

If installed to be inhibited but need not be removed from aircraft. (Includes both serviceable and unserviceable engines.)

AIRFRAME (With engines if installed)

Remove to 'graveyard'.

OUTSTANDING DEMANDS FOR SPARES

To be immediately reviewed and demands cancelled in respect of items not required.

According to the Movement Card, Form 78, we know that R4118 was 'converted to Ground Instructional' on 4 October 1944 and 'Struck off Charge' on 1 January 1947. But it is impossible to be sure of the date on which it was moved from its packing case in Bombay to that compound outside at Banaras Hindu University. What is known is that ACSEA was keen to develop a pool of skilled young Indians to staff the newly established Royal Indian Air Force, and to this end formed branches of the Indian Air Training Corps at a number of universities from February 1943. Banaras Hindu University joined the scheme some time in 1944. Records from 320 MU show that a number of Hurricane Is were 'written off to instructional' in June 1944.

The circumstantial evidence points to R4118 being sent to Banaras in July 1944. A substantial number of aircraft were 'struck off charge' on 1 January 1947, but that is likely simply to have been a recognition of a 'fait accompli'. What is certain is that little thought was given to the long-term preservation of the aircraft as the dissembled parts were laid outside on the ground. Namely, to face the ravages of heat and monsoon for the ensuing fifty-seven years.

PART

II

Restoration and Flight

The Strip

NOT a little champagne welcomed R4118 back to Abingdon on 16 July 2001. Earlier that morning Roy Noble, armed with camera, and myself, had journeyed to Thamesport in Kent to capture the moment of delivery. The workings of modern container ports are a technological wonder. Controlled from a remote computer complex, a massive gantry crane sorted our container from thousands within the 'stack' and delivered it to the correct truck in a line waiting for loading. Somehow I did not want to let it out of my sight, so we followed the lorry all the way home. It was not without some apprehension that I cut the seal on the container doors – would the aircraft still be inside, would it have been further damaged in transit?

To my great relief, despite the poor aeroplane having been 'thrown' into the container due to pressures in India, it did not seem to have suffered from its three weeks on the high seas. There was quite a party atmosphere. Despite trying to keep the aircraft a secret for the six years we were negotiating to get it out of India, my wife and I are really very bad at keeping our own secrets. Thus it was that some thirty-five people were there to greet the arrival of R4118, all of whom over the previous months had been sworn to secrecy. Pete Thorn, he of the "that's not a Spit, that's a Hurricane", sat in the cockpit with a huge smile on his face. It was twenty years since he had flown a Hurricane. With the help of a mobile crane, and Sanderson unit kindly driven by a good farmer friend, Robert Benson, the fuselage and wings were safely installed in the workshop. Incredulous at the sight of rotten pieces of metal, our visitors were put to work, carrying parts from the container to the workshop. A few bits were dropped en route but hurriedly gathered up by me, explaining that any part, however dilapidated, was valuable as a pattern.

During the previous six years I had been able not only to track down as many people as possible associated with R4118, but also to record a number of their stories on audio tape. These great men were not getting any younger, so the first thing to organise was a party to reunite them with the aircraft. On 20 September three pilots who flew R4118 in the Battle of Britain were able to sit again in the cockpit, Bunny Currant, Bob Foster and Peter Thompson. Archie Milne was unable to come from Canada, and sadly Alec Ingle had just died. We did have

Someone seems pretty happy to have R4118 back to England after fifty-seven years, even if this flight does seem somewhat precarious!

Nicholas Winton and Carolle Hanes, children of two of the 111 Squadron pilots who had flown the aircraft. Also present were Peter Parrott who had commanded 605 Squadron, Bam Bamberger and Graham Leggett, both former Hurricane pilots, and Peter Garrod who ferried Hurricanes in the Air Transport Auxiliary. Pete Thorn, who flew Hurricanes with the Battle of

Whilst unloading the port wing, the colours of South East Asia Command can be clearly seen.

Duncan Simpson OBE who was a Hawker test pilot, flew the P1127 Kestrel, which became the Harrier, an the initial flight testing following the rebuild of the 'Strathallan' Hurricane.

Britain Memorial Flight and had trained my wife, Polly, for her two solo around-the-world flights, could not be restrained from leaping into the cockpit immediately.

Then there was Duncan Simpson OBE who joined Hawkers in 1954 as a production test pilot on Hunters. He became the development test pilot on the Hunter IX and X before test flying from 1962 the P1127 Kestrel, which became the Harrier. During this time he also worked with the team and test flew the 'Strathallan' Hurricane which was rebuilt in 605 Squadron markings as Archie McKellar's aircraft. Sadly it was later destroyed by fire at Canadian Warplane Heritage. He well remembers Hawker's chief designer, Sir Sydney Camm: "If he was coming down to the pilots' office, we would get warning that he was on his way. We would then ensure certain persons of whom he did not approve were kept out of sight. His chair had to be in its right place."

Believing that a film of the story of the aircraft would be an essential record, the emotion of the occasion, particularly for the three who flew R4118 in the Battle, was recorded by our faithful camera man, Roy Noble. He was also able to capture some of Bunny Currant's more amusing memories on film.

There needed to be some serious thinking. Although I had been an enthusiastic amateur engineer most of my life, meticulously restoring vintage motor cars, I had no aero engineering experience. If we were to get R4118 back into the air before senility set in, I was going to need professional help. I had discussions with Peter Watts at Retro Track and Air who already had two Hurricane projects on the go. They appeared highly competent but I sensed their main business was moving towards the rebuilding of Rolls-Royce aero engines for which they have a fine reputation. I spoke to Tony Ditheridge at Hawker Restorations. Already two of their Hurricane restorations were flying and two others were nearing completion. Their set-up looked professional and many of the parts which would be needed were already in stock. With the help of part-time staff I decided to undertake the project within my own company. I sub-contracted the airframe assembly work to Hawker Restorations.

There was a complete set of eight Browning machine guns still in the wings. As the wings had filled with water each monsoon, the guns were in a very bad state. Bead blasting revealed manageable corrosion. After de-activation the guns were phosphated and painted. R4118 flies with its original armament.

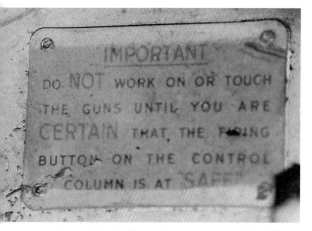

A warning to the armourers, mounted inside each gun bay.

The stripping of the aircraft was done in my workshop. And here is a moment for a confession. When we had initially found the aircraft in India, to our embarrassment (and joy!) we found all eight Browning machine guns were still installed in the wings. What were we to do? They were all rusted up solid and could clearly never work again. But they were an invaluable part of R4118's history. If we declared their presence to the Indian authorities, they would have to seize them and it would probably stop the whole deal. And if the guns were found by the UK Customs, would we be held for gun running?

We decided we just had to take the chance and leave the guns undisturbed in the wings. In the event the container was not opened by either the Indian or UK customs. But the guns then became a priority. Our son Julian spent many hours disassembling the rusted parts and blast cleaning them. Even then it was clear that the guns were quite unserviceable but we knew they should be deactivated immediately. To my intense dismay a slot was milled up each barrel and then welded, and the working parts removed. De-activation certificates were issued and each gun phosphated and painted. At least we could fly with the semblance of the original armament. Bunny Currant had some interesting reflections on the Hurricane's fire power:

In '38 the Spitfire began to come into service and, of course, during the war it was a much more glamorous name and it was a much more pretty aircraft to look at, as we all know, and it always will be. It's interesting to know that, throughout the entire Battle, the Hurricane aircraft shot down three times more enemy aircraft than the rest of the defences put together, including the Spitfires, because there weren't so many of them. The gun platform on the Hurricane was so much better than the Spitfire which had a metal wing which is very narrow, with four guns spaced out across the wing. You can't get a nice tight pattern of lead 200 yards ahead of your aircraft with guns like that. In the Hurricane, they were all four close together on either wing, and you could get this terrific pattern of lead, which, once it hit an aircraft, did all the damage.

Taking the airframe down to a bare structure was a full time job for me. I was greatly assisted by Roy Noble who photographed each stage. Two great Australians, Bill Bishop and Ross Kelly, who fly 747s for Qantas and have an insatiable appetite for old aeroplanes, fixed their rosters so that they could spend as much time as possible in the UK dismantling the fuselage. Tony Ditheridge at Hawker Restorations supplied a complete parts list and quantities of general arrangement drawings so that each part could be accurately tagged and identified with its part

The aircraft as recovered from India before stripping started. Note the armour plate behind the pilot's seat and the parachute flare tube further to the rear. The starboard fuel tank can be clearly seen inside the right hand part of the centre section.

Vandals had been at work on the cockpit instruments, but sufficient remained to ensure correct replacements were found. Curiously enough the most sensitive of instruments, the artificial horizon, could be substantially reclaimed.

All the hydraulic system was in near perfect condition including the pipework made of tungam, an almost indestructible brass alloy.

As well as being film recordist for the entire three years' restoration of R4118, including filming recovery from India, Roy Noble helped with the engineering. Here he ponders the mysteries of the BTH air pump on the Merlin III.

By now the fuselage has been stripped of the forward components and engine. After fifty-seven years, there was still air pressure in the undercarriage legs. Despite attempts to preserve originality, the air could not be saved from the tyres!

As each piece was removed, the part number and description as per the parts book were recorded and a red 'unserviceable' tag attached.

The airframe was fully overhauled before being sent to India, but these bullet holes in the port fuel tank were not discovered due to the highly effective self-sealing material applied to the outside.

number and description. As each piece was detached, it was passed to a general practitioner friend, Dr Roger Andrews. Roger spent days and days in the blasting department removing every trace of corrosion ready for each component to be examined. He would emerge looking like a coal miner, covered in blast media with a broad grin on his mouth, the only clean bit protected by a face mask.

There are literally thousands and thousands of parts on a Hurricane. Given R4118's historical provenance, we were keen to reuse just as many bits as possible commensurate with total airworthiness. The main steel longerons were clearly past their prime, as were the main spars. But most of the end fittings were salvageable, many requiring patience on the milling machine to release them from the rusted tubes. Although all the instruments were smashed, they were all there and in most cases revealed Air Ministry numbers which guided us to their accurate replacement. Virtually all the original fittings were there including many unique to the Mk I Hurricane. These included the upward firing identification device, the parachute flare tube, the early oxygen system, eight gun wings, and evidence of the earliest VHF radio (of which more later).

There was much evidence of battle damage. The webs of the main spars had been repaired in two places with riveted plates where bullets had passed through. When the fuel-sealing coverings were taken off the wing tanks, both were found to have bullet holes right through them. It is a tribute to the sealing material that these were not discovered during the aircraft's overhaul prior to shipping to India. There were several repairs to the sheet metal panels under the centre section.

But what was most revealing was the extent to which R4118 had been updated during its life. At various stages it had been fitted with Mk II undercarriage legs, tailwheel assembly, two position rudder pedals, fireproof screen aft of reserve tank, and the engine mixture control deleted. Together with its later Canadian wings, the aircraft was itself a potted history of the development from the Mk I Hurricane to the Mk II.

In addition to the eight Browning machine guns, all the pneumatic controls and heaters for the armament were there, just missing the sear and release mechanisms. The camera gun itself was not fitted, but its pneumatic switch, gimbal mount and camera door were all in place. Incidentally, Bunny Currant who flew R4118 during the Battle told me that during training they always ran the camera gun, and also on all operational sorties, but that he never saw one foot of film. The camera was always unloaded immediately on touchdown by the squadron's intelligence officer.

It was a frequent practice for airframe engineers to sign their names on major components. The wings on R4118, on which this signature appears, were built in Canada. An extensive search to trace the family has not yet been successful.

With the exception of the gun bay doors and the guns themselves, it was decided to leave the stripping of the wings to the professional rebuilders, particularly so that they could ensure everything went back together in its correct sequence. In December 2001 the wings left for the workshop in Bournemouth of Bob Cunningham, to whom they had been sub-contracted by Hawker Restorations. The airframe itself, by now looking very naked, set off in January 2002 to Hawker Restorations in Suffolk. With the initial disassembly completed, it was time to find the missing bits – and to think about the engine and propeller.

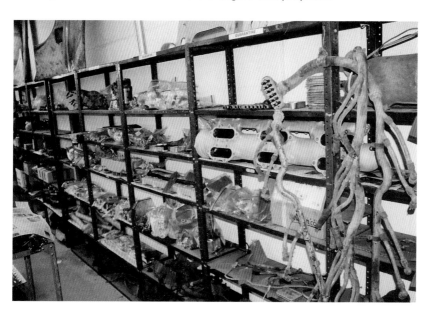

As R4118 was stripped, each part was red tagged and put into quarantine until inspected. Here a selection of engine parts await attention.

CHAPTER 13 The Search

ALTHOUGH most ancillary components were in the airframe, many were corroded beyond use. So the hunt was on for the correct original parts. All electrical equipment and all cockpit instruments were needed, mainly because of the heavy use of Bakelite which had become brittle in the Indian heat and monsoon.

Searching for parts of aeroplanes reminded me of a story told by Bunny Currant:

There was this Hurricane sitting on the airfield. We had no log books or paperwork or anything with it. Ronnie Harker was the chief test pilot for Rolls-Royce at Hucknall, had been for years, and was until he retired. He used to have to come in his car and go to all the fighter airfields during the Battle of Britain, and check on the engines for R-R, because the engines in the Spitfire and the Hurricane were totally identical. I knew him very well indeed, we all did, and he was seconded into the RAF temporarily, he wore a uniform, and he said, "Ah, Bunny, I'm getting so fed up with this, I have to do all this driving. If only I had my own aeroplane, it would be marvellous." I said, "Ronnie, if you come back tomorrow by train, you can have one." And I handed that aircraft over to him, it had no documents or anything. I said, "It's just been sitting here." He came down the next day, flew it away and took it to Hucknall. They had it for eighteen months, and he used it all the while, and it wasn't until eighteen months later that 11 Group found they'd got a Hurricane missing, and it was eventually discovered, and nobody knows how on earth that came about, they never did find out.

So even in the war they could find themselves looking for whole aeroplanes!

Trying to assemble a complete set of all the Air Ministry parts needed turned out to be a case of relying on one's ability to network. Although R4118 was sixty-three-years-old, I had to believe that somehow all the bits could be conjured up from somewhere. I started with Guy Black from Aero Vintage, a highly knowledgeable restorer who was a director of Aircraft Spares and Materials in Essex. Airsam holds a quite remarkable store of aircraft parts. Many new items were in their stock including vital parts such as a new generator, voltage regulator and obscure radio bits. Guy also helped with invaluable documentation and allowed me to copy essential Air Publications.

My next call was to Peter Elliott, the Librarian at the RAF Museum at Hendon. Apart from earlier producing the accident reports on R4118, Peter also spent hours digging out information on all the instruments, engine, propeller and radios.

So here is an appropriate moment to talk about the latter. Many early, and indeed later Hurricanes were fitted with the high

Part of the stores at Aircraft Spares and Materials Ltd who keep a vast stock of aeroplane parts. For R4118 most electrical components were available to replace the corroded pieces. A freshly overhauled generator was in its original wrapping, as were some of the early radio essentials.

frequency TR9 radio, identified externally by the aerial wire running from the top of the aerial mast to the top of the tail post. However, by July 1940, many aircraft within 11 Group fighting in the Battle in the south-east corner of England were being equipped with the new very high frequency radios. The first VHF set fitted to Hurricanes and Spitfires was the TR1133, installed in many aircraft from August 1940 onwards, which utilised the aerial mast but not the wire running from the top of it. The main components comprised a transmitter/receiver in a box weighing 26 lbs, a rotary transformer weighing a further 12 lbs and a complex hard-wired junction box wiring the pieces together. In place of the TR9's cable-operated cockpit controller, the TR1133 used a push button controller with four pre-tuned frequencies. Both radios used a master and remote contactor which transmitted an identification signal to the ground station, interrupting verbal transmission for fifteen seconds in each minute.

The Identification Friend or Foe transponder unit which could be interrogated from a ground station. On the right side can be seen a clamp under which there was a tray with an explosive charge. In the event of a prospective forced landing in enemy territory, the pilot was expected to blow up the set immediately behind his seat to prevent the IFF falling into the wrong hands!

Aircraft on operations also carried an IFF, Identification Friend or Foe. In today's world it would be called a transponder. A signal from the ground station sweeping across a band of frequencies would trigger a similar response from the aircraft if it was friendly. The IFF box weighed in at a further 12 lbs, together with a control box and an impact switch. The equipment was highly secret. To prevent it ever falling into enemy hands, an explosive charge was mounted inside the set, operated by the impact switch in the event of a crash landing, or by the pilot who could press two buttons simultaneously under a cover marked 'DANGER' in the cockpit. It must have been a brave pilot to set off an explosion just ten inches behind his seat!

While dismantling R4118 we found the junction box, wiring and placards for the TR1133 radio, together with the fittings for the IFF. I quickly appreciated that finding the original radio equipment was going to be nearly, but perhaps not quite impossible. This was where the Internet became invaluable. Reading up on wartime fighter radios I found that the TR1133 was quickly replaced by the more prolific and efficient TR1143, which in turn was made in substantial quantities in the USA under the Lend-Lease Agreement, but then called the SCR522. I located an SCR522 in Canada for a modest sum, and bought it in case a TR1133 eluded me.

In the wilds of Essex I found a TR9 set being advertised which I acquired. In Kent a delightful radio buff produced a junction box in perfect condition for the TR1133 and a master contactor. A journey to Devon produced a new boxed remote contactor.

But nowhere could I find a TR1133 radio. Seemingly the only one in existence was at the Imperial War Museum at Duxford. Then came one of those strokes of luck. Ever hopeful, I was at an aerojumble at Shoreham in Sussex and was asking a stallholder if he knew what a TR1133 was and did he know where there might be one? Overhearing the conversation was John Elvins, a great chap

The internals of the TR1133 VHF radio were an exciting world of relays clicking and cams whirring. The TR1133 was the first VHF set to be used by the RAF. They were introduced into service in August 1940 but the established TR9 HF set continued in use in many aircraft.

who took me aside and said that he knew a gentleman in the West Country who had one but who would never be persuaded to part with it. Undaunted, John gave me his name and I requested a visit, at least to see what I was looking for. I was given a warm welcome by the owner but he assured me he would never be able to let it go as it was destined for a museum.

Over the next six months I kept in contact, hopefully suggesting that the radio would be more appropriately fitted to a flying Battle of Britain machine than in a museum. At last the kind man agreed to sell it together with the all important power supply. Now I had the radio but was still looking for the IFF. I spoke to at least a dozen military radio collectors. It was quite a different world to aircraft. Most were ardent collectors of 'spy' radios, small transmitters frequently disguised in innocent looking attaché cases. I was passed from one to another until in the furthermost corner of Kent I found the IFF box and its controller. Again there was no question that its owner would part with it – until he heard that I had a TR9 radio. A swap was arranged. And so we had a complete set of original radio equipment. What was even more unbelievable was that John Elvins undertook to rebuild it so that it was actually in working condition – surely unique among flying British fighters of the Second World War.

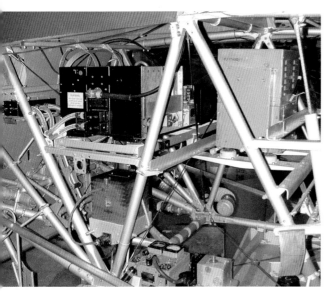

R4118 is now equipped with a full set of original radios. The large box is the TR1133 receiver/transmitter, below which in the wooden box is the master contactor. On top to the right is the IFF. Below is the IFF control panel with its meters, and to its right is the impact switch which sets off an explosive charge in the IFF to prevent it falling into enemy hands.

Assembling a full set of cockpit instruments took us to all corners of the earth. The altimeter came from Australia, the hydraulic pressure gauge from Belgium, undercarriage indicator bulbs from New Zealand, and switches from California. I found an IFF set which the Australian restorer of a Mk VB Spitfire needed – I was thrilled to be able to exchange it for a gunsight still in its wrapping after overhaul by the RCAF in 1953. I was subsequently able to find a complete TR1143 radio system for him as he was keen, like me, to have the original radio fit.

I heard of an elderly gentleman in Wales whose father had bought countless tons of aircraft surplus during and after the war. He had teams of people recovering metals from the parts. Later he traded in surplus Air Ministry items. Now the shed of bits had all but collapsed, but it yielded several essential parts, in particular the radio suppressor. I even had to sign a disclaimer in case the building fell on me! There was another tumbled down building in Buckinghamshire whose owner kindly allowed me many pleasurable hours rummaging for parts. One or two gems were found.

Having assembled the set of instruments, they all went for overhaul to Aero Vintage. The faces had the supposedly dangerous luminous paint removed and repainted in a colour to simulate the original. All were tested and put away carefully until such time as they could be fitted in the cockpit.

In September 2002 the Countryside March attracted 400,000 protesters to London, bemoaning the treatment by the Labour Government of rural communities. In the coach to London I found myself sitting next to a delightful person. We got chatting and found a common interest in old motor cars. He produced a picture of his 1936 Morris.

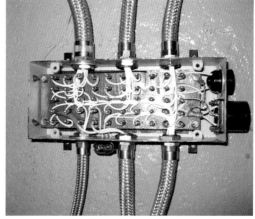

The TR1133 radio junction box after rebuilding. The sockets on the right enable ground engineers to check the system, whilst the socket below the box is connected so that the radio is cut out whilst the guns are being fired.

Later in the conversation I found he was the curator of the Royal Observer Corps Museum. I mentioned I was restoring a Mk I Hurricane, whereupon he got out the picture of the Morris again. "There you are," he said. "The rear view mirror is from a Mk I Hurricane." There and then he offered to donate it to the project. I motored to see him the following week, armed with a replacement mirror for his car.

Aren't some people fantastic?

There were a mass of other detailed parts to be made or found. There is a data plate fitted inside the cockpit on the port side in view of the pilot. This is a copy of the engine plate which gives the RPM and boost settings for take-off, cruise and all-out under battle conditions, together with oil and water temperatures and pressures. There should also be fitted a Hawker plate showing the patent numbers under which various parts of the Hurricane were protected. This was doubtless to deter the enemy from copying any of Sydney Camm's great ideas! These plates were reproduced by a fine engraver in Australia. A close study of the Hurricane I in the RAF Museum at Hendon and of early photographs revealed that the walkways on either side of the cockpit were originally covered in rubber sheeting. We mounted a worldwide search for a matching material – again a suitable replacement was found in Australia.

One of the most unexpected finds was the pair of rudder straps. Mark I Hurricanes were fitted with single level rudder pedals. However R4118 had been updated with the two position pedals. The higher position was used for aerobatic flying and included a rubber strap over each of the pedal tops to retain the pilot's feet. We had the metal ends of the straps but the rubber had long since perished away. A search had produced nothing, presumably because other straps had suffered a similar fate. However, some years ago Geoff Rayner had recovered the remains of Hurricane P3175 from the Essex marshes. He wrote up the story in his book *One Hurricane, One Raid*. Geoff presented the remains to the RAF Museum where today it stands as a vivid reminder of what happened to so many aircraft during the war. Despite its thirty-four years in Essex mud, one of the rubber toe-straps was preserved in near-perfect condition. With permission from Geoff and the museum, I carefully removed and borrowed it to make a copy. On the top of the strap the word PALMER is moulded. To reproduce this and to make the necessary mould would require tooling costing £1500, which for two straps would be hard to justify.

I was about to have a lucky break. A friend, Alan House, took me flying in his piston Provost. I looked down to settle my feet on the rudders and there, lo and behold, were two straps with PALMER on them. I mentioned my predicament to Alan who unhesitatingly said I was to have them provided I supplied a pair of leather straps as replacements.

There was just one original component which to this day we have been unable to find. Hurricane manuals refer to an Upward Firing Recognition Device. From a control (which we have) on the port side of the pilot, a cable runs to a rotating drum loaded with six cartridges. At a pull on the control handle, a flare is fired upwards, bursting through the fuselage fabric just beside the aerial mast. The device could be used to signal to control on an airfield, or to other aircraft to discourage 'friendly fire'. The relevant Air Publication calls the device a '1$\frac{1}{2}$ inch

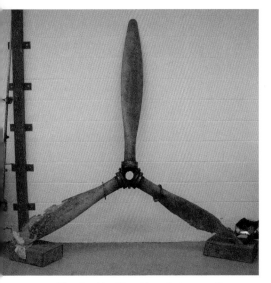

The De Havilland bracket propeller as found in India. Sadly it had been lying on the ground and subjected to monsoons for decades. It ultimately proved impossible to find an uncorroded bracket propeller. A Rotol propeller of the type also used on early Hurricanes is now fitted.

Signal Discharger'. Two Hurricane dig enthusiasts have shown me signal dischargers recovered from crashed aircraft, but these are sadly well beyond repair. The blast tube to the top of the fuselage we have already installed in the hope of ultimately finding a complete signal discharger.

The propeller turned out to be a daunting task. The original De Havilland 'bracket' (so called due to the counterweights hanging in external brackets) constant speed unit had been lying in the compound in India, covered annually during the monsoon with water. The blades were corroded beyond hope and I had little expectation of the hub. On dismantling and blasting it looked possible that it could be re-used. However, some rust pitting decided us against the safety of it to fly again. I was determined to find another identical propeller as R4118 had carried one in the Battle of Britain. I sent a letter to every museum in the UK, and to many overseas. I saw some fourteen DH propellers from Hurricanes and Spitfires, and even dismantled a number including one still on a Merlin III from a Hurricane which had crashed into the soft Fenland soil of Norfolk in 1940. But it was to no avail. They were mostly corroded, or if not, had suffered crash damage. I was forced to give up. The Hurricane I was initially fitted with a Watts 2-blade fixed pitch propeller. Then came the two position De Havilland 3-blade, followed shortly by the constant speed De Havilland 3-blade and the Rotol constant speed 3-blade. Not being able to find the De Havilland propeller, I turned

Removing this DH bracket propeller from a crashed Hurricane was one of several attempts to find a serviceable hub. Although there was little corrosion externally, internally it was quite unusable.

to the American Hamilton Standard Hydromatic which would be a cheap, effective option even though none were fitted to UK-built Hurricanes. The problem here was that the output propeller shaft on the engine would have to be changed to the coarser American spline. Ultimately I opted to fit the Rotol of which a few seemed available and was correct for the period.

The component parts of the De Havilland bracket propeller fitted to R4118. The DH bracket propeller was superseded by the Rotol which was fitted with wooden, as against metal, blades. In event of a wheels-up landing, the wood sheared, usually without damage to the engine.

A chance visit to Northern Ireland to see an enthusiast of veteran Rolls-Royce motor cars led to a meeting with the delightful secretary of the Ulster Aviation Association. There in the museum lay a Merlin III engine with an apparently perfect Rotol propeller hub. The Association most kindly agreed to my having the hub in return for my De Havilland one. Imagine my disappointment when, upon stripping it, we found it heavily corroded. I made a midnight sortie to a Gloucestershire museum where I had heard, from a chance encounter at an aerojumble, there was another hub. This turned out to be totally uncorroded but bent beyond use.

As the reader will remember, when R4118 was rescued from that compound in India, we also purchased a Rolls-Royce Griffon 66 engine, used on high-altitude Mk XIX Spitfires, which was lying unloved on the floor of an engineering laboratory. Continuing my searches for a Rotol propeller hub, Stephen Gray's Fighter Collection at Duxford suggested we might swap the Griffon for a good hub. At first sight parting with a complete engine for a hollow hub did not seem a fair exchange, but on perusing the engine further we realised that only the bottom end was in sound condition. The exchange was made.

Finding a hub was only the start of the propeller chase. Some internal parts could be rescued from the Ulster hub. Many parts were found by Peter Wood from his treasure trove. I discovered that the Australian, with whom I had swapped an IFF set for a gunsight, had made the pitch change cylinder and other parts for the propeller so these were sent from the Antipodes.

Everything was then shipped to Michael Barnett's Skycraft Services Ltd near Cambridge. The wooden blades had to be ordered from Germany! That is the only place that certified blades are being made. Michael, in conjunction with the original manufacturers, Dowty Rotol, put the jigsaw together, resulting in a totally 'as new' propeller. The constant speed unit, which controls the pitch of the propeller blades, was the subject of a huge hunt around the UK, Canada, Australia and New Zealand. Ultimately Peter Wood, just fifteen miles away came up with an original, which had to be stripped, checked and reassembled, and subsequently tested on a rig at Vintage Engine Technology.

CHAPTER 14 The Reconstruction

UNDOUBTEDLY the most difficult part of the entire project had been wresting R4118 from India. By comparison the dismantling and hunt for parts had been relatively easy. But there were challenges ahead. Initially I had intended to do most of the restoration work myself, but it became all too clear that that would be a twelve-year project and even then much work would need to be placed out. I was keen for my wife, Polly, to fly the Hurricane and also our son, Julian. Before we all got too much older it made sense to accelerate the rebuild. Having done most of the stripping myself, I decided to get more professional help with the reconstruction. We set a three-year target for completion from the time the aircraft arrived in the UK. This was certainly ambitious, but all concerned bought into the plan.

Graham Self, Chief Inspector at Hawker Restorations, consoles the owner on seeing R4118's airframe reduced to a pile of rusted tubes. In the background is a Mk II Hurricane being completed for an overseas customer.

Hawker Restorations Ltd. were the key players – and none more key than Graham Self. Graham is one of those rare engineers who can turn his hand to any task. Undoubtedly the most knowledgeable person in the world on the structure of Hurricanes, he is also a perfectionist. He supervised the entire rebuild and undertook most of the complex tasks himself. Matching Graham's skills was Mark Schofield. His particular baby, amongst many others, was the assembly of the

The new main spars assembled in the centre section jig.

tailplane. Helping Graham and Mark, turning his hand to just about anything, was Leycester Powys-Keck. HRL started with fabricating new main spars for the centre section. Each was built as the original Hawker design with two 12-sided flanged tubes and a round tube precisely encapsulated inside each other, joined by steel webs. These were the heart of the aircraft's strength. Then the fuselage longerons and other steel tubes had their ends squared and joined using special ferrules and rivets together with R4118's original stainless steel joint plates. The fuselage, centre section and engine mount were joined. The whole structure was supported and braced by the original aluminium struts and flat stainless wires. Around the framework was fitted the complex woodwork, now beautifully rebuilt by Adrian Gooderham, which gives the Hurricane its ultimate shape. Although all the steel tubes had to be replaced, virtually all the root end fittings, fuselage plates, alloy tubes and most brackets could be reused. By number of parts, some 60-70% of the original aeroplane was saved. Being such an historic machine, it was vital to preserve as much as possible. Those brackets and fittings that needed to be replaced were built by Tim Daniels who also fitted the gun structures into the wings. Future generations would be able to recognise exactly which parts had been replaced by the addition of 'HR' stamped beside the part number.

The original Hawker drawing of the fuselage allowed for 2½ inches out of true longitudinally. Hawker Restorations achieved less than ½ inch.

Brief mention has already been made of Bob Cunningham. Bob proved to be a key man in the rebuild of R4118. He and his team members, wife Simone, Steve Linden and Pat Domant, set to dismantling the wings. Taking them apart, Pat got more than he bargained for. In removing handfuls of Indian mud, he came across the skeletons of several mammals, most of which he claimed were related to the mongoose. One had to admire the skill as many thousands of rivets were drilled out without touching the sides of their holes. No less tricky was picking up the existing holes when riveting new parts with old. Being beautifully made and anodised throughout by the Canadian Car and Foundry Company, we were hopeful that most of the internal structure could be reused. However there was a degree of corrosion on some

An excellent picture showing the basic construction of a Hurricane. In the foreground, the centre section comprises steel spars top and bottom of two webs which in turn are braced across by aluminium tubes. On top of this structure is fitted a steel fuselage frame, again braced with aluminium tubes. Wooden formers and stringers add the basic shape. At the forward end is the plywood 'dog kennel' which forms the cockpit.

of the parts, so the decision was taken to replace the main wing spars, most of the ribs and all of the skins. Many pieces were also rejected, not because they were corroded but because they had work-hardened with age. Re-assembling the wings in jigs was a long and, to my ears, painful and noisy business. The result was superb. Virtually nothing of the tailplane had survived. Steve Linden made all the pieces to the original drawings, literally thousands of them.

We were most reliant on the skills and patience of Bob and Simone. Their ability to will a piece of metal into a desired shape left one speechless. Key components they made included cowlings and the radiator boat. The Hurricane is covered in an array of aluminium panels, most of which were shaped by Bob and Simone for detailed fitting at Hawker Restorations.

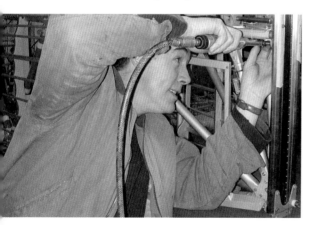

Mark Schofield drills off the tailplane spars. Note the multiface spar tubes which are curved to a central web, one of the main features of the Hurricane's construction.

With the frame and wings complete, attention turned to the hydraulics, pneumatics, electrics and coolant systems. There was a major panic as the aircraft had lost its radiator at some distant time in India. We had no pattern and only the sketchiest of drawings. With the combined help of the RAF Museum, Chris Morris at the Shuttleworth Collection and the squashed remains of a Mk I radiator kindly loaned, instructions were despatched to John Rummery in New Zealand who had previous experience of building Mk II radiators (which are very different). The radiator is a complex box of many

As Chief Engineer of Hawker Restorations, Paul Mercer signed out all the work on R4118.

components and many skills were needed to build it. John managed the project, with the individual components made in Christchurch, the cores made in Whangerei, and the whole soldered together in Auckland!

At Hawker Restorations, key players on the systems side were Phil Parish and Bob Young. The systems on Hurricanes and Spitfires are similar. Phil and Bob had years of experience on both. After stripping and inspection they were amazed to find that all the components and pipes of the hydraulic system, with the sole exception of the auto-cutoff valve, were in perfect condition. The undercarriage selector valve was quite serviceable but was replaced with the later Mk II type as being more reliable. One undercarriage leg was rejected at the non-destructive testing stage and a replacement found. The pneumatics which control the brakes, guns and camera required new pipework.

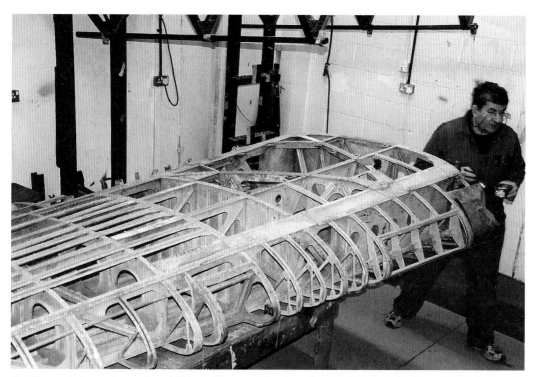

Pat Domant showed amazing skill in drilling out the rivets in the skins to reveal a remarkably sound wing structure despite years on the ground in India.

129

The electrical system was a challenge as few of the original parts had survived. Undaunted, Hugh Smith, HRL's electrical expert, began to assemble components sourced from Airsam and other places. Many of Hugh's problems arose from our desire to keep everything original whilst ensuring R4118 was safe and complied with the latest CAA requirements. Modern safety demands the use of a white cabling which looks quite out of place. After much searching we found some black aircraft-approved covering through which the wires could be threaded. The appearance to the original was excellent. Other concessions in the interest of safety and to meet modern regulations included fitting

Phil Parish, Hawker Restorations' system specialist, concentrates on a delicate job in the cockpit.

a ground/flight switch, an undercarriage horn test button, an electric fuel pump and an electric pre-oiler to ensure plenty of oil on all the engine's moving parts before starting from cold. Finding an original 12-volt undercarriage horn also proved impossible but Tony Stairs, who had rebuilt the magnetos, converted a 24-volt one.

Due to scarcity of parts, the Rotol propeller proved the most difficult item to assemble. The excellent finished job was achieved by Skycraft Services Ltd.

Leycester Powys-Keck faces the exacting task of fitting a new spinner.

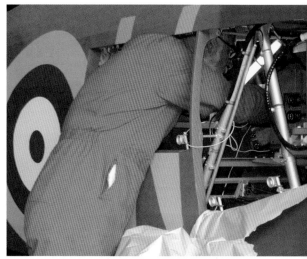

A typical pose for Hugh Smith as he sorts the intricacies of the radio wiring.

One decision will cause us major headaches. In the interest of originality, we have retained the 12-volt electrical system with the original size battery. This means that R4118 will always be dependant on ground power for engine starting – just as it did on those heady days in 1940.

Fitting the original radio equipment involved study of early Air Publications. Sadly it would not be possible to use the original VHF set as the bandwidth was too great, so we had to devise a discreet but functional position for a modern radio and transponder. A real challenge was to avoid the sight of a modern VHF aerial by utilising the original radio mast. Two radio experts from Oxford did an approved modification to tune the old mast to the new radio.

Many parts which had survived the years outside in India required careful inspection. Here Bob Young dismantles the coolant thermostat.

The Hurricane is fabricated out of a mass of tubes and brackets. Tim Daniels repaired or made new parts from original drawings.

There was a range of 'trolley-accs' in use during the war. Some were pulled manually, whilst others were fitted with tow bars. Many were dual voltage 12/24v and some had a generator mounted on the top for recharging the batteries. Colour schemes were legion – early ones were painted RAF blue, but the tops were then painted bright yellow when pilots failed to notice them when taxiing. Unfortunately the enemy found these a very good guide to spotting airfields, whereupon they were changed to olive drab. This one was restored by the Medway Aircraft Preservation Society and painted in colours typical of September 1940.

I was being pedantic in the extreme to ensure every part we installed was as it would have been in 1940, although at that time preserving originality could not have been further from the thoughts of the pilots. Bunny Currant relates:

I fitted a gun in my Hurricane at Croydon, a German gun firing sideways with the hole behind the cockpit seat in the fabric, where the gun was fitted (the armourers and the engineers fitted it) and it had a little toggle I pulled. I took it up and fired into Croydon somewhere at about 12,000 feet and it worked a treat. And I thought, when I get into a dogfight, this thing is pointing that way to cut off the angle. You see, if you were going round like that, it's no good the gun going straight back, it's got to go across, and I filled it with tracer, and I thought, "I'll give the German fighters such a fright!" No single engine day fighter had a gun, and it worked so well, but I never used it in anger because Fighter Command found out that this had been done, and boy, was I in trouble – to modify His Majesty's aircraft without permission! So we had to take it out, but I thought it was a brilliant idea – and still do!

The spade grip at the top of the control column presented a real problem. As it had been in the hands of every pilot who had ever flown R4118, I was keen to preserve it. But the ravages of time had destroyed the highly embossed original celluloid covering. Clearly I was not the only restorer to face the problem as many Hurricanes and Spitfires are flying with a cord binding around the grip. This does

The 'office' of R4118. It looks a busy place. The push-button controller for the TR1133 VHF radio is on the left. Beyond it is the camera gun footage counter.

not look original however. The most likely source of recovering, I found via the web, was a musical instrument maker in Czechoslovakia, but I was somewhat loathe to allow such an historical piece to travel that far. I did however find that the hood leather used on vintage cars had an almost identical appearance to the original celluloid if only I could get it bound tightly around the circular grip. I knew that there was a skilled man in our village who re-trimmed old motor cars. What I was to discover was that he specialised in covering the steering wheels for virtually all the UK-based Formula One racing teams. Re-covering a Hurricane grip presented few challenges.

However superbly a restoration is done, ultimately all that is seen is the exterior of the aircraft. So it was with no small relief on my part that my old friend, Bill Bishop, undertook to research exactly how R4118 looked in the Battle of Britain. For many years Bill has been a major authority on Napier motor cars. From 1906 until Napier ceased production of automobiles in 1924 to concentrate on their aero engines, Rolls-Royce had always regarded Napier as their fiercest competitor. With my interest in matters Rolls-Royce, Bill and I have a constant banter on the relative merits of the two cars.

Bill's knowledge of aeroplanes stems from being soaked in things aeronautical from the moment he arrived on the planet. His father flew, amongst many others, Super Constellations. Bill continues to fly early aircraft. He now set out to study exactly what a Hurricane built in June 1940 at the Gloster factory would have looked like.

To exercise the undercarriage and flaps, a former RAF hydraulic pump was connected to the aircraft. The system was also used for training pilots whilst R4118 remained in the hangar raised on jacks.

Left: *Unique to the Mark I Hurricane, this special funnel brings cold air from the cowling vent onto the engine-driven fuel pump.*

A rarely seen detail – the oil drain collector accumulates surplus oil from the engine breather, fuel pump, hydraulic pump and supercharger drain.

More difficult to establish would be how the 605 Squadron markings would have been applied and how the aircraft's appearance would have changed by the time of its entry into the Battle in September 1940. Very few pictures of 605 Hurricanes survive and sadly none of R4118 in the Battle of Britain period. Some of the questions to be answered were: should the camouflage be in the A or B scheme; what undersurface scheme was used and what shade of 'sky' paint was applied; what size roundels were used on the fuselage, top and bottom of the wings, and what shade of bright or dull colours were current at the time; how was the fin painted; what were the size and style of the squadron codes and the serial numbers? There were more detailed

Bill Bishop, a captain with Qantas Airlines, worked on R4118 during breaks from flying 747s. Here he faces the unenviable task of removing the self-sealing covering from the reserve fuel tank.

queries to be settled such as the colour to be used inside the wing and centre section flaps; were the inside of the undercarriage doors to be in silver or sky; and how were the gun patches to be treated?

While Bill was working on these conundrums, I concentrated on studying the stencilling on the aircraft. As time went on, more and more instructional stencils were applied, but in the Battle of Britain period not many were used. Fortunately we found an original Hawker drawing which showed those stencils required. We added a few for safety reasons, in particular instructions near the fuel fillers to show tank capacity and use of AVGAS.

A critical moment – Graham Self 'reams off' the wing taper fitting pins.

The fuselage is covered in Irish linen and treated with several coats of red and silver dope before being painted in traditional cellulose. Good dry weather is essential at this stage!

Although the original cowlings on R4118 were in reasonable condition, they had become hardened with age. To ensure longevity, it was decided to make new ones. The old cowlings could then be used for a static restoration.

April 2004 and R4118 emerges on its undercarriage with the wings for their first trial fitting. Note the camera gun in the starboard wing.

Other stencilling shows the serial numbers, and initial build and overhaul companies for each major component. The source of this information is on the data plate riveted inside the component. Thus the centre section flap would be stencilled PA/G5/132990, showing the flap serial number, the G5 indicating it was built at Glosters, Hucclecote, and PA being the overhaul shop at Parnall Aircraft, Yate. Additionally a W/T symbol was applied to indicate earth bonding to prevent wireless interference.

To undertake the fabric covering and much of the aircraft's paintwork, we turned to Clive Denney of Vintage Fabrics who had finished many warbirds previously. Close attention was paid to the original Hawker drawings for the style and method of fabric covering. The original type of Irish linen was used followed by coatings of red and silver dope. The whole aircraft was then painted in cellulose, to the camouflage B scheme, following Bill's instructions. Inevitably we did make some mistakes. An earlier study of Hurricane pictures showed that, where the top camouflage met the bottom sky paint in the leading edge of the wings, the two colours were merged into each other forming a soft edge. That was how it was painted. But that method turned out to have been introduced after December 1940. Previously the top and bottom wing colours joined on the leading edge with a sharp line. We sorely tried Clive's patience when it had to be corrected!

The camera gun was used for training sorties and in combat. The cassette contained forty seconds of 16mm film.

Every effort has been made to ensure R4118 has been finished exactly as it appeared in September and October 1940. New evidence will no doubt continue to come to light to prove if we have succeeded.

There was one other person whose presence smoothed the complex process of bringing R4118 back to life. Paul Mercer, in his role of Chief Engineer, supervised and signed off the work. He ensured that the old adage, 'It can

The gimbal mount for the camera gun. Adjustment screws allow for alignment of camera with the guns.

fly when the paperwork weighs the same as the aircraft' was almost defeated! On his shoulders lay the responsibility that the Civil Aviation Authority was happy to issue that final piece of paper – the Permit to Fly. Jenny Batley, Tony Ditheridge's PA and Pauline Ames were the final people at HRL to smooth the whole process to a successful conclusion.

I cannot speak too highly of the team at Hawker Restorations. And a real team it was, helping each other continuously, and resolving problems. They were just so enthusiastic! Maybe the excitement was generated from working on the most historic fighter from the Battle of Britain to survive, maybe because they were working with a customer who was personally involved all the way through the three years of the rebuild, or maybe because they just loved being around old aeroplanes.

The starboard wing gun compartment after restoration. The flexible pipes running from the bottom of the picture are the feeds to the pneumatic triggers.

CHAPTER 15
The Rolls-Royce Merlin III

THE engine in R4118 we knew to have been overhauled immediately before despatch to India. But in what condition were we going to find it now? After removal from the airframe, it looked quite externally corroded. We removed the rocker covers. What a sight! The inhibiting oil put in all those years ago had totally preserved the valve gear. The camshafts were like new. We were much encouraged. The two magnetos were clearly beyond use, but maybe internally the rest of the engine would be sound.

The Merlin III engine as removed from the airframe. There were at least five engines fitted to R4118 during its three years before being shipped to India.

We removed the ignition harnesses and inlet manifolds. Then shock, horror! The sparking plugs had been removed at some point in India. Wasps had nipped into the bores and ports where they had made their nests. Debris lay packed solid in every cylinder. Before further dismantling Roy Noble and I tried to blast the nests out of the inlet and exhaust ports with an airline. The mess was indescribable. Then we blew from one side and applied a vacuum cleaner to the other. This was a little more successful. We extracted literally pounds of nests from the two

The horrendous sight of wasps' nests in the bores of the engine. The insects were delighted to find a dark warm place in which to rear their young.

blocks. Steve McManus from the Shuttleworth Collection arrived armed with special tooling. We removed the supercharger and wheelcase, but it was impossible to shift either of the blocks. It appeared that the wasps' urine had welded the pistons to the cylinders. Fortunately a great friend had lent us his vintage 'Empire' rotating engine stand which was modified to take the Merlin. Thus the engine was effortlessly upended. We removed the sump and managed to disconnect the connecting rods from the crankshaft, after which the blocks could be removed with rods and pistons still in place.

The crankcase was blasted with ground walnut shells to remove external corrosion. It was then thoroughly steam cleaned. Walnut shells were used so that, in the unlikely event of any blasting material remaining, no damage could be done to the bearings.

Removing the reduction gear on the Merlin III.

Pulling the rods and pistons from the bores called for no little ingenuity. Of the twelve pistons, two came out with some judicious tugging. The rest were solid. We borrowed a hydraulic pump, fitted it to a modified spark plug and applied 800 psi to the combustion chamber. A further five pistons and rods shot out like bullets. The other five stuck fast. From those pistons we had extracted, it was obvious that the pistons had been totally corroded on their crowns by the wasps, so for the final five we resorted to desperate tactics. Each piston was tapped from below, a puller made and studs threaded into the tapped holes. Still the pistons would not move. Then we filled their insides with liquid nitrogen, thereby freezing and shrinking them in the bores. They all succumbed.

Sadly, despite all our efforts, the wasps had won. The bores were too rusted and the aluminium around the valve seats was corroded. In effect we had two useless blocks. This was all the more disappointing as we found the rest of the engine in remarkably good condition. The crankshaft, connecting rods and bearings were like new. Similarly there was virtually no corrosion inside the reduction gear and wheelcase. But nevertheless we did not have a useable engine.

During my various visits to study the Mk I Hurricane in the RAF Museum at Hendon, I had noticed two Merlin III engines on display. I tentatively approached the Director, Dr Michael Fopp, to ask if there might be any possibility of securing one of these. The trustees deliberated and most kindly proposed that an engine could be lent for a period of seven years, which would get R4118 off the ground whilst another engine could be sourced. I accepted with alacrity this most positive offer of help.

Whilst I consider myself a passable engineer when it comes to vintage motor car engines, I was not sufficiently confident in my skills to overhaul a flying Merlin. I had in the back of my mind one of Bunny Currant's stories:

I was shot down in 1940 in northern France in the Hurricane. I had knocked down a Heinkel bomber in flames, and was flying back over northern France. Suddenly the engine stopped and the propeller stopped, and there was the propeller, absolutely still, no engine, no propeller, and of course the aircraft starts to go down very rapidly then. So I thought, 'oh, I must get out', so I undid the old straps, got out on the wing root, holding onto the cockpit, and I thought, 'I can put this damn thing down', so I got back in again. I put it down with its wheels up, and it comes to a very, very sudden stop, and I hadn't had time to do my straps up again, so when it came to a sudden stop, my head hit the cockpit side, and broke my nose and cut my face, but otherwise I was alright. My No. 2 was up, circling round to see what had happened, ten o'clock in the morning, and went back to Hawkinge. I started walking, and did a very silly thing. I carried my parachute. It was damn heavy and awkward. I asked the way in the only French I knew "Ou est Calais?" I walked for hours, came to a town, found the Mayor and asked if he could find a car to take me to Calais, which he did. I think I caught the last boat out of Calais before the Germans took it. I got into the mess at Hawkinge at 11 o'clock that night. Everyone was amazed as my No. 2 had told them Bunny was somewhere in France.

To remove each of the cylinder liners, the block was immersed in a hot and steamy bath of water at 80 °C.

In the meantime Tony Ditheridge had introduced me to Maurice Hammond. It was to prove a most beneficial meeting. Maurice runs Eye Tech Engineering, a small company in Suffolk equipped with the most sophisticated computer controlled machine tools. He had substantial experience of making aircraft parts. Four years previously he had totally restored his P51 Mustang, building it from little more than a pile of pieces. The entire project had been undertaken by himself, airframe, engine, instruments, paint. He had become fully familiar with Packard Merlin engines which he had overhauled for customers at home and overseas. He had also acquired a collection of interesting flying aircraft including a Harvard and an Auster. On top of all this, he was a highly accomplished pilot. When I saw the standard of his work, I was keen for him to undertake the rebuilding of the Merlin III. But I too wanted to be closely involved. What finally clinched our agreement was that Maurice was happy for me to strip the engine myself under his watchful eye in his workshop, saving a little cost but more importantly, enabling me to be familiar with the inner details of the Merlin.

Early in 2003 I spent several weeks staying in a bed and breakfast near Eye, and working on the engine. Being such an early mark of Merlin, few of the required specialised tools existed. I stood in amazement when some complex spanner or puller was needed – Maurice would appear, vernier in hand, take a quick measurement, make a sketch on the back of an envelope, and re-appear a couple of hours later with a perfectly fitting tool. Every part had to be dismantled. Fortunately there was little wear. Of the total of about 150,000 Merlin engines built, only a small proportion was built by Rolls-Royce themselves. Ours, being an early one, was actually built by Rolls-Royce at Derby in June 1940. When we measured the components, it was hard to believe the accuracy that was achieved. The most outstanding example was the cylinder liners. These had to be removed from the blocks, inspected and re-inserted with new seals. As the gas-tight joint between the head and the liner depended on the blocks being tightly bolted to the crankcase, it was essential that the length of each of the twelve liners was identical. A liner is 11 inches long. We found their overall length did not vary by more than + or - 0.00025 inches, or half the thickness of a cigarette paper. How would we achieve such accuracy today, let alone on machine tools in the wartime conditions of 1940?

After dismantling, every component, large or small, was subjected to a spell in the stripping tank. After steam cleaning everything looked like new. Then the key parts such as crankcase, crankshaft, connecting rods, blocks, wheelcase and reduction gears were sent for non-destructive testing. I had mentioned to Steve McManus at the Shuttleworth Collection that we were working on the supercharger. Although Maurice was going to do so anyway, Steve advised us to carefully check the rotor vane as he had experienced a supercharger failure some years before when the vane had broken up. It was just as well it was NDT'd (Non Destructive Tested) as a crack was found in one of the blades. A replacement was found.

The faces of the block to which each cylinder liner abuts were precision-machined by Maurice Hammond. Under battle conditions this area presented some difficulty in maintaining a good seal, leading to the introduction of separate heads and blocks on later Merlins.

Maurice Hammond beautifully rebuilt P51 Mustang 'Janie' and the Merlin engines in both aircraft.

The main and big end bearings were perfect dimensionally but Maurice was not happy to reuse them after lying in situ for so long under unknown conditions. These, as many other components, were sourced from Aviation Jersey where Hedley Griffiths, after a lifetime spent with Merlins, offered sound advice and guidance. After NDT, the relevant components were painted (black as original) and Maurice commenced his fastidious assembly. Hundreds of micrometer readings ensured precise clearances to the original Rolls-Royce tolerances. Every reading was documented. Although most appeared serviceable, all ball and roller races in the engine were replaced.

A minor but critical modification was incorporated in the valve gear. Based on American experience of running Merlins, not infrequently to destruction in air racing, a long-standing weakness needed attention. The original rocker fingers were chrome plated to resist wear on the fingers and camshaft. This worked well until such time as the chrome started to break down, whereupon it became like a sharp file and would destroy a cam lobe in a few minutes. To obviate the problem, the old pad part of each finger was machined away, and a new tungsten carbide pad mounted in place. This was then ground and polished.

The SU AVT32 carburettor required specialist attention and was sent to Paul Sharman at Vintage Engine Technology. Although Paul had tackled the earlier Rolls-Royce Kestrels, the carburettor on the Merlin III was new to him. However his Kestrel experience proved invaluable

The overhauled blocks ready for installation.

in setting the flow and float levels and rebuilding the entire unit. The cork float required eleven coats of varnish to ensure a perfect seal.

A friend asked, "Do you have Miss Shilling's Orifice?" My initial reaction was to say "I hope not!" But then I learnt the true story. The Hurricanes and Spitfires suffered a major disadvantage against the fuel-injected Me 109s. The early Merlin engines fitted with the SU carburettor were prone to cutting out under negative G conditions. Pilots

A close view of the Merlin III valve gear after restoration.

experienced negative G in dogfights when the stick was pushed hard forward into a steep dive. The aforementioned cork float forced open the needle valve, flooding the float chamber and allowing an uncontrolled amount of fuel into the engine. This caused a rich cut and the engine stopped, not a good experience with the enemy on your tail.

The Royal Aircraft Establishment at Farnborough was tasked to come up with a solution. A young engineer, Beatrice Shilling, calculated the fuel necessary to maintain full power and added a simple restrictor into the fuel line. It consisted of a disc with a calibrated hole so that only enough fuel would pass into the carburettor. Inevitably it was known as 'Miss Shilling's Orifice'. Beatrice Shilling and engineers travelled around to the various squadrons fitting the modification. It was not a total solution but made a great improvement.

The carburettor, vacuum pump and constant speed unit were overhauled by Paul Sharman at Vintage Engine Technology Ltd. Many hours work were needed to ensure every one of the original Rolls-Royce settings were achieved.

And sure enough, when we stripped the engine, there was the fuel union with the disc inside.

Back at Maurice's workshop, the integral supercharger and carburettor was mated to the rear of the engine. The BTH magnetos were stripped, reassembled and tested by Tony Stairs. They were in 'as new' condition which was just as well because these early magnetos are now difficult to find. Dave Payne, an engineer with much experience and formal approval for the overhaul of Merlins, cleared each stage of the engine assembly. Fortunately our Merlin III had last been fully overhauled in 1943 and as such incorporated the latest modifications. Dave insisted on a few additional mods which had been found from experience to be beneficial, such as locking the magneto timing. The original magnetos had included an automatic advance from the engine controls. The other major addition to the engine was the incorporation of externally mounted dual full-flow oil filters, the wire mesh in the original built-in filters only being capable of capturing giant particles of rubbish.

Dave, Maurice and I agreed that there would be little to be gained by running the engine on a test bed. It was decided we would fit it to the aircraft and ground run for five hours, thereby testing all the systems at the same time as the engine. This made sense as it was important to check the fuel, oil and coolant systems with the engine in its operating environment.

The finished engine looked absolutely superb – and huge – sitting in Maurice's sterile engine bay. We hired a flatbed truck, carefully loaded it on and drove the twenty miles to Hawker Restorations. There Tony Ditheridge's team were all prepared with a gantry. The engine was lifted and inched into place on the engine mount of the aeroplane. It was a great day.

Suddenly the Merlin did not seem so large installed in the front of R4118.

Over the next few weeks the myriad of connections were made to the engine. These included oil and water temperature, and fuel and oil pressure gauges, vacuum lines, throttle, propeller pitch control, magneto connections, rev counter and pneumatic, hydraulic and coolant pipes. The daunting prospect for any pilot is that this lot have to be constantly monitored via the instruments whilst trying to fly the aeroplane!

A later Merlin modification was fitted at the last moment. Trying to preserve the aircraft as original as possible, we had retained the BTH air pump which provides pressure for

Left: *Maurice Hammond (left) adding the final rocker cover to his superb rebuild of the Merlin III, aided by Roy Noble who was taking time off from filming.*

Below: *The Merlin III is carefully lowered onto the engine mount.*

the brakes and guns. I thought that, as our use of the guns was likely to be severely curtailed, we should have plenty of air. But wiser heads persuaded me that prolonged taxiing and weaving on the brakes, necessary on modern airfields, could quickly exhaust the pump's capacity. On airfields in the Battle of Britain there was little taxiing – just point the nose into wind and go! So we have fitted a Haywood compressor, which is rather more involved, but once in place requires little maintenance and has a greater capacity.

CHAPTER 16 Into the Air

I'S a funny thing about a major restoration project. When it appears that it is 99% complete, one discovers there is 20% still to do! So when we believed there were only a couple of weeks to go before the engine could be started in the airframe, there were still a myriad of details to complete.

For example, the seat belt had to be sourced and fitted. Originally, a Sutton Harness was fitted. Finding genuine parts together with modern approved webbing proved difficult. Besides, the early harness was uncomfortable to say the least. We tracked down a period American harness which, when married to an acceptable webbing, looked most original. Of course we had to prove its tensile strength. Then we had to run tests on and have signed off the modern radio fit. Although the Becker radio and transponder had a German JAR approval, there was much to-ing and fro-ing to have them certified for use in the UK. Frowned upon by some pilots, provision was made for a portable GPS.

Rather akin to the old Rolls-Royce motor cars of the 1910s and 20s which I used to rebuild, the Hurricane is a big aeroplane and yet there is no room for luggage of any sort. We therefore allowed ourselves the luxury of fitting a locker to the desert equipment tray. Straightforward one might think, but no, a mass of stress calculations had to be done to show it would withstand up to 20 pounds of the pilot's personal effects and sandwiches. It was lined in green beige to prevent those annoying rattles that might just be heard above the sound of the Merlin!

There were smaller items outstanding. Modern CAA regulations require an extensive degree of placarding in the cockpit. Original fittings no longer in use, such as the oxygen system, are required to be labelled 'inoperative'. Pilots in wartime were expected to know the aircraft's maximum airspeed, flap extension speed and cruise settings. Today these have to be displayed on the blind flying panel. And is a 'NO SMOKING' sign really necessary?

The only major item still holding up completion was the propeller. Parts for these are becoming quite unavailable, so making them to original Rotol drawings is the only option. These pieces were not easy to make in quantity during the war. Producing them in tiny batches today is nigh on impossible. A lack of the pitch change eye bolts would leave our nearly-ready-to-fly Hurricane stuck on the ground. At that moment the Shuttleworth Collection came to the

This view of the Mk I Hurricane clearly shows its parentage from the Hawker bi-planes.

rescue with a loan set of bolts. Fitting the propeller took just a day. Finishing the spinner took rather longer, but ended up resplendent with the early Rotol badge. Following an original, a domed aluminium copy was machined and sent to Australia for engraving. These badges were only fitted until about November 1940, after which Britain's war effort was more economically directed.

The day came for R4118 to be weighed. I was apprehensive, not on account of the overall weight, but on the distribution of load fore and aft. We had all the equipment in the rear of the fuselage which had been fitted during the Battle. The Rotol propeller now fitted at the front weighed some 70 lbs less than the original De Havilland one. Were we going to be tail heavy? Phil Baker from Loadmasters busied himself around the aircraft, getting each wheel onto sets of low-level digital scales. The weight was fine, well within the maximum laid down by the original Hawker company. Then the tail of the aircraft was raised to its flying position and the exercise repeated. Our fears were confirmed. We had too much weight in the tail, or not enough on the nose. What could we do? Certainly the aircraft could not be flown outside its balance envelope. Nor did I want to remove from the rear fuselage the original radios and IFF equipment we had so painstakingly assembled and rebuilt. There was much head-scratching. Mark I Hurricanes flew in the Battle with Rotol propellers and the same equipment, so must have faced the same problem. At that moment Tony Ditheridge bounded up with an illustration from his Hawker archives. There was the drawing of a pair of weights for fitting on the front of the engine mount – Hawker Aircraft Company's original solution to the problem. Maurice Hammond was called upon to reduce massive lumps of steel to the shape and weight demanded. With 80 lbs of weight up front, we thought the problem was solved.

Tuesday 5 October 2004 was fine and clear. Dave Payne, Maurice Hammond, all of the Hawker Restorations team and I gathered for the first engine run. What

The engine installation is checked under the critical eye of Dave Payne.

anticipation! Check oil, water and fuel levels. Tie down R4118 securely. Connect the 12-volt supply from the trolley acc to the aircraft. Dave into the cockpit. Pre-oiler on for three and a half minutes. Fuel on. Electric fuel pump on for twenty seconds. Six strokes of the priming pump. Starter magneto on. Check all clear? Press the electric starter button. One third of a propeller revolution and the engine bursts into life. Our Battle of Britain Hurricane was running again after sixty-one years!!

That day and the next were taken up with a programme of ground running. It was most exciting. I ran it myself for an hour, gingerly exercising the controls at this early stage. Phil Parish declared the engine to be the sweetest running Merlin he had ever heard. That was a great start, but there was a problem. On engine shutdown fuel continued to drip from the air intake. It was coming from the carburettor. Whatever was done, it could not be stopped. Paul Sharman, who had meticulously rebuilt the unit, was as puzzled as the rest of the team. Unlike later pressure-fed Merlin carburettors, one could not get inside it without removing the engine, the prospect of which excited no-one. But after a couple more days and further ground runs the inevitable prevailed and out the engine had to come. I was down in the dumps.

For the next two weeks Paul struggled on the test rig with the problem of the float needle valve allowing fuel under the test pressure of three and a half pounds per square inch to pass, causing flooding. Buoyancy of the cork float seemed critical. I had two float assemblies from other engines. We were lent another from the Shuttleworth Collection, so we had four to play with. In desperation I went to see a company, C Olley and Sons Ltd, which still builds cork floats for Hobson carburettors fitted to De Havilland Gypsy engines. Peter Olley, great, great, great grandson of the founder in 1844, shook his head. The cork in the floats we had was the very best, such quality and buoyancy not being available today, but could he keep the float overnight and contact me the next day? The following afternoon I called on Peter again. He produced an identical Merlin III float! It turned out that his company made the original floats, and what was more he still had one on the shelf. It weighed exactly the same as the other floats we already had, so I did not seek to rob him of it.

About to fit the carburettor back on the engine and into the aircraft, feeling the problem had been improved but not solved, I had a phone call from Paul. Using a special lapping technique, all was now working perfectly on the test rig. We could re-install the engine with confidence. What a relief!

The delay meant that we were now into December for flight testing, not exactly the best time of year. Our original plan had been to test at Earls Colne airfield where we had been offered hangarage. But by now the hangar had been let. At that moment a very kind offer came from Terry Holloway at Marshall Aerospace at Cambridge. We could re-assemble the Hurricane in one of their huge hangars and flight test from there at Cambridge Airport. Tony Ditheridge and I met with Terry and his team. Nothing was too much trouble.

The great day arrived when we could move R4118 to Cambridge Airport. The team had to ride shotgun to protect the aircraft from overhanging trees.

R4118 was nearly ready for shipment to Cambridge. A final paintwork modification was needed. We had feathered the paint between the top camouflage and the sky underside colour along the leading edge of the wings, a feature correct on the Mk II Hurricanes. But a study of photographs of the Battle of Britain period showed a solid break line along this edge. Insistent upon complete authenticity, I persuaded Clive Denney to repaint that part of the wings, which he did with great good grace, seeing that it was not his fault in the first place.

14 December, a Tuesday, was set for the move to Cambridge. By coincidence, Bill Bishop, my Qantas pilot friend who had helped so much with the stripping of the airframe and the decisions on the paintwork scheme, had brought a 747 into Heathrow the day before. We collected a video photographer en route and arrived at Hawker Restorations at Moat Farm, Milden to find one of the two low loader trucks already stuck fast in the mud. It took three tractors to pull him out. It was clearly going to be impossible to load the Hurricane beside the workshop where it had been rebuilt, so the fuselage was towed to higher ground where it could be craned onto one of the trucks. One wing fitted under the airframe, whilst the second truck carried the other wing and the propeller.

There was one further snag. Perched on top of the truck, the Hurricane would not fit under some of the trees lining the narrow Suffolk lanes. I could already see a twig piercing the fabric. So a couple of Hawkers' engineers rode onboard, armed with saws and poles to attack offending branches. It was little wonder that the convoy arrived at Cambridge Airport somewhat after dark. However the precious cargo was soon safely unloaded and tucked up in a warm hangar.

The following week was devoted to refitting the wings and propeller. Then came the critical stage of further duplicate inspections. Dave Payne and Paul Mercer inspected every inch of the aircraft, checking the rigging and security of every flying surface and control.

The author and Tony Ditheridge from Hawker Restorations go through some of the massive paperwork related to the restoration of R4118. Every part in the aircraft was recorded according to whether it was serviceable, repaired or remade, together with all the material specifications, thus ensuring complete traceability.

The test flight was set for Thursday 23 December. I was fortunate in having been introduced to Pete Kynsey, the Chief Pilot from the Fighter Collection at Duxford. Pete had started out as a flying instructor, and then gone onto helicopters over the North Sea. For a number of years he flew with the British Aerobatic Team, culminating in becoming the British aerobatic champion. He flew business jets and his 'day' job is now flying as a captain on 767s. Since the mid 1980s Pete has flown most of the historic aircraft types in the UK. The Civil Aviation Authority requires operators of warbird aircraft to have an experienced chief pilot, a role which Pete has kindly undertaken for R4118. It is a requirement that any other pilot who flies the aircraft is authorised by the chief pilot.

Thursday morning dawned fine but windy. In a mixture of elation and trepidation I flew our Piper Dakota from Oxford to Cambridge while my wife, Polly, collected our middle son, Clive, from Heathrow. He carried a new telephoto lens to capture the moment of liftoff. Everything on R4118 was ready. But would Pete Kynsey be happy with the wind gusting to 25 knots? The decision would have to wait until the moment of taxiing out. Despite our desire to keep the first flight a quiet, low-key affair, the local BBC and ITV companies were there with cameras rolling. The aircraft was pulled gingerly from the security of the hangar. The Shell bowser drew up. Pete wanted full tanks. Hawkers' engineers fussed around the aeroplane. Pete took his time to walk around. A final check on the wind. It was all systems 'go'. Pete was into the cockpit, the hood closed, the thumbs up signal. With R4118 connected to the trolley acc by its umbilical cord, he primed the oil, primed the fuel and pressed the starter button. Instantly the engine roared into life. The aeroplane was straining at the leash. Unplug the trolley acc, pull away the chocks, let her roll.

Pete allowed the Hurricane to move down the taxiway, gingerly weaving from side to side for visibility and testing the brakes. Then quicker as confidence grew. Runups at the holding point. All seemed OK. Listening on a portable radio, there was the take-off clearance from air traffic control. All of a sudden the mighty roar of the Merlin could be heard. The small form at the distant end of the runway became rapidly bigger. R4118 was airborne – for the first time in over six decades! A cheer went up. The undercarriage retracted. Then we watched as Pete climbed to 4,000 feet over the airfield. The cloud was high enough for those on the ground to watch the whole of the twenty-five minute flight as the aircraft was put through its initial test routine within comfortable gliding distance of the field should anything have gone wrong. Those of us on the ground watched, elated but still apprehensive.

We need not have worried. The Hurricane came in to a text book landing. It taxied to the hangar. Now the applause was louder, more relaxed. The television cameras focussed on Pete as he climbed out. "What was it like?" "How did it feel to be flying an aeroplane which defended England in 1940?" The questions came thick and fast. "The Hurricane flew very well indeed," said Pete. "It was a real privilege to fly such an historic aircraft."

We adjourned to Marshalls' canteen. Hawkers' engineers gathered around Pete Kynsey for the all-important debrief. "It was a lovely aeroplane to fly," said Pete. "The engine was beautifully smooth." Inevitably there were a few problems. The aircraft flew tail heavy, so

UP-W takes off from Cambridge Airport on 23 December 2004. She carries the same livery as worn with 605 'County of Warwick' Squadron in September and October 1940.

further attention would be needed to the centre of gravity. A couple of the instruments were clearly inaccurate. One of the undercarriage legs would not lock in the up position. The harness lock needed adjustment. The RPM needed tweaking. But that was all. Quite amazing after such a rebuild and a real tribute to so many people who had played their part in bringing R4118 back to life.

The second test flight was undertaken three weeks later on a cold, clear January day. At the controls was Stuart Goldspink. Stuart flies 767s for the same company as Pete Kynsey, Britannia Airways. Initially learning to fly in New Zealand, Stuart flew Chipmunks as glider tugs before spending some years crop-spraying on Pawnees in the UK. He has flight-tested several rebuilt early aeroplanes and has flown half the world's population of presently airworthy Hurricanes.

This test was in front of an invited audience, all of whom had been closely involved one way or another with R4118. Guest of honour was Bob Foster who had flown nine operational combat sorties in R4118, resulting in one Ju88 shared destroyed and two Ju88s damaged, a staggering 33% success rate. Mimi and David Thompson, wife and son of Peter Thompson; James Churchill, son of Walter Churchill; Nicholas Winton, son of Denis Winton; and Mike Ingle, nephew of Alec Ingle, were all there. It was an emotional moment for them all as the Hurricane, flown in a former time by their close family members, took to the skies. The event was supported by many skilled engineers and enthusiastic amateurs, all of whom had contributed to the moment. Seated in the aircraft's cockpit, Bob Foster had a new story to tell:

Pilot Officer (later Wing Commander) Bob Foster reunited with the aircraft in which he damaged and destroyed three enemy aircraft during the Battle of Britain. His log book records each sortie in R4118.

One day after a dogfight above the clouds I came down and found myself over the Channel. I headed towards the coast and flew inland looking for familiar landmarks. I checked my instruments, and the compass seemed to be all haywire, pointing in the wrong direction. I thought no more of it and continued inland. Suddenly puffs of black smoke started bursting around me and the penny dropped. I had indeed crossed the coast, but it was the French coast, and I was heading south towards Paris, not north towards London. I turned and came back fast and low, I was lucky to get away with it.

Stuart flew for thirty minutes. He had a large grin on his face when he climbed out of the cockpit. Most of the problems encountered on the first test flight by Pete Kynsey had been fixed, but still the undercarriage could not be relied upon to lock in the retracted position. There was no trouble in locking the undercarriage in the down position though, quite a relief!

There is only one other Hurricane Mk I flying in the world. The Mk IA Sea Hurricane belonging to the Shuttleworth Collection is flown by Andy Sephton. Tony Ditheridge thought it would be highly beneficial to have an opinion as to how our Mk I flew compared with Shuttleworth's. Fortunately Andy is a test pilot with Marshall Aerospace where the Hurricane was hangared. He instantly agreed to test ours. Just the day after Stuart had done the second test, Andy flew R4118 for thirty-five minutes. He made a number of points, including finding that the north arrow on the compass pointed south! His comparisons with the Sea Hurricane were all favourable. His report concluded: "Suffice to say that the comments are only minor, the general state of the aircraft is excellent and the restoration is perhaps the most sympathetic that I've seen so far. Please pass my congratulations on to all involved."

Flight testing of these wartime aircraft is an exacting business. The Civil Aviation Authority lays down a rigid test schedule. Pete Kynsey and Stuart Goldspink put R4118 through all sorts of hoops to check that it flew 'to the book', and to detect any abnormal characteristics. The ultimate test was to dive the aircraft at 380 miles an hour to establish the Vne (never exceed speed). The wings did not fall off, so the trial was deemed successful!

Testing continued for a total of five hours. After a final inspection the CAA granted a Permit to Fly. R4118 was born again. These historic aeroplanes are committed to our care during our brief lives, but we hope that this gallant fighter will long remain a token to the memory of those whose brave deeds in 1940 preserved Britain's freedom.

Following the first test flight, I had sent Bunny Currant a photograph of the take-off. He should have the last word:

What a beautiful sight to see R4118 in flight 65 years since 1940 and my flight in her from Drem to Croydon on 7 September. What a simply beautiful photo it is. I am so thrilled through and through. Thank you, may it give you and many such joy. And when does Polly hope to fly it? Good luck and I hope you will be so thrilled with the experience. Bless you both and R4118. Yrs aye, Bunny (93 a few days ago).

The R4118 connection: Nicholas Winton, son of Denis Winton; David and Mimi Thompson, son and wife of Peter Thompson; Kaethe and Bob Foster; James Churchill, son of Walter Churchill; and Mike Ingle, nephew of Alec Ingle. Shown in the winter sunshine for the second air test on 13 January 2005.

CHAPTER 17
The Great Day

AS I stood watching that first flight, a raft of mixed emotions welled up inside me. Dear wife Polly was jumping up and down in excitement, but being a typical male, I was rather less demonstrative. Besides, my initial concern was for the pilot of this first sortie. I was apprehensive in case something should happen to R4118 after the years of blood, sweat and tears getting it from India; and the not inconsiderable cost that had gone into it.

I also felt for all those who had been involved in the rebuild. They had put so much into it. Their labours had looked superb, but now here was the ultimate test of their skills – would it fly? It flew alright, but we could see a degree of smoke coming from the exhausts. It was running rich. I had a portable two-way radio with me. Should we call the pilot back? Then the smoke stopped. I breathed again.

Then Pete Kynsey brought R4118 safely down with a perfect three-point landing. I was elated – the same feeling as when we opened the container in July 2001 and saw that the aircraft had indeed arrived back home. I allowed myself a moment of pride. The photographs show me grinning from ear to ear. Polly and I had a big hug, then handshakes all round.

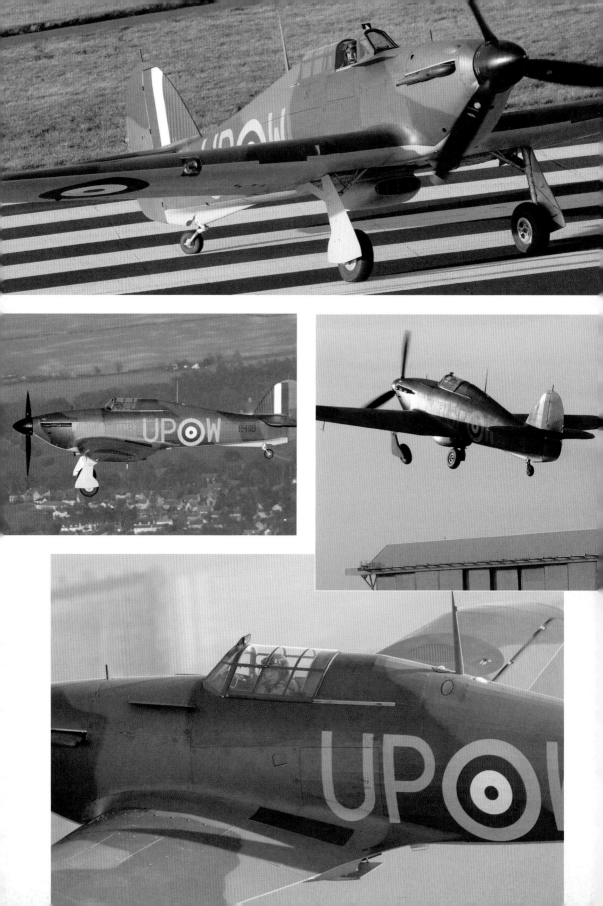

CHAPTER 18
Living with a 75-year-old Warbird

OPERATING a second world war fighter in the United Kingdom environment has been an experience! Having completed the flight testing, we were given space at Oxford airport in a blister hangar. In those early days the fire crews kindly pushed R4118 from the hangar to the apron. The airport management was most helpful, but an increasingly busy airport was not the ideal place to keep and maintain a warbird.

We had a stroke of good fortune. One day in 2005 an enterprising estate agent sent some particulars of a property through the post. I opened the envelope, glanced at the contents and shot them across the breakfast table to Polly. Here was a 140-acre farm with a grotty bungalow, but with a hangar and runway. What was more, it was only seven miles from our existing home and a bungalow could always be fixed. Polly leapt up, saying she was ringing the agent, although it was only 8 am, to demand to see the property by midday. I said that if we appeared too keen, we would pay through the nose. We did! But it gave us the perfect place to keep the Hurricane and Polly's Piper Dakota in which she had done two solo world flights. The maintenance of the Hurricane was initially done under Hawker Restorations' Civil Aviation Authority approval, but now here was an environment in which we could have our own CAA approval. We erected a hangar, and wrote the required exposition document which set out how and by whom R4118 would be maintained. With what I regarded as great flexibility, the CAA approved myself to work on the aeroplane and sign it out although I had no aeronautical engineering licences. They looked at the restoration work I had done on three vintage Rolls-Royces and were apparently impressed. In reality our A8-20 approval was granted because we had Paul Mercer as our Chief Engineer and Dave Payne as our Deputy Chief Engineer, both highly respected by the CAA. Their main involvement was at the annual inspection while I did the day-to-day servicing. We were required to have a Chief Pilot, without whose approval no-one could fly. Throughout my ownership Pete Kynsey undertook that role, approving Stu Goldspink, Carl Schofield and Keith Dennison as our regular pilots. Al Pinner, Phil O'Dell and Dave Harvey also displayed the aircraft. All seven pilots showed R4118 at its best, and more importantly, flew it safely. Our son, Julian, did twelve hours in a Harvard in Florida and was checked out by Pete Kynsey to fly R4118.

A rare event produces a heart-stopping moment. Hurricane R4118 flying with Spitfire P7350, the only two surviving flying fighters from the Battle of Britain, at Dunsfold in June 2005.

"David Cameron and Prince William outflank the Battle of Britain veteran Bob Foster during a 70th anniversary flypast at Westminster Abbey yesterday." The Times, 20 September 2010.

So that was the aeroplane and pilots sorted. Now the airshows and private displays. Much of my time towards the end of each year was writing to organisers in the hope that they would want R4118 to perform. If invited, the pilot's details would be forwarded including flying licence, medical certificate, display authorisation, and certificate of re-validation together with the aircraft's permit to fly, certificate of validity and insurance. We carried £15 million third party cover. Operating a warbird is horribly expensive, so income from airshows made an essential

Photographer John Dibbs catches the wingman's view of R4118 returning from a sortie over the Channel.

contribution but by no means covered the annual cost. Two other income streams were from film and television, and from private air displays. R4118 starred in several films including one about Churchill in which a pilot is seen leaping into R4118, from which with the wonders of modern computer technology, it was possible to create the scramble of an entire squadron. In another, 'Battle of Britain' featuring Ewan McGregor with his brother, Colin, learning to fly a fighter with the same training as second world war pilots, there was a break in filming. We adjourned to the local pub with the camera crew and were joined by two of 'The Few', Bob Foster and Geoffrey Wellum. It made good television. Over another weekend our hangar was converted into a 'green' film set. With clever digital manipulation, R4118 was used in a running video 'The Scramble Experience' in the Wing Museum at the Battle of Britain Memorial at Capel-le-Ferne. For some years we held a small event for 1000 people at our home strip to thank the inhabitants of the local villages for putting up with our flying activities. Participants included variously Spitfires, Hurricanes, Tiger Moths, and a host of other aircraft including the Battle of Britain Memorial Flight. Over the years we had numerous complaints – that they did not see enough of Hurricane R4118!

One of our favourite events was the annual Battle of Britain Dining-in Night at RAF Benson. Carl Schofield or Keith Dennison would display R4118 over the Officers' Mess to the assembled guests as the sun went down, navigation lights on, land at the base, and remove flying suits to reveal their dinner jackets, ready for dinner. Bob Foster was twice guest of honour as was an old friend, Don Chadwick who flew photo-reconnaissance Mosquitos from Benson in 1944. Bob held the rather younger RAF officer-audience spell-bound with experiences in the Battle. Walking into the Benson Officers' Mess for the first time since 1944, Don commented that not much had changed – except there was a new carpet. In response to my raised eyebrow, he said

"O yes, we used to play a game. Two teams of two competed. One team at the far end of the room each had a fire extinguisher. The other team had a broom and a bucket of paraffin. The broom was dipped in the paraffin, set alight and hurled to the other end. If the fire was put out by the chaps with the fire extinguishers before it hit the carpet, they won. If it hit the carpet, the broom team won!" Perhaps we are over-controlled today?

Supporting the aircraft at shows was highly dependent on the help of volunteer groundcrew. We had two teams, one at base to pre-flight and see off the pilot and machine, our regulars being Rick Chase

Propeller blade damage from loose light on the runway.

and Gavin Selwood. Awaiting arrival were our airshow team of Simon Steggall and Liz Maxim and others. They travelled all over the country ready to look after the needs of pilots and aeroplane. Without their dedication and sheer enthusiasm, R4118 would not have been seen and its remarkable story told.

Keeping a Battle of Britain veteran aircraft in the air is not

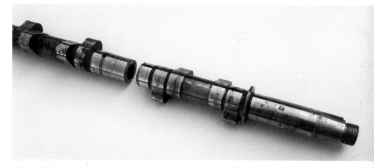

The offending camshaft which caused the forced landing on 18 July 2010.

always a bed of roses. As we have seen, each aeroplane had two full-time crew keeping it in flying trim when on squadron operations. In our civilian world all those years later, the aircraft still needs constant attention and one has to cope with the unexpected. On 19 August 2007 Carl Schofield was displaying R4118 at the Shoreham airshow in the usual simulation of a Battle of Britain tailchase. It was a superb show, but after landing a large gash was found in one of the propeller blades. Apparently a taxiway light had been previously dislodged and the wash from R4118's propeller had whipped it up. The propeller had to have a new blade and be zero-timed. The engine had to be checked, but with the benefit of wooden rather than metal blades, no damage was done.

Keith Dennison experienced another incident, flying between the Royal International Air Tattoo at Fairford and en route to the Farnborough Airshow. The story can be read in the accompanying copy of the Occurrence Report. The cause was a broken camshaft, leaving the engine running on seven of its twelve cylinders. It was subsequently discovered that Merlin III engines had experienced loose brackets holding down the camshafts, causing them to flex and break. We found the drawings for the subsequent Rolls-Royce modification which was then incorporated on the engine. On another occasion we found small drips of water coming from an exhaust port. This was discovered to be from a hairline crack. Fortunately there was a Rolls-

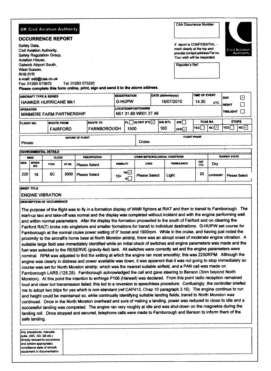

Royce repair scheme for this, by welding. The prospect of welding a 75-year-old block was not attractive until we found a new and advanced technique of laser welding. Using a laser, the weld could be targeted to a restricted area and used only a small amount of localised heat, thus avoiding any distortion to the block.

I never did more than taxi the Hurricane myself, but had enormous pleasure in doing all the engineering to keep it in the air. I used to joke that the pilots bent it each weekend and I mended it each week. There was no truth in it, but it was time-consuming to keep it in perfect condition.

Left: *Keith Dennison's Occurrence Report following a broken camshaft in the Merlin III on 18 July 2010.*

In perfect echelon. From the top: *The Battle of Britain Memorial Flight's PZ865 (The Last of the Many), The Historic Aircraft Collection's Z5140, R4118 and the BBMF's LF363.*

The 90th anniversary of 'Tremblers'. Both aircraft flew with 111 Squadron and celebrated with a formation sortie on 13 June 2007, R4118 being flown by Pete Kynsey.

CHAPTER 19

The Pilot's View

Keith Dennison, who has regularly flown Hurricane R4118, has kindly contributed this article which first appeared in the March 2015 edition of Flyer.

Keith Dennison gives us a detailed checkout on a wonderfully restored Hurricane. Climb into a five-kill survivor from the Battle of Britain, a few feet behind that roaring 1,030hp Merlin for a 250mph flight of a lifetime.

PETER Vacher, the owner of Hawker Hurricane Mk1 R4118 UP-W, has invited you to fly his beautifully restored and historically significant aircraft. My purpose is to brief you for your flight and to give you a few of the hints and tips for flying the Hurricane that I've picked up during eight years of flying the aircraft on the display circuit in the UK and Europe.

Now, you have a reasonable number of hours in other aircraft, and you've done your differences training for both retractable undercarriage and variable-pitch propellers. You've done a conversion to tailwheel aircraft and I'm pleased that you have taken my advice and got some experience in a Harvard, one of the best ways of preparing to fly any single-seat warbird for the first time. So I won't spend too much time on the fundamental differences between the Hurricane and the aircraft you are mainly used to flying.

I think it's far better to do this brief at the aircraft, so let's walk across to Peter's hangar. Don't forget your kneeboard with the checklist I gave you – there's nowhere to put anything down in the Hurricane and as there's no floor as such, if you do put something down it'll probably end up sculling around in the bilges, so anything you take with you needs to go in a flying suit pocket or to be strapped securely to your knee. Bring your helmet too. You'll find it's very noisy in there and, with the canopy open, there can be some airflow buffet in the cockpit, so your helmet will need to be more secure and give you effective ear protection – you'll need it!

Approaching the aircraft you'll gradually realise that it's big. Indeed, if you ever see a Hurricane and a Spitfire parked together you'll notice that the Hurricane is notably bigger than the Spitfire. It stands much taller; everything about it is chunkier. The size of the aircraft and the height of the cockpit will mean that the flare height and hold-off height before landing will look considerably higher to you than in a light aircraft, although your time on the Harvard will have prepared you well.

Doing the walkround is surprisingly conventional; despite the size and vintage of the aircraft,

166

you are really looking for the same things as you do on a light aircraft – panels all done up, leaks, damage, pitot cover off, control surfaces free – the oil will have been topped-up by the ground crew as it's a tricky process and you don't want to overfill. The lubrication of the supercharger in the Merlin III was by a total-loss system, so Merlin III-engined aircraft are always a bit oily after flight but if you overfill the tank you'll waste oil and have an even bigger clean-up job. The coolant will also have been checked for you. I always enjoy walking round R4118 and revelling in the superb attention to detail including all the codes on wings, tailplanes, control surfaces, every part of the airframe, that faithfully record each component's place of manufacture and its servicing history – this aircraft just exudes history and it is a tremendous privilege to fly her.

Let's get you in the cockpit and I'll brief you on the start and the flying. Right foot in the stirrup that drops down from the fuselage behind the port wing-root, right hand in the handhold high on the fuselage side and then heave yourself up to put your left foot on the wing-root walkway and grab the cockpit sill with your left hand. The wing-root is steep, so hold onto the cockpit sill as you walk up alongside, particularly if it's wet. You'll see a kick-in footstep in the fuselage side, right foot in there and step onto the seat and get yourself settled in.

Up to your neck

The first thing that will probably strike you is that you're up to your neck in aeroplane, the cockpit sides are high and the nose slopes up ahead of you, denying a view straight forward; the forward view is actually much better than in many warbirds, but you'll still have to weave when taxying to clear your path. The seat is adjusted by a big, handbrake-like lever on the starboard side of the seat.

Keith Dennison in the 'office', Cosby Victory Show 2013.

I adjust my sitting height to align the straight edge at the base of the windscreen with the horizon, that gives a great reference for the three-point attitude when you come to land and a small amount of clearance between the top of your helmet and the canopy.

Strapping into the seat-pack parachute and the four-point harness is straightforward. The harness can be set into locked, or a sprung, go-forward mode using a small selector mounted on a longeron on the right cockpit side. A similar lever on the left side locks the canopy open, but not closed; you'll find the airflow will shut the canopy by itself if you leave the canopy anything more than half-forward – it seems very strange when you first see it happen. Make sure the canopy is set to locked, but about three inches forward of fully-back; I'll tell you why later.

The pre-start checks are easy to do, just follow the checklist. However, I'll give you a couple of tips. It's best to start the aircraft from Peter's genuine 1940 12V trolley-ac, so we'll get that plugged in. R4118 has an original 12V electrical system – many restored warbirds are given 24V systems, which are more powerful and have much more capacity – the 12V system will give you three good start attempts, but after that it will be getting tired, so using the trolley-ac is a good idea if it's available. If the aircraft has flown within the last 24 hours, then you don't need to pre-oil the engine; at all other times you must pre-oil the engine using the electrically-driven, pre-oil pump – the switch is on the left cockpit shelf just below your left shoulder next to the generator, fuel pump switches and the voltmeter. The pre-oiler pumps oil around the engine and ensures that everything is lubricated before you start turning – you should see a steady build of oil pressure to about 30psi while the pump is running. Run the fuel pump for 30 seconds before priming the engine for start and then use the Ki-Gass primer pump, below the instrument panel in front of your right knee, to prime the engine. Unscrew the large brass head of the pump and then slowly pump. The first few strokes will be very soft – these strokes don't count – but eventually the pump will become hard to push in and this is when you are really pumping fuel. With a cold engine you'll need four good, hard strokes of the pump.

Priming Merlins when they are anything other than cold is a tricky judgement, too little and it just won't go, too much and you get the spectacular, but worrying, gouts of flame from the exhaust stacks – if that ever happens to you in the future just keep turning the engine until the flames subside and you've burned off the excess prime in the safest possible way. Four strokes when the engine is cold is accurate and reliable; the engine can usually be regarded as 'cold' about an hour after shutdown, and if the engine is hot, no priming is required. But what to do in the vague middle-ground of a warm Merlin? I found the best advice in the memoirs of a Battle of Britain pilot – his advice was to guess the prime and err on the low side, then after setting the throttle a crack open, starter magneto on and with stick held hard back you press the starter. If the engine hasn't fired after three blades then pump the primer like billyo until it does. Flick the magnetos on as soon as the engine fires. I've adopted this advice ever since reading it and it has never failed me.

Three hands

You'll notice that your left hand will need to push the starter button, as well as flicking the mags on, while your right hand is standing by to prime and your third hand is holding the stick back – yes, it's best to work out exactly how you are going to accomplish everything before you go for your first start.

The Merlin will settle into a slow idle initially; leave it there for a minute while all the pressures settle down, complete the few after-start checks and then set a smooth, faster idle for warming up – it's about 1,200rpm, but the rpm gauge doesn't start to read until 1,600rpm so you just have to find the fast idle where the engine sounds happy. You need 15°C on the oil temperature and 60°C on the coolant temperature before you can run-up; this will take about five minutes. On hard man-made surfaces, or hard grass that is sufficiently smooth, you can taxi when the coolant temperature is 40°C so that you are, hopefully, arriving at the hold short by the time the engine is ready to run up. To taxi you'll need a squeeze of power to get her moving but then she will move along quite nicely with that same fast idle setting you had before.

Steering is by differential use of the pneumatic brakes. The amount of braking is set by squeezing a bicycle-type brake lever mounted within the circular grip at the top of the stick. If you leave the rudder pedals neutral, then braking will be equal to each wheel and you will brake in a straight line; by applying full rudder in the desired direction of turn, the brake pressure is applied only to that wheel and you turn. The brakes are not powerful, so keep your taxi speed down and anticipate the need for manoeuvring. At very low speed, a bit of power and full asymmetric brake will allow you to spin the aircraft around very tightly. Holding short of the runway and with the engine up to temperature, align the aircraft into wind, hold the brakes on with the stick hard back and smoothly set 2,000rpm for the engine checks. A full check involves setting zero boost (about 2,350rpm) and even full power, but it's best to do such checks with chocks in and groundcrew assistance to ensure the tail stays down; using 2,000rpm gives a good check for routine purposes. You'll be pulling quite hard to keep the stick back, but it's not for long, so man-up! Check the magnetos first in the usual way; you're looking for not more than 80rpm drop on each mag, then exercise the constant speed unit by smoothly moving the rpm lever back (it's on the left cockpit wall above the throttle), reducing the engine rpm by 300rpm and then return the lever to fully forward and check that the rpm is restored; do this three times.

The engine will be hot by now and you cannot dally before getting airborne otherwise, particularly in the summer, you can overheat on the ground. Complete the pre-take-off checks. Take note of the control for the undercarriage and flaps as it can catch you out. The control is against the right cockpit wall outboard of your right knee, so you have to swap hands after take-off to retract the undercarriage.

Make sure that you have plenty of throttle friction applied else, as you swap hands to do this after take-off, the throttle will probably move fairly smartly towards idle, resulting in a frantic bout of hand-swapping in an attempt both to stay airborne and get the wheels up – this amuses onlooking pilots but frightens both you and the owner to death!

The combined undercarriage and flap control consists of something that looks like a car gear lever that moves in an H-shaped slot. In the left-hand vertical slot the lever controls the undercarriage, in the right-hand slot it controls the flaps. Have you spotted the gotcha? Yes, it's all too easy after landing, basking in the success of your latest display, to select the gear-up rather than the flaps – it happens, be warned! There is a little catch at the base of the upper-left slot that is designed to prevent this particular error and you will move that out of the way as part of the pre-take-off checks so that you can move the lever left and forward to retract the undercarriage.

Leave the flaps up and the canopy open. You can set 28° of flap if a shorter take-off is required but on most runways no flap is required – not only that, not having to worry about the flaps will slightly reduce the drama after your first take-off! Set the fuel selector to the reserve tank that sits right in front of the cockpit and will gravity-feed fuel to the engine if the mechanical fuel pump fails; its capacity is a mere 28 gallons, which you can use quite quickly if you get enthusiastic, so you must remember to select the main wing-tanks shortly after take-off.

One deafening Merlin

OK, you're ready to go in this amazing, five-kill survivor of the Battle of Britain. It's a lovely day and there's a classic ten knots down the strip. The period Royal Air Force Pilots' Notes give a crosswind limit of ten knots and this is good advice for both take-off and landing until experience is gained. However, with experience, up to 20kt of crosswind can be tolerated with the handling on grass being a little better than on a hard runway. Holding some aileron into wind helps on both the take-off and landing rolls.

With the stick held hard back, start the take-off by smoothly advancing the throttle to +4psi of boost; this should give about 2,650rpm early in the take-off roll but will increase quickly to 2,850rpm as the airspeed increases. And now you'll feel the aural and physical assault of the Merlin six feet in front of you in full force – it will vibrate more than you are used to; a 27-litre capacity and that much metal whirling and reciprocating at high speed is difficult to keep entirely vibration free, and wow! What a noise! It's not the glorious sound of a Merlin that is held dear in every British heart, it's a deafening, roaring cacophony of sound quite unlike the symphony being enjoyed by those watching us.

Full power at +6¼psi of boost and 2,850rpm can be used if really required but, in deference to her age and to keep R4118 flying for as long as possible, full power is rarely used and +4psi gives entirely adequate although not exciting take-off performance – many higher performance light aeroplanes accelerate just as quickly.

There's very little swing, considering the power of the engine and the size of the propeller, but the Hurricane's wide-legged stance and design give it very benign handling during take-off and landing. What little swing there is, is to the left and a small squeeze of right rudder is all that is required to keep her straight.

At 40mph, move the stick forward to raise the tail, you may need almost full forward stick to get the tail moving, and then set a take-off attitude in which you can just see the end of the runway over the nose. There's no perceptible swing as you raise the tail, unlike the Gloster Gladiator for instance, which will swing viciously if you attempt to raise the tail on take-off either too early or too quickly – again, the Hurricane is being kind to you.

The Hurricane will get airborne at about 75mph, but on a grass surface with any undulations and bumps the exact lift-off speed can vary; the key is, if you hold the attitude as I've told you, there's no need to pull her off the ground, she'll tell you when she's ready to fly.

After lift-off, hold the nose attitude briefly to allow the airspeed to increase to above 90mph, then raise the nose to limit the rate of further acceleration – you need to get the undercarriage up by 120mph. The aircraft will feel a bit vague in pitch, as if you are connected to the elevators by weak elastic – we'll discuss this later – but stick with it as you prepare to bring the undercarriage up. Swap hands on the stick so that you can work the undercarriage lever. Remember you are going to move the lever left and forwards to retract the undercarriage; there's little trim change as the wheels move up. If you look down into the bottom of the cockpit, just behind and outboard of your feet you'll see two small windows, one each side, and you will see the wheels swinging up and into the bays. You can also see and check the undercarriage uplocks, but these are details; what you really want to see is two red lights on the undercarriage indicator that indicate that the wheels are up and locked.

Once the undercarriage is up and locked you must return the undercarriage and flap control lever to the central position in the H. The system applies a lock to keep the lever in each of the four corners of the H if it is put there; to release the lever, you will need to press a small thumb-catch mounted on the lever on the inboard edge. If you don't return the lever to neutral, nothing bad will happen in the short-term, however, the hydraulic pump will continue to run and the hydraulics will steadily overheat. You'll find this out when you come to put the undercarriage down to land and the overheated hydraulics just won't play. Then you'll have to lower the undercarriage on the emergency, gravity-drop system, which is reliable but it can be tricky to get the wheels locked; this involves side-slipping vigorously to get the wheels to 'fly' out – not something that you'll want to be doing on your first trip.

Demanding handling

So, with the wheels up and the lever back to neutral you can now give the engine a break by bringing the rpm back to 2,600rpm for the climb at 170mph and +4psi of boost – the cacophony reduces to very slightly smaller cacophony. You'll remember that I earlier told you to leave the canopy about three inches forward of fully back, this is why. You now need to reach back to pull the canopy forward and shut. Two techniques are available; either reach back above your head or reach across yourself to behind your opposite shoulder to grab the forward canopy edge and pull the canopy forward. Neither technique is easy and, if you left the canopy completely back, almost impossible. Once the canopy is shut, change the fuel tank selector over to the main tanks. Congratulations! You're airborne in Hurricane R4118.

The climb is quicker than most light aeroplanes, but not spectacularly quicker, maybe 2,000-2,500fpm. The main thing you will notice – apart from the noise – is that you'll try to trim but it will never seem to be right. You'll get the sense of having trimmed correctly but then every time you release the stick the aircraft will either pitch up or pitch down, sometimes quite markedly. This is because the Hurricane Mk1 is, at best, neutrally statically stable in pitch and, depending on the exact equipment fit and build standard, quite likely to be statically unstable. This means that, unlike a conventional, statically stable aeroplane, which returns to its trimmed condition if disturbed (by the pilot's inputs or a gust), the Hurricane will diverge from trim if disturbed. This means that you have to actively control the Hurricane in pitch at all times, it will not trim to fly hands-off, and this is also the source of the vague, connected-by-elastic feeling that you had just after take-off. That feeling – or more correctly, this poor handling quality – is worst at low airspeeds and subsides as the speed increases. It makes flying formation at low airspeeds quite a wallowy affair with a need for good anticipation and occasionally vigorous but precise use of the pitch control at airspeeds below 140mph. Mk2 Hurricanes with their longer, heavier nose are stable and trim-up and fly very nicely by comparison.

When you reach your desired cruising altitude, level off and allow the aircraft to accelerate to 190mph then reduce the boost to 0psi and the rpm to 1,900rpm; the noise reduces to simply 'very noisy'. The best economical cruise is at 190mph; with those engine settings you will be consuming a miserly 35gph. More enthusiastic flight or display flying is best done at +4psi boost and 2,600rpm. At those settings the aircraft will settle in level flight at 240-250mph.

For planning purposes, I allow ten gallons for a ten-minute display, so about a gallon a minute seems about right. By modern fighter standards, the roll control is heavy and the roll rate is ponderous, but it does roll somewhat quicker than many typical flying school aircraft.

Directional control with the rudder is powerful but does have a quirk: applying significant rudder in either direction causes the nose to drop abruptly due to the change of airflow over the tailplane. This is normally not a problem as the rudder is powerful at cruising speeds and the small rudder deflections used to balance turns do not cause the problem, but a display pilot who tries to get a bit more

We welcome all who supported the participation of Hawker Hurricane at NATO Days in Ostrava & Czech Air Force Days

On the occasion of the 70th anniversary of the Battle of Britain and to honour the pilots who fought in this battle, we have decided to invite

Hawker Hurricane Mk I with the marking R4118,

that is the direct participant of the Battle of Britain.

Because of this special occasion, we have for the first time in the history of NATO Days in Ostrava agreed to cover the costs of the airplane participation in the amount of £15,000. Due to free entry to the show we are not able to cover this by ourselves.

So we have decided to ask you, our supporters, to contribute and some of you already did. If you decide to support the participation of this unique aircraft by the amount of

159 Kč,

as a gratitude we offer:

- **unique collector print** issued in limited numbered edition
- entrance to the **Hurricane Zone**, where you can closely see this aircraft and take pictures of it
- **meeting the owner** of the plane Peter Vacher **and its pilot** Air Commodore Keith Dennison, and gaining their signature

Thank you for your support. Please enter.

The poster advertising R4118's appearance at the NATO Air Days at Ostrava in the Czech Republic.

bank on his topside pass by cheating with a bit of top rudder will find the aeroplane bunting abruptly and turning his hero moment into a rather untidy affair. Similarly, in the heat of battle, trying to rudder a few bullets on a target would not have worked out well. The Hurricane, legendarily, turned very well at slow speeds.

However, while the turning performance is good, the associated flying qualities are poor. It comes back to that pitch instability. In the turn, and particularly if you lose speed in the turn, the aircraft tends to want to increase the turn rate and g of its own accord; this means that, maybe in a display, in a slow-speed, 360° turn a firm push on the stick will be required to stop the aircraft from trying to swallow its own tail. This is also why some high-speed, topside display passes can look a bit threepenny-bitty as the pilot fights the instability with alternating forward and aft stick forces in his attempt to keep a steady turn. This is the worst characteristic of the Hurricane Mk 1. It's not difficult to master, so it is not dangerous as such, but it does make flying accurate turns quite challenging and would have made our young fighter pilots' task very demanding in the dark days of autumn 1940.

Over the hedge

Time to go back and land. Fly to the field at cruise power, the view forward and downwards isn't great due to the nose and the wings, so you might need to bank to identify features below you, but as the height comes down the view directly forward is good, allowing accurate navigation. At the field, fly a break from 500ft and cruise conditions. As you turn to downwind, ease the power back, about -4psi boost should do, not idle, open the canopy and as the airspeed falls through 150mph put the rpm lever smoothly up to maximum – you'll hear the rpm rise – and the deceleration rate will increase significantly.

At 120mph put the wheels down. When you have the two green lights indicating the wheels are down and locked you will probably be halfway down the downwind leg. Take the undercarriage and flap lever and move it up and over from the back left-hand corner to the back right-hand corner of the H; this will start the flaps travelling down. You can leave the lever in the back right corner; the time it will be there will not be enough to overheat the hydraulics and its position in the right (flap control) track of the H will help to prevent the error of mistakenly bringing the wheels rather than the flaps up after landing.

As the flaps travel fully down, there's a marked nose-down trim change and you will need a good few handfuls of aft trim. Yes, mercifully, in the approach configuration the aircraft trims out conventionally because in this configuration it is statically stable. You are looking to be at about 100mph to 85mph abeam the touchdown point; use the throttle conventionally to

"They'll never catch him!" Keith Dennison in formation with a SAAB Gripen (top left) and Sukhoi Su35 at the NATO Air Days in Ostrava, September 2010.

achieve this and as you come abeam start a gentle, continuous, descending turn onto final at 85mph, in trim. You should turn continuously round final to arrive 'over the hedge' with only a few seconds of straight flight before touchdown. It's good fun, it looks very Battle of Britain… and it'll be good practice for your Spitfire sortie – but the view over the nose on the approach in the Hurricane is good enough to do straight-in approaches if necessary.

Over the hedge, begin to smoothly reduce the power to idle and flare gently but progressively to the three-point attitude. Your aim is to arrive at 'skimming the daisies' height at idle and in the three-point attitude (if you set your seat-height correctly, align the base of the windscreen with the far horizon) and then allow the aircraft gently to settle. The aircraft runs straight and there's little need for steering or braking if the wind is down the strip. However, the brakes are weak and fade easily, so, particularly in a crosswind, you should reserve your use of the brakes for steering, not for stopping.

With ten knots down the strip and no braking before taxi speed, the aircraft will roll out in 500m. Bring the flaps – not the gear! – up after you have stopped, or turned off the strip and taxi back. Once parked, allow the engine to idle for a minute or so at the slowest smooth-idling rpm, to allow the temperatures in the engine to equalise, and then stop the engine by pulling the carburettor cut-off control beneath the instrument panel in front of your left knee. When the engine has stopped, switch off the mags and complete the post-shutdown checks.

Congratulations, you have flown a genuine Battle of Britain Hurricane. How was it for you?

The Story Continues

This chapter is kindly contributed by James Brown,
R4118's new owner.

38,000 feet above the Atlantic is not a bad place to contemplate the wonders of flight. So, having cleared my emails and prepared the presentations I needed for the week's trip to the US, I folded my laptop shut and pulled a freshly-purchased copy of *Flyer* out of my bag.

Having had a lifelong passion for aircraft, and a PPL since the late 90's, I enjoyed taking a couple of hours to indulge my love of flying during a business trip and always made sure I had ample aviation-themed reading material before I left the airport. Today's trip was no exception, so I packed away all reminders of work and laid the magazine on the small folding table in front of me. Above the tantalizing headline 'How to Fly a Hurricane' was a stunning photograph of Peter Vacher's Mk1: R4118. Of course, I'd seen her at air shows many times over the years and, with her unique Battle of Britain history and glorious early Merlin, she was already a personal favourite. We had two hours remaining before touchdown in Philadelphia, so I topped up my wine glass and turned to the article.

Within a couple of sentences, I was immersed in the Hurricane. Keith Dennison – who had been flying R4118 on-and-off for the previous eight years – took me through the full sortie from walk around to shut down and his easy, matter-of-fact style made flying the Hurricane seem an attainable goal, even for a low-hours PPL like me. But it was the small panel at the end of the article pronouncing R4118 for sale that really caught my eye. This unique Battle of Britain veteran, this genuine piece of Britain's heritage, was on the market and I might – just – be in a position to buy her.

It was February 2015, and this was my third trip to the US that month. Although I'd started my software company some 14 years earlier, the last couple of years had been frantic. The business now employed almost 200 people with offices across the US, Europe and Australia. But it was the events of the previous few weeks that made Hurricane ownership a possibility. We'd been approached by a potential buyer for our company and, although negotiations were at an embryonic stage, if the sale could be agreed, there was the glimmer of a chance that my life-long ambition of owning a British warbird could be achieved. Selling a company, however, is a fraught business at the best of times, and there could be no guarantee of when – if ever – we might close a deal. The possibility of completing the sale before R4118 was snapped up by a US warbird collector seemed vanishingly small but, with nothing to lose, I flipped open my laptop again and wrote a short, caveat-laden, email to Peter to express my interest in his beautiful aeroplane.

Two days later not only did I get a reply from Peter, but also an invitation to meet at his farm in Oxfordshire and see the aeroplane. With a great deal of excitement, and more than a touch of apprehension over what I might be getting myself into, I gladly accepted.

And so, on a grey and blustery March morning I arrived to a warm welcome from both Peter and Polly – a welcome I would later come to realise was a trademark of this wonderful couple. While Peter ushered me through to the conservatory, past paintings of Hurricanes hanging from their walls, Polly prepared tea and cake for us both, while their slightly over-exuberant standard poodle – Nelson – continued the Vacher tradition of warm welcomes.

Peter and I sat and talked for a good hour. I explained my interest in his aeroplane, and the somewhat tenuous situation we were in with the sale of our business, whilst he in turn talked me through the story of R4118's discovery in India and subsequent repatriation and restoration back in the UK (a story I was later to fully appreciate upon reading his fantastic book). It was clear from the moment Peter started talking that his knowledge of the Hurricane was encyclopaedic, and his passion for originality shone through. Wherever possible, every component fitted to R4118 was either a part that had been recovered from India with the remarkably-complete airframe, or was a genuine Mk1 Hurricane part that he'd tracked down through his extensive network of colleagues and friends around the world. Only where airworthiness issues prevented original components being used, he explained, were new parts manufactured to original specifications.

I was mesmerised by Peter's enthusiasm. The more he talked, the more I realised what an enormous part of his and Polly's life the Hurricane had become and, I suspected, how emotional any eventual sale would be for them both. The thought quickly dawned on me that owning a Hurricane, especially *this* Hurricane, would be a huge responsibility. Here was an aircraft that, not only had flown 49 sorties during the heat of the Battle of Britain, shooting down or damaging five enemy aircraft, but one that was now a unique airworthy survivor into which Peter had poured almost 20 years of his life. An aeroplane that was famous as being one of the most original survivors of the entire second world war; and an aeroplane that was a tangible link to the bravery and sacrifice of the men of Fighter Command who gave so much during the summer of 1940.

As we finished our tea, and started the short walk across the back garden of the Vacher's home towards the hangar where R4118 was kept, it occurred to me that this was not going to be a typical buyer / seller transaction. The Hurricane was clearly a much-loved member of the Vacher family and, even if I could produce the funds required for the purchase, I knew that finding the right owner for R4118 was more important to Peter and Polly that the cash her sale might generate. However pleasant that last hour had been, I realised that I'd probably just been 'interviewed' for the job of R4118's new owner. I just hoped I'd passed!

Invisible from the house, a large modern hangar appeared from behind a row of trees at the edge of the Vacher's garden. Crossing a neat hard-standing, Peter guided me into the building through a side door and switched on the lights. There, sitting in front of us was R4118. I was speechless.

With her tail positioned towards us, she looked bigger and more purposeful than I'd imagined. A pair of fuselage panels had been removed and lay on the floor beneath her starboard wing and, through the openings they exposed, I could see her tubular steel structure and the mass of internal bracing wires that distinguished her construction from the monocoque skin of her more famous counterpart, the Spitfire. We walked slowly around the aeroplane, with Peter guiding me through the genius of Sir Sydney Camm's masterpiece. Occasionally he'd stop and describe a marking or component. "This," he said, "is the original retractable foot stirrup. Can you believe that Wing Commander Bob Foster actually stood on that as he scrambled to intercept Ju88s over Beachy Head on 28 September 1940? This is R4118's Merlin III that we recovered from Banaras along with the airframe. It was filled with the remains of a hornets' nests when we brought it back to the UK but Maurice Hammond managed to restore it to airworthy condition for us."

For the next half hour, Peter explained the meaning of the various stencils painted on the flying controls; the aluminium part numbers visible through small Perspex windows at the root of the fin; and numerous other components, the provenance of which he knew intimately. Eventually he paused. "Would you like to sit in her?" he asked. The answer was written all over the grin on my face and a few minutes later I settled into the parachute padding of her seat and slid the canopy closed. There, in the seat Bunny Currant had used as he ferried R4118 from Drem to Abingdon on 7 September 1940; holding the very spade grip, complete with the gun button Archie Milne had pressed to despatch a Me110 three weeks later; my mind was made up. I would do whatever I could to buy R4118 and keep her in the UK where she belonged.

In the months that followed, Peter, Polly and I met regularly. They invited me and my family to their 'Air Day' where R4118 flew a beautiful display; we assembled a team to conduct a pre-purchase survey of the aeroplane which, needless to say, she passed with flying colours; and Peter and I discussed the engineering support I would

The handover. James looks delighted, Peter a little wistful.

For the last time, Peter signs out R4118 – on the rear fuselage panel.

need to ensure that she remained in the superb condition she was in that summer.

Gradually, a plan for the transfer of ownership of R4118 emerged and, under the headline of a newly-formed company – Hurricane Heritage – I engaged the support of a new Chief Engineer (Matt Pettit) and Chief Pilot (Paul 'Shents' Shenton), as well as agreement from Peter's groundcrew to continue working on the aeroplane once any sale went ahead. Importantly, we decided to make The Shuttleworth Collection at Old Warden Airfield the base for our Hurricane operation. With such a unique and historic pedigree, I wanted R4118 to be based at an airfield where the public could see her. With a grass runway and superb collection of vintage aircraft, Shuttleworth was the perfect location, not only enabling the public to visit aircraft housed within the museum on non-flying days, but also hosting a fantastic series of events throughout the year.

Finally, on a sunny morning in early October 2015, just days after the sale of our company had completed,

The early type hydraulic pump. The failure of this rare item grounded R4118 for much of its first season with James Brown.

Peter, Polly and the Hurricane Heritage team held a formal hand-over ceremony at the Vacher's airstrip in Oxfordshire. It looked like the whole village had come to wave goodbye to their famous neighbour and, after speeches had been made, photographs taken and gifts exchanged, Dave Harvey gave a spectacular farewell display before departing to R4118's new home at The Shuttleworth Collection. As I jumped aboard my Cessna 182 to follow R4118 as she routed to the north, I looked to my right to see Peter and Polly at the edge of their airstrip watching R4118 disappear over the treeline. Their achievement had been truly remarkable: not only had Peter navigated the complexity of Indian bureaucracy to facilitate R4118's return to the UK; he'd managed one of the world's most authentic warbird restorations; returned a Battle of Britain veteran to the air; operated her on the air show circuit for more than 10 years; and negotiated a sale that enabled her to remain in the UK. Now it was my turn to take on the role of custodian of this remarkable veteran and I just hoped I could do half as good a job as Peter and Polly had done.

As I write these words in March 2017, over two years have passed since Peter and I first met, and 18 months since we acquired R4118. Despite an early hydraulic pump failure, which took several months of detective work by our Chief Engineer to resolve, we've had a very successful first season filled with unforgettable experiences. I've had the privilege of flying alongside R4118 on a photo sortie as she climbed through broken cloud and soared amongst gleaming white cumulous above the green fields of England; I've met the Battle of Britain Memorial Flight pilots and learned about Hurricane operations from them; and I've had the enormous satisfaction of watching R4118 thrill the crowds at air shows across the country.

But above all, the most memorable experience of owning R4118 has been the impact she has on ordinary members of the public. With R4118 based in her new home at The Shuttleworth Collection, I frequently meet veterans, relatives of pilots or groundcrew and enthusiasts, all of whom have the same emotional response to our Hurricane. Occasionally, for people with a personal connection to the Hurricane, we'll sit them in the cockpit and as we slide the canopy closed, there's invariably the odd tear that gets wiped away as the enormity of going into battle in her sinks in. Our Hurricane – R4118 – with her incredible history provides an almost unique link to the Battle of Britain and, under our custodianship, we're determined to tell her story to the next generation of up-and-coming pilots, historians and enthusiasts.

With this aim in mind, we've harnessed all the tools of my children's generation to tell the story of R4118. With a presence across a range of social media platforms, a website filled with photos and videos, and a new schools' education programme, our goal is for the Hurricane to become as famous and well known as the Spitfire. She may not boast quite the same graceful lines as her more famous counterpart, but the Hurricane force accounted for more enemy aircraft destroyed than the rest of our defences combined throughout the Battle of Britain and, for my money, I'd take a Hurricane into battle every time.

As for my personal ambitions for R4118, I'd love to fly her: to experience the power, noise and sheer thrill of piloting this incredible machine myself. To help make this dream a reality, I've assembled a team of engineers and pilots who have designed a training programme which

The old and the new. Clockwise: Nelson, Polly, Peter, Matt Pettit (new Chief Engineer), Dave Harvey, James, and Rick Chase and Gavin Selwood who helped Peter with R4118 as groundcrew and now continue with James.

will hopefully take me from 600-hour PPL to Hurricane pilot over the next couple of years. Along the way, we've built an extraordinary collection of aircraft, each of which have their own stories to tell and their own lessons to teach a pilot like me: a 1944 Piper L4 Cub with D-Day history and the battle damage to prove it; a 1942 Harvard IIB that was used by the Royal Canadian Air Force to train Commonwealth pilots throughout the war and, of course, the ultimate Hurricane in the form of R4118. Every hour of training is a joy, and I want to be fully ready for the day I sit alone in the cockpit, open up the Merlin and fly her. And, if it turns out my flying skills aren't up to the job and that day never arrives, just being the custodian of this magnificent machine, and carrying on Peter's great work, is enough of a thrill that I won't be disappointed.

Peter Vacher adds:

Polly and I were thrilled that R4118 could stay in the United Kingdom and even more delighted that it has gone to James Brown, a man with just so much enthusiasm for the part played by these aircraft in defending our shores in 1940. To find that it is now kept at The Shuttleworth Collection, where it can be seen by so many visitors, was the icing on the cake. Thank you, James.

On 3 October 2015 R4118 was flown by Dave Harvey to its new home at The Shuttleworth Collection, via the dreaming spires of Oxford.

605 Squadron Crest
as used on their Annual Dinner menu
3 June 1939, three months before
the outbreak of war.

Squadron Scramble

Jimmy was new to the squadron, athletic, nineteen and with ginger hair.
A likeable sort, quietly confident, freshly trained – so in need of a prayer!
We sat by our huts in a Kentish field near to our runway of cut grass.
Soon and yet again we will meet the Luftwaffe en masse.

The raging sun warned us of the Devil's final sting
Do the bells of hell go ting – a – ling – a – ling?

Scramble! Squadron Scramble! Scramble!
Who will live and who will die in life's flighty gamble?
I ditched my pipe and sprinted towards my Hurricane.
Familiar faces tightened my parachute and helped strap me in again.
A flick on the ignition switch, good contact.
A Merlin cough – swirl of smoke – a reassuringly agreeable pact.
I'm soon encapsulated as nervous hands closed the cockpit hood.
Plug in for transmission, hope for clear messages that can be understood.
Gun sight on, oxygen on, all instruments addressed.
Brain totally focussed for the oncoming acid test.

Chocks away. I turned into the wind and pushed the throttle forward.
Faster; still faster until powerful wings mastered flight and took me skyward.
Wheels up, I pulled hard on the stick desperate to gain height.
We always tried to attack out of the sun, give the bandits a fright.
Our controller announced '100 plus bombers at 15,000 feet'.
'Steer 195 degrees, Angels 15' then a Tally-ho for a meet.

I suddenly spotted them, a large formation, about 5,000 feet below.
My heart pounded as I assessed the situation and called 'Tally-ho'
I kicked the rudder; banked sharply and gave the stick a push.
Rapidly gathering speed we dived for a real adrenalin rush.
Gun button to fire. I led a ravenous attack.
A three second burst put a Junkers 88 on the rack.

SQUADRON SCRAMBLE

All around I saw flashes of flame and trails of smoke.
Young Jimmy, a 90-degree attack, a two second burst.
Like a hot wire through cheese, he'd bagged his first.
A Messerschmitt 109 was diving vertically in a fit of death throes.
It looked like a wounded wasp with a yellow nose.
Jimmy, Jimmy, behind you I yelled!
But he bought it, went down like a tree just felled.
Out of ammunition, low on fuel, returned to base.
Another set of parents to be informed of a missing face.

The raging sun warned us of the Devil's final sting.
Do the bells of hell go ting – a – ling – a – ling?

Tom was new to the squadron, tall, and nineteen with black hair.
A likeable fellow, chirpy, bright, freshly trained – so in need of a prayer!
We sat by our huts in a Kentish field near to our runway of cut grass.
Soon and yet again we will meet the Luftwaffe en masse.

Co-written by:
Wing Commander C F 'Bunny' Currant DSO, DFC and Bar,
CdeG, and Michael Kendrick,
inspired by a friend. April 2001

A Closer Look at R4118

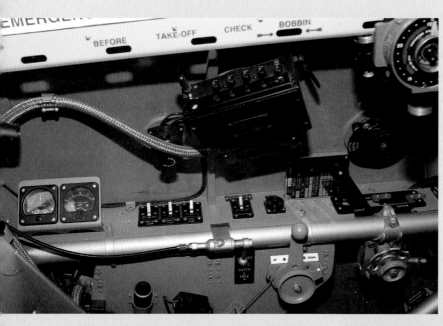

The port side of the cockpit with the push button controller for the TR1133 VHF radio, and the ammunition counter below which are the prop control and the throttle. The green lever adjusts the direction of the landing lights.

When the Browning guns were fired, the links between the cartridges together with the spent cartridge cases simply dropped through these apertures in the underside of the wings.

The powerful landing light in the port wing.

Rarely, if ever, seen on a restored aircraft, the aerial for the Identification Friend or Foe runs to the tailplane on both sides.

The markings on the side of the cockpit were applied when R4118 was overhauled by David Rosenfield Ltd, Manchester. The 'G5' indicates that the aircraft was built by Gloster Aircraft Company, followed by their manufacturer's serial number. 'CX' is the Cellon finish, whilst 'WIT' is the wireless telegraphy bonding symbol.

Four items of interest: one of two oxygen bottles, the TR1133 radio introduced in August 1940, the IFF set and the parachute flare tube for illuminating the ground when necessary for night landing.

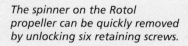

The spinner on the Rotol propeller can be quickly removed by unlocking six retaining screws.

APPENDIX I
Camouflage and Markings

HOWEVER meticulous has been the rebuilding of R4118, ultimately what is seen is the external appearance. It has been a severe challenge to ensure that the finished aircraft looks as near as possible in every detail as it did in the Battle of Britain. I am grateful to Bill Bishop for the many hours of work he put into researching every nuance of colour and marking. The reader may therefore be interested in the following notes compiled by Bill.

These notes have been prepared to assist in the painting of R4118/UP-W/G-HUPW. As no photograph of this aeroplane during the Battle of Britain has come to light, the decisions have been reached after extensive reference to sources listed below and to the few photographs of 605 Squadron aeroplanes available. They cannot therefore be considered as a finite description of the aircraft in September 1940, but the best estimation that can with present sources be achieved.

1] UPPER SURFACES
Dark Earth and Dark Green. Unless evidence shows to the contrary, to be in B scheme applicable to even numbered aeroplanes. A yellow gas detector patch on the left hand wing could possibly have been applied.

DECISION: DARK EARTH AND DARK GREEN IN B SCHEME. Note Hawker drawing #116520 shows A scheme, B scheme is a mirror image. No gas patch.

2] UNDER SURFACES
Much more difficult to be definite as to what colour should be applied. It can be shown what PROBABLY SHOULD have been on R4118 BUT NOT what WAS on R4118.

Glosters were advised on 11 June to apply **Sky** on under surfaces from that date. R4118 was not delivered until 17 August 1940 so this could be assumed to be the colour it was delivered in, however Sky is not thought to have been readily available until August and was in common use in September 1940.

NOTE: Archie McKellar's aeroplane V6879 in which he was shot down on 1 November 1940 is known to have had Sky under surfaces, however the date on which this colour was applied is not known.

Unless there is evidence to the contrary Sky would be the most appropriate and you could paint the underside of the port wing in Night, which was reintroduced for recognition purposes around October 1940.

DECISION: SKY AS CURRENTLY APPLIED TO SOME COMPONENTS, including the underside of both wings.

3] LANDING GEAR
Having looked at hundreds of photos in all the books covering Hurricanes I can find, I would feel quite confident in suggesting **Silver/Aluminium** for the gear legs including the tailwheel strut and wheel hubs.

Interior surfaces of the gear doors are a little more difficult to tie down. The great majority of photos tend to show these areas left in **Natural metal/Aluminium** but some were definitely painted to match the under wing colour.

Natural metal/Aluminium is the most likely colour to apply and certainly easier to keep clean if natural metal.

DECISION: ALUMINIUM TO INSIDE OF GEAR DOORS AND WHEELWELLS.

4] SERIAL NUMBERS
Painted in Night, 8" high. Gloster are recorded as having their own style of numbers and this will need to be used for the Battle of Britain period of its service.

DECISION: NIGHT/BLACK 8" HIGH AND 5"WIDE IF POSSIBLE IN GLOSTER STYLE *(Ref 5 pg 27)*. Top edge of numbers to be 8" below centreline of tailplane and rear edge to be 5" forward of a line drawn vertically downward from the leading edge of the tailplane. Width of strokes to be 1" *(Ref 8 pg67 Hawker Drg No E 116520 but with stroke width 1" as per other references)*.

5] FUSELAGE ROUNDELS
35" Diameter **Red/White/Blue/Yellow. (Bright shades)** The roundel was to be centred on the intersection of side former #5 and the 5th stringer up from the bottom *(Ref 8 pg 51)*. This results in the front edge of the roundel coinciding with a line drawn vertically downwards from the leading edge of the aerial with the aeroplane in the flying attitude.

NOTE: Glosters are known to have continued the use of pre-war bright colours for the red and blue long after it had been replaced by the wartime dull colours and R4118 would very likely have been finished in these bright colours. R4116 of 615 Sqn was shot down on 28 August 1940 and some parts of this aeroplane are at the Hawkinge Museum. These show that this had the roundels painted in the bright shades of blue and red. It is known that some aeroplanes were repainted at squadron and MU level, however it is unlikely that there would have been time to carry out such minor work prior to the end of the Battle of Britain.

DECISION: 35" TYPE A1 ROUNDELS POSITIONED AS ABOVE USING BRIGHT PRE-WAR COLOURS AS PER GLOSTER PRACTICE.

6] WING ROUNDELS

Upper wing: 49" Blue/Red again most likely in the brighter shades as per the fuselage roundels.

Lower wing: It appears that these came and went with the phase of the moon and you will have to determine the date that you want the markings to represent to come up with what should have been applied. Not all squadrons were equally diligent in reacting to changes of markings when orders were issued as not only did they have a war to fight, but also materials and manpower were often not available. Officially, under wing roundels were deleted with the introduction of Sky undersides on 6 June 1940 and then reintroduced on 1 August 1940. They were to be **50" Type A** roundels.

I doubt that anyone can tell you that you are wrong either way, however for most of its time with 605 Sqn, R4118 should have carried underwing roundels.

DECISION: UPPER SURFACES: 49" TYPE B RED/BLUE ROUNDELS CENTRED 80" IN FROM WINGTIP (in bright colours as applied by Gloster).

LOWER SURFACES: 50" TYPE A RED/WHITE/BLUE ROUNDELS CENTRED 80" IN FROM WINGTIP (in DULL COLOURS as they would have been applied by Squadron or MU after delivery from Gloster).

7] SQUADRON CODES

UP-W should be in **Medium Sea Grey**, orders called for 48" high letters but most appear to have used the alternative **30" high** letters, as 48" simply did not fit. This applied to most squadrons equipped with single engined aeroplanes.

DECISION: 30" LETTERS IN MEDIUM SEA GREY. Width of stokes to be ⅛th of letter height ie: 3.75". Style to be as depicted in the drawings provided, however the height of the centre bars of the letter W is open to discussion.

8] PROPELLER and SPINNER

Both finished in Night as standard, with the outer 4" of the propeller tips and pitch limit data near the hub in **Yellow**.

NOTE: Night is not Black.

DECISION: NIGHT AND YELLOW AS INDICATED ABOVE.

9] FIN FLASH

Red, White and Blue bands each 8" wide and 27" high were authorised for use from 1 August 1940 and advised to all commands on 11 August. A lot of variation is noted in photographs of the period. The photograph of R4118 as JU-J appears to show it with the 9" wide white and blue stripes with red covering the leading area of the fin and this also can be seen on photos of other 605 Sqn aeroplanes. V6701 JU-F was similarly marked in February 1941. This is not in keeping with the instructions of the time.

DECISION: 9" WIDE WHITE AND BLUE STRIPES WITH LEADING AREA OF THE FIN IN RED. (Extending from the top of the tailplane fillet to the top of the fin, colours do not extend over the rudder horn balance). ALL TO BE IN BRIGHT PRE-WAR COLOURS. *(Ref 5 pg27 upper righthand fin, and Ref 7 pg124).*

10] GUN PATCHES

These were not a painted rectangle as often depicted, but a patch of fabric doped over the gun openings to keep out dust and more importantly rain, which could freeze, blocking the barrels and mechanisms.

DECISION: Fabric patches of a slightly irregular shape to be doped over gun openings with RED OXIDE dope as used throughout the airframe exterior as a primer. Edges probably not having frayed or pinked edges, but simply torn edges.

11] FABRIC PATCHES

Fabric patches of a production nature would be of a higher standard than those applied at squadron level to make good damage etc.

DECISION: Cut edges to patches applied during manufacture.

12] PAINT

The process including number of coats of dope, undercoats and colour coats to be in accordance with current aircraft finishing practice and will be the subject of further discussion.

DECISION: Subject to discussion, however CELLULOSE to be used throughout.

REFERENCES:
1] *The Hawker Hurricane*, Francis K Mason, Crécy.
2] *Profile #111 Hurricane Mk I*, Francis K Mason, Profile Publications.
3] *Famous Airplanes of the World #28*, Unknown [Japanese], Bunrindo Co. Ltd.
4] *Camouflage and Markings #2*, Paul Lucas, Scale Aircraft Monographs.
5] *Combat Colours #2*, H C Bridgewater, Guideline Publications.
6] *Hurricane in Action*, Jerry Scutts, Squadron/Signal Publications.
7] *The Hawker Hurricane*, Richard A Franks, SAM Publications.
8] *Camouflage and Markings, RAF 36-45*, James Goulding, Ducimus.
9] *British Aviation Colours of WWII*, J.Tanner RAF Museum, Arms & Armour Press.
10] *605 Squadron*, Ian Piper, Louis Drapkin Ltd.

COLOURS: Quoted from Reference #4

	Colour match BS 381C	Colour match FS 595
Red (bright)	538 Post Office Red/Cherry	11140
Red (dull)	none quoted	30109 (FS 595B)
Blue (bright)	110 Roundel Blue	15056
Blue (dull)	none quoted	35948
Yellow	none quoted	33538
Medium Sea Grey	637 Medium Sea Grey	36270
Dark Earth	450 Dark Earth	30118 (FS 595B)
Dark Green	241 Dark Green	34079 (FS 595B)
Night	642 Night	37030 (FS 595B)
Sky	210 Sky	34424 (FS 595B)
Aluminium	none quoted, use Aluminium as used on aircraft structure	

STENCILLING:

If determining the camouflage and markings was a minefield, establishing just what stencils were and were not used on an aircraft in September 1940 has been no less difficult. Modern rebuilds representing aircraft of the Battle of Britain era have tended to use the accumulation of stencils from later in the war. For example, DTD (Directorate of Technical Development) specification numbers were applied from late in 1941 when aircraft began to be painted in more than one type of paint (cellulose and synthetic). Earlier aircraft did not carry DTD numbers. Certain instructional stencils such as 'IS YOUR OXYGEN CYLINDER TURNED ON?' cannot be seen in 1940 photographs, nor do they appear on the Hawker drawings. All stencils were painted in 'Night', not black.

We therefore decided to follow the Hawker drawings of the period and to include the following instructional stencils:

FIRST AID – BREAK HERE
ELECTRICAL CONNECTIONS INSIDE
CONTROL LOCKING GEAR HOLDING DOWN RINGS & STOWAGE FOR HOOD COVER INSIDE
DO NOT FORCE – TO OPEN PULL DOWN STEP
AILERON CONTROL USE 50-50 OIL (DTD 201) & PARAFFIN plus TURN

In the interest of safety we added:

AVGAS 100LL CAP 33 GALS (x2)
AVGAS 100LL CAP 28 GALS
COOLANT MIXTURE 30% GLYCOL 70% WATER

Apart from instructional stencils, serial numbers of major components were carried in one inch high characters, usually together with a W/T emblem indicating the electrical bonding to minimise Wireless Telegraphy interference. The letters and numerals have the following significance so far as R4118 is concerned, and are taken from the original data/modification plates riveted inside each structure:

41H/   The Air Ministry code for all Hawker aircraft

G5/   Components made by Gloster Aircraft Company Ltd, Hucclecote

G8/   Components made by Gloster Aircraft Company Ltd, Brockworth

CCF/   Components made by the Canadian Car and Foundry Company

CX   Cellon doping treatment for fabric surfaces

AF   Unknown factory

S2   Hawker's shadow factory at Brockworth

PA   Parnall Aircraft Ltd

RAS   Rollason Aircraft Services, Croydon and Tollerton

LMSD   London Midland & Scottish (Railway), Derby, controlled by
        Scottish Aviation Ltd, Prestwick, but wings rebuilt at LMS, Wolverton

TAYR   Taylorcraft, Rearsby

DRLM   David Rosenfield Ltd, Manchester

R4118's component serial numbers are:

Rudder
TAYR/S2/G5/93914 plus W/T

Fin
G5/41H/134925 plus W/T

Fuselage (aircraft's serial number)
DRLM/G5/92301/CX plus W/T

Aileron Port
G8/84540 plus W/T

Aileron Starboard
G5/41H/86702 plus W/T

Wing Port
LMSD/CCF/41H/14136 plus W/T

Wing Starboard
LMSD/CCF/41H/10127 plus W/T

Outer Wing Flap Starboard
AF/G5/41H/116797

Outer Wing Flap Port
PA/41H/174079

Tailplane
RAS/41H/94903 plus W/T

Elevator
PA/41H/93644 plus W/T

Centre Section Flaps
PA/G5/132990 plus W/T

Centre Section
G5/41H/92195/CX plus W/T

Movement Card Form 78

HURRICANE R4118 was one of the second production batch of one hundred aircraft delivered between May and July 1940 by the Gloster Aircraft Company, Hucclecote, Gloucestershire, to Air Ministry Contract 19773/39. Production ran at about two aircraft per day. The Merlin III engine number recorded on the card is A167621. The same Air Ministry number and the equivalent Rolls-Royce number 24927 were on the engine plate when the aircraft was recovered from India. The Form 78 plays a vital part of the aircraft's history:

18.07.40	Allotted to 22 Maintenance Unit (MU), Silloth
23.07.40	Taken on Charge (TOC) 22 MU, Silloth
17.08.40	TOC 605 Squadron 'County of Warwick', Drem
22.10.40	FBO (2) 'Flying Battle Operational'
23.10.40	TOC Austins, Service Aircraft Section (SAS), Hurricane Repair Organisation
03.12.40	Allotted to 18 MU, Dumfries
17.12.40	TOC 18 MU, Dumfries
18.01.41	TOC 111 Squadron, Dyce
26.04.41	TOC 59 Operational Training Unit (OTU), Crosby on Eden
14.10.41	Cat B damage (beyond repair on site, but repairable at a Maintenance Unit or at a contractor's works) TOC Taylorcraft, Civilian Repair Organisation (CRO), Leicester
12.12.41	Repaired Aircraft Awaiting Allocation (RAAA) at CRO
22.12.41	TOC 44 MU, Edzell
23.02.42	Cat AC damage (repair is beyond the unit capacity, but can be repaired on site by another unit or a contractor)

01.03.42	Repaired On Site (ROS)
01.04.42	TOC 44 MU, Edzell
23.05.42	Allotted to 56 OTU, Tealing
24.05.42	TOC 56 OTU, Tealing
05.04.43	Repaired In Works (RIW), David Rosenfield Ltd (CRO), Manchester
28.05.43	Awaiting Collection (AW/CN) CRO
16.06.43	TOC 5 MU, Kemble
11.11.43	TOC 52 MU, Cardiff
12.12.43	To Bombay, India aboard SS *Singkep*
06.02.44	Arrived Bombay, India. Mov 3 (sic) 12.02.44
04.10.44	Converted to Instructional
?.?.47	Struck Off Charge (SOC). Branch Instruction No. 38

Operational Records with 605 and 111 Squadrons

Day to day operations of R4118 during the Battle of Britain, as detailed in the 605 Squadron Operations Record Book

From Dawn	To Dawn	Pilot	Up	Down	Duty
07.09.40	08.09.40	P/O Bunny Currant	1430	1640	Drem to Abingdon
07.09.40	08.09.40	P/O Bunny Currant	1740	1820	Abingdon to Croydon
08.09.40	09.09.40	S/Ldr Walter Churchill	0925	0955	Croydon to Kenley to Croydon
09.09.40	10.09.40	S/Ldr Walter Churchill	1655	1835	Operational patrol in combat
12.09.40	13.09.40	P/O Alec Ingle	1350	1400	Operational patrol
13.09.40	14.09.40	P/O Bob Foster	1410	1505	Operational patrol and combat-Ju88 dam
17.09.40	18.09.40	P/O Alec Ingle	1530	1700	Operational patrol
18.09.40	19.09.40	P/O Jock Muirhead	0935	1035	Operational patrol
18.09.40	19.09.40	P/O Jock Muirhead	1245	1415	Operational patrol
18.09.40	19.09.40	P/O Jock Muirhead	1545	1645	Operational patrol
18.09.40	19.09.40	P/O Jock Muirhead	1710	1750	Operational patrol
19.09 40	20.09.40	P/O Jock Muirhead	1420	1530	Operational patrol
20.09.40	21.09.40	P/O Jock Muirhead	1100	1225	Operational patrol
20.09.40	21.09.40	P/O Jock Muirhead	1420	1505	Formation flying
21.09.40	22.09.40	P/O Jock Muirhead	1800	1910	Operational patrol
23.09.40	24.09.40	P/O Jock Muirhead	0915	1015	Operational patrol
23.09.40	24.09.40	P/O Jock Muirhead	1150	1235	Operational patrol
23.09.40	24.09.40	P/O Jock Muirhead	1735	1845	Operational patrol
24.09.40	25.09.40	P/O Jock Muirhead	0815	0920	Operational patrol
24.09.40	25.09.40	P/O Jock Muirhead	1120	1235	Operational patrol
24.09.40	25.09.40	P/O Jock Muirhead	1540	1720	Operational patrol and combat – Do215 dest

26.09.40	27.09.40	P/O Archie Milne	1150	1310	Operational patrol
26.09.40	27.09.40	P/O Archie Milne	1415	1435	Redhill to Croydon
27.09.40	28.09.40	P/O Archie Milne	0915	1000	Operational patrol and combat – Me110 dest
27.09.40	28.09.40	P/O Archie Milne	1145	1305	Operational patrol
28.09.40	29.09.40	P/O Archie Milne	0935	1100	Operational patrol and combat
28.09.40	29.09.40	P/O Bob Foster	1230	1300	Patrol
28.09.40	29.09.40	P/O Bob Foster	1310	1410	Patrol and combat
28.09.40	29.09.40	P/O Bob Foster	1500	1540	Patrol
28.09.40	29.09.40	P/O Bob Foster	1735	1830	Patrol and combat – Ju88 damg
29.09.40	30.09.40	P/O Archie Milne	1625	1720	Patrol
30.09.40	01.10.40	P/O Archie Milne	1055	1130	Patrol
30.09.40	01.10.40	P/O Archie Milne	1300	1415	Patrol
30.09.40	01.10.40	P/O Bob Foster	1635	1805	Patrol
01.10.40	02.10.40	P/O Bob Foster	1305	1440	Patrol and combat– Ju88 dest
01.10.40	02.10.40	P/O Bob Foster	1605	1730	Patrol
02.10.40	03.10.40	P/O Bob Foster	0835	1000	Patrol
05.10.40	06.10.40	P/O C E English	1600	1710	Patrol
07.10.40	08.10.40	P/O C E English	0935	1055	Patrol and combat
08.10.40	09.10.40	Sgt Charles Sones	1035	1115	Patrol and combat landed at Gatwick
08.10.40	09.10.40	Sgt Charles Sones	1430	1440	Gatwick to Croydon
15.10.40	16.10.40	P/O Alec Scott	1440	1450	Air test
15.10.40	16.10.40	P/O Alec Scott	1535	1655	Patrol
19.10.40	20.10.40	P/O Derek Forde	1415	1445	Patrol
20.10.40	21.10.40	P/O Peter Thompson	1125	1315	Patrol
21.10.40	22.10.40	P/O Derek Forde	1430	1445	Patrol
22.10.40	23.10.40	P/O Derek Forde	1025	1055	Patrol landed at Kenley
22.10.40	23.10.40	P/O Derek Forde	1350	1400	Kenley to Croydon
22.10.40	23.10.40	P/O Derek Forde	1410	1450	Patrol and combat

Day to day operations of R4118 February to March 1941, as detailed in the 111 Squadron Operations Record Book

Date	Pilot	Up	Down	Duty
03.02.41	S/Ldr Biggar	1055	1115	From Dyce to Montrose
04.02.41	Sgt Stein	1330	1340	To Edzell
10.02.41	W/O Blaize	1045	1055	From Edzell
10.02.41	Sgt Seaman	1215	1300	Man. for Combat
10.02.41	W/O Blaize	1400	1430	Scramble
10.02.41	Sgt Haine	1510	1540	Camera gun
10.02.41	Sgt Haine	1605	1645	Camera gun and formation
10.02.41	P/O Winton	1835	1905	Dusk Landings
11.02.41	Sgt Haine	1035	1125	Climb 25,000 feet
11.02.41	P/O Winton	1235	1315	Man. for Combat
11.02.41	W/O Blaize	1345	1435	Scramble
11.02.41	P/O Wainwright	1520	1600	Formation (Kucera P3318)
11.02.41	Sgt Seaman	1640	1720	Formation (Haine P3524)
11.02.41	P/O Wainwright	1800	1835	Dusk Patrol
14.02.41	P/O Winton	1125	1155	Formation (Hanes P3701)
14.02.42	W/O Blaize	1220	1245	Formation (Stein P3701)
16.02.41	Sgt Haine	0940	1025	Man. for Combat
16.02.41	Sgt Spencer	1215	1240	Air Firing
16.02.41	Sgt Haine	1325	1355	Air Firing
16.02.41	P/O Wainwright	1415	1435	Air Firing
16.02.41	P/O Winton	1445	1515	Air Firing
16.02.41	Sgt Haine	1620	1655	Formation and weaving
16.02.41	Sgt Seaman	1540	1600	Air Firing
18.02.41	Sgt Stein	1000	1035	Formation practice (Kucera P3318)
18.02.41	Sgt Haine	1355	1440	Formation (Hanes P3524)
18.02.41	Sgt Haine	1720	1825	Formation (Mansfeld V6701/Hanes P3524)
21.02.41	Sgt Stein	1025	1110	Dog Fighting (Kucera V6701)
21.02.41	Sgt Stein	1140	1220	Scramble
21.02.41	Sgt Haine	1345	1510	Formation (Winton P3524/ Hanes P3701)
24.02.41	Sgt Seaman	1335	1350	To Edzell

09.03.41	P/O Winton	1135	1145	From Edzell
09.03.41	P/O Winton	1220	1230	To Edzell
09.03.41	P/O Winton	1240	1250	From Edzell
09.03.41	P/O Winton	1315	1345	Scramble
09.03.41	Sgt Stein	1520	1630	Scramble
10.03.41	P/O Winton	0700	0800	Dawn patrol
10.03.41	P/O Winton	1005	1105	Scramble
10.03.41	P/O Winton	1820	1845	Formation (Wainwright V6606)
11.03.41	Sgt Hanes	1020	1050	Practice formation (Stein V6606)
12.03.41	Sgt Hanes	1215	1240	Scramble
13.03.41	P/O Wainwright	1030	1055	Scramble
13.03.41	P/O Winton	1405	1525	Scramble
13.03.41	P/O Wainwright	1550	1715	Patrol
13.03.41	F/Lt Simpson	1825	1835	Air test on new machines
14.03.41	Sgt Seaman	1145	1230	Formation
14.03.41	Sgt Seaman	1450	1540	Formation (Blaize R4086/Haine P3046)
15.03.41	Sgt Spencer	1120	1125	Scramble
15.03.41	Sgt Spencer	1200	1315	Patrol Firth of Forth
16.03.41	Sgt Haine	1130	1225	Scramble. Landed at Dyce
17.03.41	Sgt Haine	0930	0935	From Dyce
18.03.41	Sgt Spencer	0855	0920	Scramble
18.03.41	Sgt Hanes	1430	1515	Cloud flying
18.03.41	Sgt Haine	1605	1655	Formation changing (Wainwright P3524/Seaman V6984)
19.03.41	Sgt Spencer	1015	1100	Formation practice (Kucera P3318/Seaman R4086)
19.03.41	Sgt Seaman	1415	1455	Formation changing (Kucera P3318/Winton V6984)
19.03.41	Sgt Hanes	1520	1535	To Dyce
19.03.41	Sgt Hanes	1800	1830	From Dyce
19.03.41	Sgt Hanes	1930	2000	Dusk landings
20.03.41	Sgt Seaman	1155	1235	Scramble
20.03.41	Sgt Seaman	1345	1425	Formation (Wainwright P3524/Spencer V6696)

21.03.41	Sgt Seaman	1040	1140	Formation (Wainwright P3524/Haine P3046)
21.03.41	Sgt Seaman	1450	1605	Scramble
22.03.41	Sgt Haine	1225	1330	Scramble
22.03.41	Sgt Stein	1440	1515	Scramble
23.03.41	Sgt Seaman	1400	1445	Scramble
23.03.41	P/O Winton	1625	1705	RT and Dogfight
23.03.41	Sgt Haine	1930	2050	Dusk patrol
23.03.41	Sgt Haine	2215	2310	NF practice
24.03.41	Sgt Haine	0720	0800	Dawn patrol
24.03.41	Sgt Seaman	1050	1125	Scramble (combat report)
24.03.41	Sgt Spencer	1525	1550	Camera gun
24.03.41	Sgt Stein	1815	1845	Scramble
25.03.41	Sgt Spencer	1135	1150	Flight formation (Simpson W9179/Winton P3524/ Kucera V6696/Mansfeld V6701)
25.03.41	Sgt Seaman	1640	1700	To Dyce
25.03.41	Sgt Seaman	1730	1745	To Edzell from Dyce
25.03.41	Sgt Seaman	1750	1800	To Montrose from Edzell
25.03.41	Sgt Spencer	2000	2035	Night flying practice
30.03.41	Sgt Stein	0905	0955	Scramble
30.03.41	Sgt Stein	1435	1505	Scramble
30.03.41	Sgt Stein	1735	1755	Scramble

APPENDIX IV

Engine History

STUDYING which, and how many engines were fitted to R4118 has required some serious detective work. I am grateful to Peter Kirk at Rolls-Royce for much information gleaned from their archives.

R4118 was built in May/June 1940 with, it can be assumed, a Merlin Mark III engine (engine 1). The aircraft was not taken on charge until 23 July 1940 by 22 MU at Silloth. From there it moved to 605 Squadron on 17 August 1940. The first record of it flying with 605 Squadron was on 7 September 1940 when it was flown from Drem to Croydon during the height of the Battle of Britain. There would have been little reason to change the engine during this period.

On reaching Croydon, it immediately became operational and was in such continuous use during the Battle that it is unlikely that any engine change was made before it suffered 'flying battle operational' damage on 22 October 1940.

We know some of the history of two of the replacement engines. The earlier of these two had its Air Ministry engine no. A174794 recorded as being in the aircraft at the time of an accident on 23 February 1942. A174794 was a Merlin III, Rolls-Royce no. **31725**, one of a batch of 500 built at Derby, Order no. 4980C, Contract no. B58634/39. It was built on 30 September 1940, tested on 2 October 1940 and despatched on 3 October 1940 to 7 MU at Quedgeley. They certainly did not hang around! Rolls-Royce have pointed out that sending it direct to an MU means it was consigned as a spare engine, not one to go into a new airframe.

By the time this engine was fitted to R4118 it had already been in another aircraft and had a partial overhaul at De Havilland which was completed on 9 August 1941 and sent to 14 MU. Rectification work was carried out by Sunbeam Talbot on 25 May 1942.

A later replacement engine was still fitted to the aircraft when it was found in India. This is Rolls-Royce no. **24927** which, according to Rolls-Royce's records corresponds with Air Ministry no. A167621. A167621 is the number recorded on the Form 78 Aircraft Movement card. This confirms that the aircraft is indeed R4118. Engine **24927** (A167621) was in a batch of Merlin IIIs nos. 23591-25229 built to Order no. 4980 at Crewe between 23 June 1940 and 12 October 1940 under the same contract number as above, B58634/39. At the same time 500 identical engines were ordered from Derby under Order no. 4980/A.

Engine **24927** was tested week ending 29 September and despatched on 3 October 1940. It was overhauled by Alvis on 16 April 1943. Rolls-Royce's records usually indicated if the engine was damaged beyond repair or taken out of service. No such record exists, possibly indicating that its aircraft was not recorded as being written off.

Thus we know we had an unrecorded original engine and at least two replacement engines to which we will refer by their Rolls-Royce nos., **31725** and **24927**. Compiling the history is not helped by the Air Ministry's practice of writing the engine number on the Form 78 in pencil which was simply rubbed out and re-written every time there was a change of engine.

So, how many engines did R4118 have? As one of the few Hurricane Mark Is to have survived, it had unusual longevity. Correlating the engine history with the Form 78 Aircraft Movement card, we can deduce that R4118 had at least five engines at various times, and possibly more.

We have seen that R4118 was unlikely to have had an engine change prior to it joining 605 Squadron, nor during the Battle of Britain with that squadron. By the time the aircraft was damaged on 22 October 1940, it had flown fifty-two sorties in the Battle totalling 52.8 hours with an average sortie time of sixty-one minutes. The aeroplane was repaired at Austins and taken on charge at 18 MU at Dumfries on 17 December 1940. Although the required time between major overhauls of the Merlin III was not to exceed 300 hours, few engines reached that limit. Under battle conditions a more average life was eighty hours. So it is probable that a replacement engine (engine 2) would have been fitted at Austins or 18 MU after the stresses and strains of the Battle.

On 18 January 1941 R4118 was taken on charge by 111 Squadron at Dyce, with whom it did seventy-seven sorties by 30 March 1941 totalling forty-eight hours, an average sortie time of thirty-seven minutes. By 26 April 1941 it had moved to 59 Operational Training Unit at Crosby on Eden, without passing through an MU, so is unlikely to have had an engine change in between.

Between April and October 1941 there is still no mention of the aircraft passing through an MU, so no further engine could have been fitted.

The next we know of the aircraft is from an accident record card (Form 1180) recording Cat B accident damage on 7 October 1941. Flt Lt F J M Palmer, a New Zealander, was unable to avoid a lorry driving onto the runway when he was landing at 59 OTU. Although accident record cards usually recorded the engine number, sadly it is missing on this.

Following its ordeal with the lorry, the aircraft was taken on charge by Taylorcraft at Rearsby, Leicester, on 14 October 1941. After repair it moved to 44 MU on 22 December 1941. Whilst with this maintenance unit it barely survived two months before another accident. The record card shows that on 23 February 1942 R4118 hit a snow bank on landing with no brake air pressure, flown by Flt Lt Alistair Bannerman Lennie (sadly killed in another flying accident on 8 December 1942 only six weeks after being married). This time the engine (engine 3) number is recorded – A174794, i.e. Rolls-Royce no. **31725**.

From the Rolls-Royce records of engine **31725** we know that it had a partial overhaul completed on 9 August 1941 and must therefore have been fitted to R4118 at Taylorcraft between October and December 1941, or at 44 MU between December 1941 and February 1942. Indeed the accident on 23 February 1942 occurred at the end of a test flight – could it have been a test of the new engine? The accident damage was 'repaired on site'.

The aircraft remained at 44 MU until allocation to 56 OTU, Sutton Bridge, on 23 May 1942. But this is interesting. On 29 May 1942 engine **31725** underwent 'rectification' at Sunbeam Talbot. Therefore this engine must have been removed before R4118 went to 56 OTU. So yet another engine (engine 4) must have been fitted at 44 MU. But this could not have been engine **24927** which is in the aircraft now, as that did not come off overhaul at Alvis until 16 April 1943.

There is then a long period of unrecorded detail from May 1942 until April 1943, during which time the aircraft appears to have been in the uninterrupted care of 56 OTU. Whether any engine change happened in this period is unknown.

On 5 April 1943, R4118 was 'repaired in works' at David Rosenfield Ltd, Barton, Manchester, moving to 5 MU at Kemble on 16 June 1943. Engine **24927** (engine 5) must have been installed by one of these two organisations before R4118 left 5 MU on 11 November 1943 for 52 MU at Cardiff, a packing station for aircraft being sent overseas. On 12 December 1943 the aircraft was shipped to India.

Hawker Modifications

Being those mods incorporated in R4118 up to the time of its despatch to India.

Modification no.	Description
AIRFRAME	
11	Automatic hydraulic system
44	Armour protection front
52	Rudder
67	U/C wheel, brake and drum strengthened
69	Hydraulic pressure gauge provision
72	Wheel housing rear fairing strengthened
74	Fixed parts to TR1133 introduced
77	Unknown
81	Unknown
105	Regulator, suppressor and mod generator
119	Rudder
125	Unknown
128	Armour protection against stern attack
132	Exhaust glare shields introduced
136	Cooling duct for fuel pump
139	Excessive pressure in oil system reduced
143	Slow running cut-out control introduced
151	Unknown
160	Starboard flare tube and control deleted
163	Repositioned oxygen bottle and existing equipment moved forward
173	R3002 IFF introduced
176	Windscreen de-icing introduced

179	Rear view mirror introduced
185	Heywood compressor introduced
188	Armour forward of header tank
190	Two position foot pedal
193	Upward firing recognition device
214	Emergency crowbar introduced
217	Fireproof screen aft of deck tank introduced
218	New tailwheel and shock strut introduced
224	Oxygen economiser introduced
225	Additional oxygen cylinder introduced
267	Reinforced oxygen cylinder
273	Formation keeping lamps deleted
275	Engine mixture control deleted
331	G45 camera in lieu of G42B
373	Generator failure warning light introduced

WINGS

149	Structural change
175	Structural change
280	Structural change

TANKS

58	C/S tanks chafing strip
165	Self-sealing fuel tanks
172	Reinforcing fuel tanks fixed
197	Corrosion inhibitor in C/S tanks
255	Revised method of covering S/S tanks

Operational Aircraft during the Battle of Britain

At the time that R4118 entered the Battle of Britain, pilots, not aircraft, were in critically short supply as the following analysis shows:

BATTLE OF BRITAIN

FIGHTER COMMAND – OPERATIONAL AIRCRAFT AND CREWS AS AT

	10 July 1940				8 August 1940				31 October 1940			
	Sqdns.	I.E.	Service-able a/c	OPERATIONAL (Serviceable with crews)	Sqdns.	I.E.	Service-able a/c	OPERATIONAL (Serviceable with crews)	Sqdns.	I.E.	Service-able a/c	OPERATIONAL (Serviceable with crews)
Hurricanes	27	432	582	344	28.5	568	645	370	34	544	561	399
Spitfires	19	304	320	226	19	328	335	257	19	304	294	227
Gladiators	-	-	-	-	0.5	8	7	7	0.5	8	9	8
Defiants	2	32	39	24	2	32	30	20	2	32	39	10
Blenheims	6	96	92	62	6	96	83	66	6	96	61	40
	54	864	1033	656	56	1032	1100	720	61.5	984	964	684

Source: PRO AIR 20/4174

Index

INDEX